THE BROKEN ESTATE

THE BROKEN ESTATE

Essays on Literature and Belief

JAMES WOOD

JONATHAN CAPE
LONDON

Published by Jonathan Cape 1999

2 4 6 8 10 9 7 5 3 1

Copyright © James Wood 1999

James Wood has asserted his right under the
Copyright, Designs and Patents Act 1988 to be identified
as the author of this work

First published in Great Britain in 1999 by
Jonathan Cape
Random House, 20 Vauxhall Bridge Road,
London SW1V 2SA

Random House Australia (Pty) Limited
20 Alfred Street, Milsons Point, Sydney,
New South Wales 2061, Australia

Random House New Zealand Limited
18 Poland Road, Glenfield,
Auckland 10, New Zealand

Random House South Africa (Pty) Limited
Endulini, 5A Jubilee Road, Parktown 2193, South Africa

Random House UK Limited Reg. No. 954009

A CIP catalogue record for this book
is available from the British Library

ISBN 0-224-05294-2

Papers used by Random House UK Limited are natural,
recyclable products made from wood grown in sustainable forests.
The manufacturing processes conform to the environmental
regulations of the country of origin

Typeset by Deltatype Ltd, Birkenhead, Merseyside
Printed and bound in Great Britain by
Creative Print and Design (Wales), Ebbw Vale

To C. D. M.
and to Leon Wieseltier

Just as Saul went out to look for his father's she-asses and found a kingdom, so the essayist who is really capable of looking for the truth will find at the end of his road the goal he was looking for: life.

— Lukács, *Soul and Form*

And in these books of mine, their distinctive character, as essays on art, is their bringing everything to a root in human passion or human hope.

— Ruskin, *Modern Painters*

Contents

Introduction:
The limits of not quite

The real is the atlas of fiction, over which all novelists thirst. The real is contour, aspiration, tyrant. The novel covers reality, runs away with it, and, as travellers will yearn to dirty their geography, runs from it, too. It is impossible to discuss the power of the novel without discussing the reality that fiction so powerfully discloses, which is why realism, in one form or another and often under different names, has been the novel's insistent preoccupation from the beginning of the form. Everything flows from the real, including the beautiful deformations of the real; realism is not a law, but a lenient tutor, for it schools its own truants. It is realism that *allows* surrealism, magic realism, fantasy, dream, and so on. 'All writers believe they are realists', writes Alain Robbe-Grillet in *Pour un nouveau roman*.

There are writers for whom reality is torn into existence, abruptly birthed, such as Céline, Dostoevsky; and there are others, such as Tolstoy and Proust, for whom reality seems to be born calmly, as it were, in an open ward, in white view. We respond, as readers of fiction, to a massive variety of realities. Yet in all fiction those moments when we are suddenly moved have to do with something we fumblingly call 'true' or 'real'. One such moment occurs in *A Portrait of the Artist as a Young Man*, when Stephen Dedalus hears his father sing an old song ('the tender tremors with which his father's voice festooned the strange sad happy air'), and then his father exclaims: 'Ah, but you should have heard Mick Lacy sing it! Poor Mick Lacy! He had little turns for it, grace notes he used to put in that I haven't got.' This moves us – why? Because it is like life? Certainly, for although it may not exactly resemble our lives, it brings to our heart a plausible loss; we have all felt our own version of 'You should have heard Mick Lacy sing it!' It is moving because an experience that Stephen Dedalus believes is original to him – wistfully hearing his father hear a sad air – is revealed, so gently, to be not original to him, and is revealed as actually a much fiercer and more complicated experience for his father. Behind one reality lies a deeper, more private reality, which is always lost.

But the moment is also *like Joyce* as well as like life; if we exclaim 'How real, how true', we do so because our idea of what is real and true has been partly constructed by Joyce. 'How true that a character in Joyce would feel like this', we say to ourselves. (Stephen hearing his father is like Gabriel hearing his wife speak of Michael Furey, her first love, in 'The Dead'.) In Christina Stead's novel, *The Man Who Loved Children*, we encounter this sentence about halfway through the book: 'Sam was always anxious for morning.' We delight at the truth of this observation only because it is absolutely 'true' about the character Sam, whose reality Stead has so powerfully furnished. Thus moments of truth in fiction may be only in small part related to the lifelike; rather, they flow toward and withdraw from the lifelike. In *The World As Will and Representation* Schopenhauer remarks that Dante got his fantasy of hell from the world. Readers of fiction should base their theories of realism on that remark. He means that Dante's hell is real, and feels real, not that it is 'realistic' or 'lifelike'. Indeed, Schopenhauer means that life is hell-like, that it resembles Dante's hell. Dante's reality is a maddened version, a black hypostasis of life. But our sense of this reality comes largely from Dante's capacity to convince us of this sense, rather than from the world.

Fiction is real when its readers validate its reality; and our power so to validate comes both from our sense of the actual real ('life') and from our sense of the fictional real (the reality of the novel). A lovely example of this occurs in Joseph Roth's great novel of the Austro-Hungarian empire, *The Radetzky March*. The hero, a feckless young lieutenant named Trotta, is in debt. His loyal batman, a poor peasant named Onufrij, decides to give his master all his painfully earned savings. He goes to the piece of land where the money is buried in a cloth, and digs his savings out of the ground. Haltingly, he brings them to Trotta, and offers them. 'Herr Lieutenant, here is money!' Trotta takes one look at the money and declines it. 'It's against regulations, do you understand?' says Trotta. 'If I take money from you, I'll be demoted and drummed out of the army, do you understand?' He sends Onufrij away.

Roth remarks that Trotta had read about 'golden characters' like Onufrij in sentimental literature, and had never quite believed them. Yet, Roth assures us, such 'uncouth boys with noble hearts' do not just exist in sentimental books, they also 'exist in real life'. He reminds us that 'a lot of truths about the living world are recorded in bad books; they are just badly written.' The passage is very moving, because it seems true, real, lifelike – not least in its comical pointlessness: the money excavated, proudly donated by Onufrij, and then proudly refused by Trotta. But one notices the movement here: Roth assures us that such people as Onufrij exist in real life. And we believe him. But why? Only because we have just encountered him in such reality in the novel. We have no sense of Onufrij in real life; only a sense from the novel. The character is thus the best proof of the authenticity of the technique that just created him. Onufrij is the ombudsman of his own production. We are the jury. Roth asks us to validate the reality of his writing by believing it. In this sense, fiction is proved by what it discloses, and is thus always a running test-case of itself. Like a travelling assizes, moving from county to county, a novel always brings its own criteria for judgment with it. Every novel is its own reality and its own realism. It is its own evidence and its own court.

Nevertheless, the reality of fiction must also draw its power from the reality of the world. The real, in fiction, is always a matter of belief, and is therefore a kind of discretionary magic: it is a magic whose existence it is up to us, as readers, to validate and confirm. It is for this reason that many readers dislike actual magic or fantasy in novels. As I write in my discussion of Toni Morrison's fiction, 'the creation of characters out of nothing, their placement in an invented world, is chimerical; and for this reason one rarely wants the novelist further to ripen these chimeras in a false heat . . . Fiction demands belief from us, and this request is demanding in part because we can choose not to believe. But magic – impossible happenings, ghoulish returns – dismantles belief, forcing on us apparitions which, because they are beyond belief, we cannot choose not to believe. Belief is a mere appendix to magic, its unused organ . . . This is why most fiction is not magical, and why the great writers of magical tales – E.T.A. Hoffmann, Gogol, Kafka – are so densely realistic.'

The gentle *request* to believe is what makes fiction so moving. Joyce requests that we believe that Mick Lacy could sing the tune better than Stephen's father. Joseph Roth requests that we believe him when he remarks that Onufrij was a real person, not the character in a bad book. It is a belief that is requested, that we can refuse at any time, that is under our constant surveillance. This is surely the true secularism of fiction – why, despite its being a kind of magic, it is actually the enemy of superstition, the slayer of religions, the scrutineer of falsity. Fiction moves *in the shadow of doubt*, knows itself to be a true lie, knows that at any moment it might fail to make its case. Belief in fiction is always belief 'as if'. Our belief is itself metaphorical – it only *resembles* actual belief, and is therefore never wholly belief. In his essay 'Sufferings and Greatness of Richard Wagner', Thomas Mann writes that fiction is always a matter of 'not quite': 'To the artist new experiences of "truth" are new incentives to the game, new possibilities of expression, no more. He believes in them, he takes them seriously, just so far as he needs to in order to give them the fullest and profoundest expression. In all that he is very serious, serious even to tears – but yet *not quite* – and by consequence, not at all. His artistic seriousness is of an absolute nature, it is "dead-earnest playing".'

Fiction, being the game of not quite, is the place of not-quite-belief. Precisely what is a danger in religion is the very fabric of fiction. In religion, a belief that is only 'as if' is either the prelude to a loss of faith, or an instance of bad faith (in both senses of the phrase). If religion is true, one must believe absolutely. And if one chooses not to believe, one's choice is marked under the category of a refusal, and is thus never really free: it is the duress of a recoil. Once religion has revealed itself to you, you are never free. In fiction, by contrast, one is always free to choose not to believe, and this very freedom, this shadow of doubt, is what helps to constitute fiction's reality. Furthermore, even when one is believing fiction, one is 'not quite' believing, one is believing 'as if'. (One can always close the book, go outside, and kick a stone.) Fiction asks us to judge its reality; religion asserts its reality. And this is all a way of saying that fiction is a special realm of freedom.

The essays in this volume pace the limits of the 'not quite', in both fiction and religion. It will become clear that I believe that distinctions between literary belief and religious belief are important, and it is because I believe in that importance that I am attracted to writers who struggle with those distinctions. Around the middle of the nineteenth century, those distinctions became much harder to maintain, and we have lived in the shadow of their blurring ever since. This was when the old estate broke. I would define the old estate as the supposition that religion was a set of divine truth-claims, and that the Gospel narratives were supernatural reports; fiction might be supernatural, too, but fiction was always fictional, it was not in the same order of truth as the Gospel narratives. During the nineteenth century, these two positions began to soften and merge. At the high-point of the novel's triumph, when people felt it could do anything, the Gospels began to be read, by both writers and theologians, as a set of fictional tales – as a kind of novel. Simultaneously, fiction became an almost religious activity (though not, of course, with religion's former truth-value, for this was no longer believed in). Flaubert, a pivotal figure here, began to turn literary style into a religion while Ernest Renan, in his *Vie de Jésus*, began to turn religion into a kind of style, a poetry. It became no longer possible to believe that Jesus was who he claimed to be; he was now a 'character', almost the hero of a novel. Of course, the seeds of this shift lay in earlier times, in the deism of the eighteenth century especially. Gotthold Lessing, for instance, was both a theologian and an aesthetician, and in the 1780s was reading the Gospels as historical narratives. He distinguished sharply between what he called 'the religion of Christ' and what he called 'the Christian religion'; the first was a set of claims made by a man in an historical text; the second was the 1700-year accretion of dogma. Lessing passed into English thought through Coleridge, whose posthumous book, *Confessions of an Inquiring Spirit* (1840) paraphrased – and emblazoned – the German theologian. Coleridge strove to be one of those readers who might 'take up the Bible as they do other books, and apply to it the same rules of interpretation'. Just as fiction supplies, and constitutes, the only evidence for our belief, so Coleridge felt that 'the Bible and Christianity are their own sufficient evidence'. If we are to believe the Scriptures, Coleridge seems to argue, it will be because of the novel-like effect those writings have on our hearts, and not because the Church has simply asserted that they are supernatural and infallible. For Coleridge, like Lessing, the Scriptures were writings, or as we would say now, texts, and susceptible to our individual torque. It is a mark of how literary – how novelistic – such thinking had become, that Coleridge used the Book of Job as his clinching argument for the fallibility of the Scriptures. God could not have written a story that was such an argument against Himself, says Coleridge. Only a human being could do that. In other words, Coleridge might have added, God is not a novelist, he does not have negative capability.

For some of the writers discussed in this book – Melville, Gogol, Renan, Arnold, Flaubert – the difference between literary belief and religious belief was not always clear, and was often an excruciation. It is no surprise that this happened at the high moment of the European novel. For it was not just science, but the novel itself, which helped to kill Jesus's divinity, when it gave us a new sense of the real, a new sense of how the real disposes itself in a narrative – and then in turn a new scepticism towards the real as we encounter it in narrative. Ultimately, this 'break' was good neither for religion nor perhaps for the novel, although it was perhaps a beneficial moment in our progress from superstition. For Christianity, instead of disappearing, merely surrendered its truth-claims, and turned itself into a comforting poetry on the one hand, or an empty moralism on the other. Truth slipped away. (The heirs of Renan and Arnold are everywhere in contemporary Christianity.) And the novel, as I suggest in my discussion of Flaubert, having founded the religion of itself, relaxed too gently into aestheticism.

Nevertheless, there have always been writers great enough to move between the religious impulse and the novelistic impulse, to distinguish between them and yet, miraculously, to draw on both. Melville and Flaubert were such novelists, and so were Joyce and Woolf. For Virginia Woolf, fifty or so years after the convulsions of the nineteenth century, and the daughter of a celebrated agnostic, there was no formal agony of religious withdrawal. The hard work had been done. For her, a kind of religious or mystical belief and a literary belief softly consorted – and yet, for her, the novel still retained its sceptical, inquisitorial function. In her writing, the novel acts mystically, only to show that we cannot reach the godhead, for the godhead has disappeared. For her the novel acts religiously but performs sceptically.

I hope that these essays may do something similar.

Sir Thomas More: A man for one season

It may be better to be a John Knox than an Alcibiades, but it is better to be a Pericles than either.

– Mill, 'On Liberty'

Thomas More, the scrupulous martyr, is the complete English saint. But no man can ever be a saint in God's eyes, and no man should be one in ours, and certainly not Thomas More. His image has been warmed by different breaths. He is seen as a Catholic martyr because he died opposing Henry VIII's divorce from Catherine of Aragon and the King's robbery from the Pope of the leadership of the English Church. But he is also seen as a lawyer-layman caught in the mesh of presumptuous ecclesiology, an English Cicero of the pre-Reformation who nobly gave his head to forces beyond his control. Most absurdly, because of Robert Bolt's screenplay, this barrister of Catholic repression is widely envisioned as modernity's diapason: the clear, strong note of individual conscience, the note of the self, sounding against the authoritarian intolerance of the Early Modern state. Thomas More died in defence of an authoritarian intolerance much more powerful than a mere king's, however, for he died believing in God and in the authority of the Pope and the Catholic Church. As Lord Chancellor, he had imprisoned and interrogated Lutherans, sometimes in his own house, and sent six reformers to be burned at the stake, and he did not do this so that he might die for slender modern scruple; for anything as naked as the naked self. This drained, contemporary view of More, which admires not what he believed but how he believed – his 'certainty', only – is thinly secular, and represents nothing more than the retired religious yearning of a non-religious age.

I

Peter Ackroyd's dignified biography offers a picture of More which is a combination of Catholic admiration and modern scholarly determinism. Ackroyd soaked himself in late medieval history; happily, he does not pretend to conduct a historical séance, as he has in earlier work. (He does not walk down the Old Kent Road arm in arm with 'cockney More'.) He gives a reliable, indeed moving, account of ordinary religion in sixteenth-century England, and synthesizes a vast body of material. But his book is partial, merciful and sentimental where it should be total, unforgiving and grave. Ackroyd is evasive about More's evasions. He invariably gives him the benefit of the doubt in his battle with the Lutheran heretics, and is dreamily naive about More's Machiavellianism at court. He is gentle with the incoherent and frantic tattoos that More beat out in the enormous anti-Lutheran tracts of the 1520s. At no point does he properly examine the justice of the Protestant case, either doctrinally or politically, preferring to see its progress deterministically, in high doom, as the inevitable 'birth of the modern age'. His book is mild Catholic elegy. This not only clothes More in stolen righteousness, but delays once again a truly secular judgment of More (as opposed to the drained secular view), in which the zealous legalist might be seen for what he was, in all his itchy finesse of cruelty.

More's life, in particular its quick, morbid promotion towards martyrdom, is as compelling here as elsewhere: Ackroyd narrates it with royal fatalism. Here is the gentle house in Bucklersbury, where Erasmus, More's 'darling', wrote *In Praise of Folly* in 1509. We encounter again More's hairshirt, worn quietly underneath his public vestments so that only his daughter discovered it by chance, and the knotted straps with which he flagellated himself. His extended family, as Holbein's sketch reveals, existed as a *collegium* for the new humanism. More taught his children to read Greek and Latin by affixing letters to an archery-board and encouraging his pupils to fire arrows at them. The prosecutor of later years could bear to chastise his children only with a peacock-feather. He and his wife, Alice, played the lute together, like ideal woodcut spouses. More was one of a number of humanists who believed that the liberal arts, especially the study of Greek and Latin literature, needed renovation. With Erasmus he translated the satirical and highly irreligious writer, Lucian, from Greek to Latin. He wrote, in 1518, that one should 'build a path to theology' through the great secular authors. He believed that the Church needed to be reformed, and was not obscure about the clerical abuse that was turning the people against the priesthood. Out of this world came his beautiful lament, *Utopia* (1516), whose lovely ironies would come to seem self-ironies, and whose playful negatives would curdle into the mean calculations of More's later years. For in the inverted island world of Utopia, divorce is permissible, and the inhabitants can follow any religion they like; these would become the two determinants of More's later fixity. The founder of Utopia, writes More, could see that religious differences sowed discord. Thus he allowed freedom of worship. He himself 'might do the best he could to bring others to his opinion, so that he did it peacably, gently, quietly and soberly . . . If he could not by fair and gentle speech induce them unto his opinions, yet he should use no kind of violence and refrain from displeasant and seditious words.' This was not, alas, portable wisdom; More would punish religious dissent not only with 'displeasant' words, but with state violence, and would come to say that he would rather not have written *Utopia* than see one heretic prosper.

Utopia is Saturnalian. It satirically turns custom upside down, so that in our own world we see the pompous altitude of custom, in its arbitrariness. The inhabitants of Utopia, for instance, make their meanest objects out of gold and silver, and give precious gems to their children as toys. In a beautiful jest, More writes that ambassadors, unaware of Utopian customs, once arrived at the island finely dressed in gold chains. The islanders took the visitors to be slaves, and assumed that their simply dressed servants were the actual emissaries. This kind of inversion is the rocker-switch of all moral satire; it is there in

3

Lucian, in Montaigne's *Utopia*-like essay 'On Cannibals', and in Swift. In Lucian's *Menippus*, which More translated, the hero travels to Hades to find that death has undone all the pointless hierarchies of life: Philip of Macedon is stitching rotten sandals to earn money, Xerxes is begging, and so on. But the point of Lucian's lesson is made clear earlier on, when Menippus tells us that *on earth* things have already become sadly inverted: 'On observation I found these same people practising the very opposite of what they preached. I saw those who advocated despising money clinging to it tooth and nail . . . and those who would have us reject fame doing and saying everything for just that, and again pretty well all of them speaking out against pleasure, but in private clinging to it alone.' In this light, Hades corrects these inversions by reinverting them, and in the same way, the island of Utopia is the comic inversion of the uncomic inversion of rectitude we practise in life. Accordingly, Utopia is not an ideal society so much as a comic one. More did not intend us to live in Utopia, so much as to be logically mocked by it: the Shakespearean Fool is the near equivalent.

It is difficult to reconcile the author of *Utopia* with the heretic-hunter of the mid-1520s, who personally broke into Lutherans' homes and sent men to the stake. It is true that Luther's challenge, from 1519 onwards, and Henry's proposed divorce, menaced More with visions of schism, and that the literal defence of the realm became More's necessary objective as Lord Chancellor. (He likened the fight against heretics to the fight against the Ottoman Empire.) But certainly, the shift from Utopian to prosecutor, in the space of ten years, is a bewildering one. Perhaps we should read *Utopia*, despite its play, more tragically – as not only Lucianic satire, but as a darkly ironic vision of the impossible. The Utopians are pagans, and thus live without knowledge of original sin. It is impossible, so More would have thought, for Christians to get back to this Eden, and indeed we should not attempt to, because we have Christ's plan to save us, not Utopia's. Yet what would a world without the *need* of Christ's rescue look like? Perhaps it would resemble

Utopia. The tiniest flickering of a tragic blasphemy, a yearning to be other than we are, is what enriches *Utopia* and gives it its air of mournful surmise. Whatever the explanation, the spirit of *Utopia*, whether comic or tragic, was left behind by More. At times, he seems to have known exactly what lay ahead. In his *History of King Richard III* (1513), he wrote that 'kings' games . . . were stage plays, and for the more part played upon scaffolds.' The 'More part', indeed. At other times, only we, in the harness of retrospect, can see how the ironies of this life buckle. Who could have invented, for instance, the irony of a line which blares at the reader from More's *Responsio ad Lutherum*, a tract written against Luther and in support of Henry VIII's own anti-Lutheran treatise, *An Assertion of the Seven Sacraments*? The sentence issues triumphantly from More as he traps Luther in argument: 'the King has you cornered.' As the 1520s progress, the dance of king and subject becomes emblematic, almost stagy. We watch as More and Henry circle around each other, exuding deadly perfumes: on the first day of January 1532, More presented Henry 'with a walking stick inlaid in gold leaf and in turn he was given a great golden bowl'. (The stick would strike, and the bowl would break.) And the final months are deeply moving; the loyal public servant, confined in the Tower for seven months, now selflessly bearded and long-haired, the body dying but also unconstrainedly living, become something natural. More was returning to spiritual childishness; his last words to his daughter are especially lovely: 'God maketh me a wanton, and setteth me on His lap and dandleth me.'

The darker More eclipses the saint, however. More was drawn into the defence of the Catholic realm early in the 1520s, while still a royal counsellor. He wrote the *Responsio ad Lutherum* in 1523, and from then until his death in 1535, the battle against reform was his obsession. In 1526, Tyndale published his pocket-sized English translation of the New Testament. Heretical books were being imported from the continent. An English tendency towards anti-clericalism seemed in danger of fattening into the grossest Lutheranism and rebelliousness. Thomas More struck. A series of vicious arguments and counter-arguments streamed from his pen. Tyndale was 'the beste', and Luther and his wife were 'Friar Tuck and Maid Marion'. Unlike the twilit *Utopia*, these were written not in Latin but in brazen English: the *Dialogue Concerning Heresies* in 1528, *The Supplication of Souls* in 1529, the massive *Confutation of Tyndale's Answer* in 1532 and 1533, among whose half-million words can be found More's promise that if anyone translate into English *In Praise of Folly,* or works 'that I have myself written', he would burn them with his own hands 'rather than folk would . . . take any harm of them, seeing them likely in these days to do'.

As Lord Chancellor, which he became in October 1529, More, though a layman, was soon the Church's most eager agent. With the help of John Stokesley, the Bishop of London, More personally broke into the houses of suspected heretics, arresting them on the spot and sometimes interrogating them in his own home. He imprisoned one man in the porter's lodge of his house, and had him put in the stocks. He raided the home of a businessman called John Petyt who was suspected of financing Tyndale; Petyt died in the Tower. Six rebellious Oxford students were kept for months in a fish cellar; three of them died in prison. More was now a spiritual detective, a policeman in a hairshirt, engaged in 'what would now be called surveillance and entrapment among the leather-sellers, tailors, fishmongers and drapers of London'. Six protesters were burned under More's chancellorship, and perhaps forty were imprisoned. Ackroyd is admirably detailed about these activities. But he resides in the sympathetic assumption that 'it might be argued that his severe stance was a reaction to the menaces of the period', and so he barely examines the compromised intellectual foundations of More's defence, and too often treats the anti-heretical tracts as just the grapes of heady sixteenth-century rhetoric.

Luther wanted to reorient theological certainty so that it could be grounded in Scripture. He regarded many of the practices of the Church as no more than human inventions, now subject to gross abuse by clergy and laypeople alike. For example, Luther felt that the Eucharist, which commemorates Christ's last supper, had become a superstition. Early sixteenth-century worshippers consumed the Host (the communion bread) only once or twice a year. For the rest of the time, it was sufficient simply to gaze on the Host as the priest elevated it above his head, at daily or weekly masses. To look upon the Host sufficed because the bread had become a crude visual proof of Christ's existence; it *was* the body of Christ, and diligent worshippers might boast that 'I see my Maker once a day.' This was one of the Church sacraments that Luther attacked. He felt that a partial biblical truth had been humanly corrupted. He could find no evidence in the New Testament for the doctrine of the transubstantiation. He concluded that people only believed such a thing because the Church told them to. Instead, Luther saw this sacrament as a divine promise, a symbol rather than a proof. Elsewhere in the Church, Luther found similar reifications of the spiritual. More had been in favour of reform as a young man. But time was now drawing in. Reform was not the same in the age of Luther as in the age of Erasmus. More truly believed that Luther presaged the arrival of the Anti-Christ; Suleiman the Magnificent and the Ottoman hordes were grazing the edges of Europe. The King's divorce threatened the unity of the Church. Now the heretics had to be crushed. More's essential defence was traditional. In the *Responsio* (1523), he used Augustine's argument that the Church, and not only Scripture, has authority. We accept the Gospels themselves only because the Church tells us to; why then, he complained to Luther, is it not 'reasonable to believe certain truths only on the authority of the Church'? More's idea of the Church was like his idea of the customary law, a body of continuous and exercised truths. Like the early Church Fathers, he appealed to 'what has been believed everywhere, always, and by all'. He trusted in the accumulated wisdom of 'the whole corps of Christendom', and it can be fairly said that he died not in blind defence of the sovereignty of the Pope, but in reasoned defence of the primacy of the common Church and its ancient head. Yet into this traditional argument he squeezed tinctures of rage and untruth. Ackroyd largely ignores this, providing extracts from More's works which are too small to allow proper judgment. In fact, More was unscrupulous, greasy, quibblingly legalistic. In the *Dialogue Concerning Heresies* he blamed the sack of Rome, and the attendant atrocities, on Luther's followers. Ackroyd repeats this, forgetting to mention that Rome was in fact taken by mercenaries of the Catholic emperor Charles V. More was astonishingly disingenuous. Throughout the late 1520s, he claimed that anticlericalism was identical with heresy, when he, an early anticlerical, knew this to be untrue. In reply to one Simon Fish, who had argued that England's travails had to do with the greed and idleness of the clergy, More claimed that things were much the same in the country as they had always been, and then appealed to Henry VIII's vanity as defender of the faith to stamp out the unpatriotic anticlerical heretics. When More was not lying, he was dissembling. Two examples will be sufficient. (Neither is quoted by Ackroyd.) In the *Dialogue Concerning Heresies*, More attempted to answer the charge of the reformers that it was not Christian for the Church to burn heretics. The Church did not burn people, replied More; the state burned them. This was strictly true, because the ecclesiastical courts tried heretics and the state courts sentenced them. But More's language is disingenuous. The Church, he writes, would never want to kill anyone. 'It is not the clergy that laboreth to have them punished to death.' The 'spiritual law' is 'good, reasonable, piteous, and charitable, and nothing desiring the death of any therein'. The Church asks the heretic to repent; if he does not, the Church excommunicates him, at which point 'the clergy giveth knowledge to the temporalty, not exhorting the prince, or any man else, either, to kill him or to punish him.' The Church does not urge anyone to punish the heretic; it 'leaveth him to the secular hand, and forsaketh him . . .'

Ackroyd remarks at one point, fairly perhaps, that More was 'no different from most of his contemporaries' in supporting burning. But More's wriggling in this passage is unseemly. First, if he is so keen to absolve the Church of this punishment, then he cannot hold the practice in very high moral esteem, and it is simply legalistic to argue that it ceases to be repulsive once the state performs it. But moreover, More knew perfectly well that though formally Church and state dealt separately with the heretic, practically both sides worked together. He knew this because this was his own working experience. The Church, said More, never 'exhorted' a prince to burn anyone. Perhaps not in so many words, except that the Church performed the equivalent of exhortation every time it excommunicated and 'forsook' heretics. (Three hundred years later, in *The Idea of a University* [1852], Cardinal Newman would employ a similar argument, that the Spanish Inquisition 'in no proper sense belonged to the Church. It was simply and entirely a State institution . . .') And it should be remembered that the defender of the Church in this passage was not a clergyman but a politician – a representative of the very 'temporalty' to which he neutrally transfers the blame of burning. This is More the lawyer, truthful only in letter. It is the same More who told Thomas Cromwell in 1534 that he had 'written nothing' since 1527 against the King's divorce; again, precisely true perhaps, except that More was one of the leaders, behind the scenes, of Catherine of Aragon's faction. Ackroyd rather meaninglessly comments, on More's duplicity at court, that it was 'a difficult as well as an ambiguous role and More was the only man in the kingdom who could have played it'. But a more cold-eyed scholar, Alistair Fox, has written that it 'gives evidence of a political endeavour in More so subtle and devious as to set not only Machiavelli, but also Richard III and Iago to school.'

When More could not win an argument, he slid into puerility. For example, in his tract *The Supplication of Souls* (1529), More tries to beat the reformers ('this lewd sect') with a flurry of numbers: 'if ye consider how late this lewd sect began . . .

and how few always' they have been, 'and then if ye consider on the other side how full and whole the great corps of all Christian countries'. And not only numbers are on our side, continues More, but quality: 'match them man for man, then have we . . . Saint Austin against Friar Luther, Saint Jerome against Friar Lambert, Saint Ambrose against Friar Huskin, Saint Gregory against priest Pomerane, Saint Chrysostom against Tyndale.' If these heretics include their wives in the battle, then they might seem to have an advantage; but we have 'blessed women against these friars' wives'. For we have 'Saint Anastasia against Friar Luther's wife, Saint Hildergaarde against Friar Huskin's wife . . .', and so on.

Ackroyd reads the tracts as rhetorical dressage rather than as doctrinal ordnance. For him, More is a Londoner, a man of the people defending popular tradition, who used vernacular English and earthy taunts to defeat his opponents. Of one tract, he writes warmly: 'he uses the language of London as a way of refuting the more impersonal objections of his opponent.' Of the *Dialogue*, he comments: 'The whole theme and purpose of his *Dialogue Concerning Heresies* had been to celebrate that common culture which was under threat.' And near the end of his book, he provides us with a mournful reminder of that 'common culture' which was about to pass: 'a time, soon to come, when there would be no more lights and images, no more pilgrimages and processions, no guild plays and no ringing for the dead, no maypoles or Masses or holy water, no birch at midsummer and no roses at Corpus Christi.'

This is very hazy. To begin with, in what sense was More a man of the people? His very defence of Catholicism rested on the rejection, in part, of the politics of the people. The so-called new humanism had always espoused a somewhat stoppered radicalism, in which elites reformed elites. Luther, by contrast, wanted to aerate the elite. Erasmus complained to Justus Jonus in 1521 that Luther 'is making even cobblers aware of things which used to be discussed only amongst the learned, as mysteries and forbidden knowledge . . . above all I would urge that one avoid disorder.' Like Erasmus, the More of the 1520s and 1530s was against disorder. In 1533, in his *Apology*, he wrote that it would be better to have no reform at all, even 'though the change might be to the better', if it involved public complaint against the law. Although, in 1528, he wrote in favour of translating the Bible into English, by 1530 he had decided against it. And even in 1528, in the *Dialogue*, he warned that an English Bible must not get into the wrong hands. It is especially dangerous when 'men unlearned . . . ensearch and dispute the secret mysteries of Scripture'. Things should be as they were in the Book of Exodus, writes More, when Moses ascended Mount Sinai and talked to God. The people, unlike Moses, 'ought to be content to tarry beneath, and meddle none higher than is meet for them'. The priest on the hill, privy to mysteries, and the people beneath, coddled in obscurity – there might be no better image of the old Catholic curtain, the antique Scholastic protectorate.

On one issue, More was right: Luther's belief that faith alone, without good works, justified one in the eyes of God, was a cruelty that not only demanded an inhuman mental loyalty, but which, brought to its logical end, abolished the purpose of Christian conduct on earth. Yet because More had so sternly set himself against the essential plea of Lutheranism, he could never see that Luther's type of fideism did not arrive out of nothing, but owed its hard extremity to the Church's superstitions of corporeality. Luther was opposing grey with white, in overreaction. For although the Reformation did indeed end a common calendar of feast-days and processions, as Ackroyd charges, the religious share of that calendar had become a bullied almanac of rote and rite, the codification of mass ignorance. The evil lay not just in the pagan animism of certain corruptions – of believing that a pardon from the Pope might speed a soul from purgatory to heaven, or that the sprinkle of holy water, like that of salt, banished demons. It lay in the systematic withdrawal of Scripture from the people: psalms had been reduced to one or two verse extracts; at the Eucharist, the canticles had been starved to only one; priests were preaching fewer sermons; the amount of Scripture read publicly was in decline. More would not admit this. He refused to examine the proposition that if the Church acts merely humanly, then its authority is merely human, not divine. Despite the thousands of words he wrote against Luther, he turned his eyes from the awful challenge of Luther, which was to move God back from the visible while simultaneously expanding our invisible encounter with God. It was this challenge of absence, an admittedly cold challenge, which received its formal English statement when Latimer, in 1536, ordained that religious images were 'only to represent things absent'. But More also turned his eyes from the political petition of the reformers, which was that the Church, again in Latimer's words, had 'deluded the people'. (The 1549 book of Common Prayer stated, as one of its expressed aims, the edification of the people.)

Yet the Protestant case against More, for all its power, is too easily made in the late twentieth century, and represents a rather blank triumph. One should avoid sounding like such propagandists of the Renaissance as Jacob Burckhardt, who writes, in *The Civilization of the Renaissance in Italy:* 'That religion should again become an affair of the individual and of his own personal feeling was inevitable when the Church became corrupt in doctrine and tyrannous in practice, and is a proof that the European mind was still alive.' One will make Protestantism sound like a modern secret that More was simply too old to catch, and thus make More a doomed historical villain, because he could not have acted differently – or a hero, if one is approaching this inevitability from the side of Peter Ackroyd's velvet reaction. This idea of More's entrapment by history or by the inevitable forward march of 'the European mind' must then represent the point at which Catholic admiration joins hands both with Protestant excoriation and with modern, secular admiration. Indeed, it represents the point at which Protestant criticism of More becomes identical with Protestant admiration.

For if More is doomed, then he is always something of a hero, from any vantage.

But More could have acted differently, and it is on this presumption that a secular case against him should be made. Yet what does it mean to say that he could have acted differently? What are these belated assizes that could possibly convict More almost five hundred years after the time? Would that not be meaningless? The secular case is not acutely an argument with More the historical actor so much as with the category of sainthood. To argue that Napoleon could have acted differently at Borodino is a meaningless wrestle with a *fait accompli*, and was properly mocked by Tolstoy. But to argue that a saint could have acted differently is always to argue that he *should* have acted differently; it is to argue with the Church that blesses his actions as deeds outside history and beyond the *fait accompli*. The Catholic claim for More as a saint is transhistorical and universal; More was saintly then, and is saintly now and for all time; for the Church, it is calendrically trivial that More happened to be canonized only in 1935. The secular argument against More can only match the religious argument for More if it too deploys transhistorical and universal categories. The Church says, in effect: this is how More should have acted, and we are well pleased with him, and we can pronounce this blessing at any moment in providential history because our values are timeless; the secularist must parry: this is not how he should have acted, and we must be able to say this at any moment in profane history because the only ground on which we can denounce More is on the ground that he betrayed certain timeless and universal ideals of secular human conduct. That is to say, the religious defence of More issues from one belief-system, and the secular argument against issues from another, and these two systems of thought are still at war. There is hardly any need to describe these two systems; a detail is offered by two books which appeared within five years of each other: Cardinal Newman's *Apologia Pro Vita Sua* (1864) and John Stuart Mill's *On Liberty* (1859). Newman's position is hardly different from

More's, three hundred years earlier. Newman argues that the Church should control what is known and discussed, because the Church has final authority over truth. Earlier, Newman wrote in *The Idea of a University* that 'Liberal Knowledge' can be allowed slightly to prosper precisely because religious truth can never be assailed: 'truth never can really be contrary to truth . . . error may flourish for a time, but Truth will prevail in the end.' Mill's essay, which wrestles incessantly with Christianity, argues that truth is only tested, and is actually constituted and proved, by its 'collision with error', and that all opinions must thus be admissible. In a sense, Mill had already 'won' politically at the time of writing, and Newman never had the political power that More possessed. But the struggle between Newman's idea of sanctioned truth and Mill's idea of released error has not finished, and is never finished as long as Christianity, or any other system of sanctioned truth, exists.

The secular argument against More, then, is both premised on the infinity of this battle and is another episode in it. To this end, the secularist is bound to remark that a system of sanctioned truth has three defects germane to a criticism of Thomas More's conduct. First, it tends to deprive people of the means by which they might censure, and then adjust, their own behaviour, because it does not believe in correction by error; it is a circular system – 'if we would solve new questions, it must be by consulting old answers', writes Newman, adding that the notion of new doctrinal knowledge 'is intolerable to Catholic ears'. Second, and flowing from this, if error is neither extended the possibility of occasionally being true, nor allowed to express itself when merely untrue, then a system of sanctioned truth must inevitably produce a category of punishable heresy, a category which might as easily imprison Jesus or Thomas More as Tyndale or Cranmer. Third, sanctioned truth must imply the dominance of the Church's truths over the state's, and the Church's struggle to maintain its authority over the state. These three characteristics of Catholic belief, and not merely More's 'integrity', imprisoned him; just as, three hundred years later, that same circularity mentally imprisoned Cardinal Newman. Later in the *Apologia Pro Vita Sua*, Newman writes icily in defence of sanctioned truth, that there is a correct time for everything, and that sometimes a protester against the Church who might seem to a later age 'a bold champion for the truth and a martyr to free opinion' is in fact 'just one of those persons whom the competent authority ought to silence'. Newman meant people like Luther, of course; but those who believe in the forceful silencing of dissent, as More did, may well be silenced themselves, and we should shed no tears that they have been circularly revenged upon by their own beliefs.

So it is enough for secular criticism to argue that More should have acted differently, and in asserting only this, secular criticism gives birth to itself. It is enough for the secularist to say that there are categories and modes of being which possess a transhistorical and universal status equivalent to sainthood's, and by which it is therefore permissible to judge More's actions. This is surely what Mill meant, though he was not discussing More, when he wrote: 'There is a different type of human excellence from the Calvinistic; a conception of humanity as having its nature bestowed on it for other purposes than merely to be abnegated. "Pagan self-assertion" is one of the elements of human worth, as well as "Christian' self-denial". There is a Greek ideal of self-development, which the Platonic and Christian ideal of self-government blends with, but does not supersede. It may be better to be a John Knox than an Alcibiades, but it is better to be a Pericles than either . . .' We do not have to be as sublimely wild as Nietzsche (though it is tempting), and condemn More's obedience to God as the typical product of 'slave-morality'. We can simply observe that in all of history other men have believed as strongly as More in God or in gods without sending people of differing opinions to the stake. More was nothing like his supposed example, the gently latitudinarian Cicero, for instance: Cicero's philosophical and religious dialogues (as opposed to his legal and political speeches, of course) often read as if he delighted in being contradicted, while More's are spittingly conclusive. Closer to More, Erasmus, though slippery and haughty and decidedly anti-Lutheran, was not touched with More's love of power, and shrank from his legalistic bombardments. Erasmus's 'humane middle ground', writes Euan Cameron in *The European Reformation*, 'opposed alike to scholastic obscurities, vulgar superstitions, protestant dogmatics, and popular disorder, was steadily deserted by both sides'. On one of those sides was Sir Thomas More, cruel in punishment, evasive in argument, lusty for power, and repressive in politics. He betrayed Christianity when he led it so violently into court politics, and he betrayed politics when he surrendered it so meekly to the defence of Catholicism. Above all, he betrayed his humanity when he surrendered it to the alarms of God.

Jane Austen's Heroic Consciousness

Jane Austen founded character and caricature at the same time – which is the essentially satirical, essentially English approach to fictional character. From her, Dickens learned that characters can survive on one large attribute and still be fat with life. From her, Forster learned that characters do not have to change to be real; they must merely reveal more of their stable essence as the novel progresses. Yet at the same time, the first stirrings of what would become Woolf's stream-of-consciousness are found in Austen – she invented a new, rapid semaphore for signalling a person's thought as it is happening. It is this innovation, the discovery of how to represent the brokenness of the mind's communication with itself, that constitutes her radicalism.

Jane Austen was a ferocious innovator, and her innovations were largely complete by the time she was twenty-four. This tells us something about the elusive mixture of application and instinct in her writing life. On the one hand, she shocked fiction forward from Samuel Richardson's epistolary mode; on the other, she left behind barely a word about her idea of fiction, of aesthetics, or of religion. We have only 160 letters by her, and most of them are rather tedious: the futile daily plough of seedless social events. But one can tell that she was a natural revolutionary in fiction. Almost as soon as she started writing squibs and family sketches as a teenager, she began to find new ways of representing fictional characters. These young experiments would soon bear fruit, as Austen began to create the room of heroines for which she is admired and loved.

Austen's heroines do not change in the modern sense, because they do not really discover things about themselves. They discover cognitive novelties; they probe for rectitude. As the novel moves forwards, certain veils are pierced and obstacles removed, so that the heroine can see the world more clearly. In the course of that process, more and more of the heroine's stable essence is revealed to us. Thus plot is inherently rational and problem-solving in Austen ('rational' was one of Austen's favourite words, and is used often by her heroines). The habitual stance of the Austen heroine is that of the reader, one who reads and reflects upon the material of the novel before her, and, when all that material is complete at the end of the novel, makes her decision. It is probably for this reason that readers so adore Austen's heroines – not because they are especially real or 'rounded', but because, like us, they are readers of the novel in question, and *thus on our side*. Elinor Dashwood in *Sense and Sensibility*, like Fanny Price in *Mansfield Park*, craves 'the relief of quiet reflection'. Elinor describes this process of reflection several times in *Sense and Sensibility*. When she reappraises Willoughby, she is 'resolved not only upon gaining every new light as to his character which her own observation or the intelligence of others could give her, but likewise upon watching his behaviour to her sister with such zealous attention, as to ascertain what he was and what he meant . . .' Elizabeth Bennet, at the end of *Pride and Prejudice*, finally sees Darcy as he really is, not as she mistook him – that is her triumph; she does not learn anything really decisive about herself. She is, perhaps, less proud and judgmental, but she has hardly transformed herself. Likewise Fanny Price. Fanny is, in some ways, a caricature of goodness, unchangeably good. The novel, showing its origins in stage-conventions (despite the fact that it is a book that appears to censure the stage), lays a stable characterological foundation within its first fifteen pages, and never deviates from it: Mrs Norris appears, and is wicked and garrulous; Lady Catherine de Burgh enters, and takes up the posture she will maintain for the rest of the book, 'doing some long piece of needlework, of little use and no beauty, thinking more of her rug than her children, but very indulgent to the latter, when it did not put herself to inconvenience'; and Fanny Price will not deviate, either, from Edmund's early assessment: he is 'convinced of her having an affectionate heart, and a strong desire of doing right'.

Emma Woodhouse is the nearest Austen came to creating a character who discovers something about herself. Like Elizabeth Bennet, she must rationally solve a problem – which is the problem of who is right for whom, and ultimately, who is right for her – and the novel allows her to conduct several disastrous experiments. To that extent, she learns, at the end of the novel, what we have always known about her, that she is blind, headstrong, and foolish. But she too is essentially stable, for she is incorrigible. Indeed, is not the incorrigibility of Austen's heroines what makes them so appealing? Do we not imagine that Emma will continue to act foolishly in the future, even with Mr Knightley by her side? One of the reasons that we know from the beginning of the novel that Emma is essentially good but wilful (as opposed to bad and hapless) is that we sense that Mr Knightley loves her, and we feel that Mr Knightley is a repository of the novel's highest values. A fairy-tale cradle protects Emma from real harm. A comparison may be made with a modern heroine, Isabel Archer in *The Portrait of a Lady*. Ralph Touchett is Isabel's higher understanding, her Mr Knightley. Yet in James's tragic, psychological vision, Ralph cannot save Isabel from herself. She must make mistakes for herself. Emma, by contrast, makes mistakes on behalf of others; for herself, she makes the right choice, and chooses Mr Knightley. In an early conversation, Mrs Weston says to Mr Knightley that Emma 'will never lead any one really wrong'. This observation the novel is about to prove untrue. But in the same conversation Mrs Weston says that 'she will make no lasting blunder', which is quite correct. Within this capsule, Emma's subjectivity rides.

Austen's heroines do not discover, then, what is best in themselves; they discover what is best *for* themselves and for others. Austen's work is not therapeutic but hermeneutic. As it happens, hermeneutic study was given its fullest development at this time by Friedrich Schleiermacher, the German theologian. But we know from contemporary texts that the words 'hermeneutical' and 'hermeneutics' were in wide currency in English long before Schleiermacher, and that they were applied to people as often as to the study of texts. Someone who understood other people, who attended to their secret meanings, who read people properly, might be called hermeneutical. Schleiermacher himself stressed repeatedly that hermeneutics could be applied to ordinary conversation as well as to the Scriptures. In 1829, in his Academy Address 'On the Concept of Hermeneutics', he referred to the art of reading 'significant conversations', and added: 'Who could move in the company of exceptionally gifted persons without endeavouring to hear "between" their words, just as we read between the lines of original and tightly written books? Who does not try in a meaningful conversation, which may in certain respects be an important act, to lift out its main points, to try to grasp its internal coherence, to pursue all its subtle intimations further?' This is what the Austen heroine does. Even the wild and undisciplined Emma is such a reader. When Mr Knightley finally proposes to Emma, Austen writes: 'While he spoke, Emma's mind was most busy, and, with all the wonderful velocity of thought, had been able – and yet without losing a word – to catch and comprehend the exact truth of the whole.'

This is the hermeneutic task of the Austen heroine, to which is added a distinctly Protestant, or even Evangelical, bent. For Austen's heroines also read themselves, and carry their spirit inside them. Henry Crawford asks Fanny, in *Mansfield Park,* for advice, and she replies: 'We have all a better guide in ourselves, if we would attend to it, than any other person can be.' Our inwardness is our God and our guide; we apply to it for aid. The inwardness of Austen's heroines is precisely what makes them heroic in the novels. This is measurable, because Austen maintains a hierarchy of consciousness: the people who matter think inwardly, and everyone else speaks. Or rather: the heroines speak to themselves, and everyone else speaks to each other. The heroines are the only characters whose inner thought is represented. And this speaking to oneself is often a secret conversation, which Austen almost invented a new technique, a precursor of modernist stream-of-consciousness, to represent. We can watch the development of this technique. Her first novel, *Sense and Sensibility* (1811), has almost none of this kind of stream-of-consciousness. *Sense and Sensibility* abounds in passages like this one, in which Austen's notation of excited thought seems to strain to outgrow itself, yet which stays inside conventional narrated thought: 'What felt Elinor at that moment? Astonishment, that would have been as painful as it was strong, had not an immediate disbelief of the assertion attended it. She turned towards Lucy in silent amazement, unable to divine the reason or object of such a declaration, and though her complexion varied, she stood firm in incredulity and felt no danger of an hysterical fit, or a swoon.' Lucy has just told Elinor that she is engaged to Robert Ferrars's brother, and Elinor is revolving this shock in her mind. But Austen stays outside Elinor, noting her change of colour, and calming the reader, as it were, with the promise that Elinor will not become hysterical. The reference to an external change – a change of colour – is significant, for it suggests that Austen is using the idea of the stage, that a character will physically register a shock, on the outside. Austen's point, of course, is that Elinor is not like one of these stage-actors; Elinor is too calm to register agitation as anything more than an almost invisible change of colour. She thinks 'in silent amazement', and is therefore inaccessible to us. ('What felt Elinor at that moment?') Elinor, in this sense, anticipates the later Austen heroines: from an almost invisible blush, it is only a small increment for the novelist into the very mind of a character. Nevertheless, at this moment in Austen's development, we cannot enter Elinor's mind; her 'silent amazement' is actually silent.

Pride and Prejudice (1813) allowed Austen to burst into the interior of her heroine, Elizabeth Bennet. But she rations a gradual increase in the reader's access. At first, Elizabeth resembles Elinor; she does not speak to herself, except in Austen's indirect report. Slowly, her intensity deepens, and Austen's registration of Elizabeth's self-conversation begins to gather its mass. When she first hears that Darcy has separated Bingley and Jane, she goes to her room, where 'she could think without interruption of all that she had heard'. Here, Austen begins to expand the range of Elizabeth's mental revolutions, and we witness Elizabeth 'exclaiming' to herself bitterly about how poorly Jane has been used: 'All liveliness and goodness as she is! Her understanding excellent, her mind improved, and her manners captivating.' But this self-exclamation soon ends, the agitation having brought on a headache (a headache, tears, or sleep, will often end the representation of female inwardness in early Austen). Only twenty pages later, Elizabeth is unbound. Darcy has written to her, and she has taken the letter with her on a walk. She is alone. As she reads it, she is burnt with shame, and her speech to herself is rapidly broken up into different stumbling inroads:

> 'How despicably have I acted!' she cried. – 'I, who have prided myself on my discernment! – I, who have valued myself on my abilities! who have often disdained the generous candour of my sister, and gratified my vanity, in useless or blameable distrust. – How humiliating is this discovery! – Yet, how just a humiliation! – Had I been in love, I could not have been more wretchedly blind. But vanity, not love, has been my folly. – . . . Till this moment, I never knew myself.'

This, in essence, is the stage soliloquy. In the course of

Mansfield Park (1814), and *Emma* (1816), Austen uses it with ever greater sophistication, dispensing with quotation marks, and blending the heroine's soliloquy with her own third-person narration, so that she is able to move in and out of a character as she pleases. At the same time, her heroine's mental speech loses the last tinctures of the staginess that still clings to Elizabeth's ('How despicably have I acted!'), becoming looser and more conversational. Fanny Price is seen thinking to herself much earlier in *Mansfield Park* than Elizabeth is seen doing the same in *Pride and Prejudice*; and of course, Emma fills the entire book with her lively self-disputations: *Emma* is one large mental chamber. Where before, Elizabeth had to roam outside to express her thoughts, Emma's thought arises in the most ordinary and domestic settings, among her puffs, powders and billets-doux. Austen novelizes the soliloquy, in effect:

> The hair was curled, and the maid sent away, and Emma sat down to think and be miserable. – It was a wretched business, indeed! – Such an overthrow of everything she had been wishing for! – Such a development of everything most unwelcome! – Such a blow for Harriet! – That was the worst of all. Every part of it brought pain and humiliation, of some sort or other; but, compared with the evil to Harriet, all was light; and she would gladly have submitted to feel yet more mistaken – more in error – more disgraced by mis-judgment, than she actually was, could the effects of her blunders have been confined to herself.

This is immensely supple, Austen marvellously extending what is sometimes called free indirect style, in which the author describes the heroine's thoughts with such sympathetic agitation that the heroine seems to be writing the novel. In free indirect style, though narration is still in the third person, the heroine seems to flood the narration, forcing it onto her side. ('It was a wretched business indeed! – Such an overthrow of everything she had been wishing for!') In her later novels, Austen tends to alternate free indirect style with a first-person stream-of-consciousness. *Mansfield Park* abounds in examples of the latter. Near the end of the book, Fanny, in Portsmouth, receives a letter from Edmund. She is sure that Edmund will marry Mary Crawford:

> As for the main subject of the letter – there was nothing in that to soothe irritation. She was almost vexed into displeasure, and anger, against Edmund. 'There is no good in this delay,' said she. 'Why is not it settled? – He is blinded, and nothing will open his eyes, nothing can, after having had truths before him so long in vain. – He will marry her, and be poor and miserable. God grant that her influence do not make him cease to be respectable!' – She looked over the letter again. ' "So very fond of me!" 'tis nonsense all. She loves nobody but herself and her brother. "Her friends leading her astray for years!" She is quite as likely to have led *them* astray. . . . "The only woman in the world, whom he could ever think of as a wife." I firmly believe it . . . Edmund, you do not know *me*. The families would never be connected, if you did not connect them. Oh! write, write. Finish it at once. Let there be an end of this suspense. Fix, commit, condemn yourself.'

In this superb passage, quite characteristic of the later novels, Austen combines third person narration ('She looked over the letter again'), first-person soliloquy ('Edmund, you do not know *me*'), and scraps from Edmund's letter which are not quoted in first-person, but which Austen turns into free indirect style in order to hurry the effect of the passage, and to stamp on the reader the sense of *Fanny's* thought, of *Fanny* having taken and converted Edmund's words into her own. As the paragraph develops, so third-person narration falls away, and we entirely enter Fanny's mind. This writing, moving between different modes, hurriedly capturing the very stammer of ratiocination, makes Austen a more radical novelist than, say, Flaubert.

Flaubert never allows Emma Bovary quite such a broken self-conversation. Unlike the smoothly controlling Flaubert, Austen wants to capture the difficulty of solitary thought, and in this her modernity lies.

This thought is a kind of concealment in all of Austen's novels except in the free and open *Emma*. Austen's heroines withdraw, or wait until visitors have departed, or go on walks, in order to think. (The two enormous modern changes that are found in Woolf and Joyce are that a character need go nowhere particular to think; and that thought need not have the gravity of emergency or agitation in order to earn its place. Thought is as natural as narration, and has in fact become narration.) Austen's heroines are separate, different from everyone else in the novels by virtue of their ability to speak to themselves. In *Mansfield Park* Mary Crawford asks Edmund if the young Fanny is 'out, or is she not?' Mary means presentable, socially adult, and Edmund replies that his cousin is an adult, 'but the outs and not outs are beyond me.' Mary comments, reprovingly, that 'it is much worse to have girls *not out*, give themselves the same airs and take the same liberties, as if they were . . .' Mary decides that Fanny is '*not out*', and seems obscurely irritated by the challenge that Fanny's being 'not out' represents. Austen no doubt implies another kind of 'out' or 'in', the 'out' of outwardness and the 'in' of inwardness. We might think of Austen's heroines, despite their vivacity, as always 'in', insofar as they are the only characters who hoard their thought, and who are seen to do so.

It is through inwardness that we get to know a character. Emma complains (to herself) that Jane Fairfax is 'so cold, so cautious! There was no getting at her real opinion. Wrapt up in a cloak of politeness, she seemed suspiciously reserved.' If Jane Fairfax seems reserved to us, as well as to Emma, it is because Austen never shows her speaking to herself. We feel we cannot 'get at her real opinion', because we do not witness her thinking it. But we are always close to Emma's real opinion, even if it is the wrong one. In this sense, Emma's reality is what is most right about her. We delight in the rightness of her reality even when she is wrong. When one says, then, that Austen's heroines are 'in', it is not that they are like Jane Fairfax, who seems lost to herself; rather that they are real to themselves, and thus to us. And they are heroines *because* of this quality of being 'in'. Austen refers to Emma as being in 'mental soliloquy', and while Austen's heroines are soliloquists, the obviously bad people in the novels are monologists, people who speak *at* others. Mr Collins, Mrs Norris, Miss Bates, Mrs Elton (who 'only wanted to be talking herself', writes Austen), all speak as if on stage, to an audience. Austen's heroines, by contrast, speak to themselves, like people in a novel. Her heroines belong to the novel; her villains belong to the stage.

Her heroines belong to the novel; and indeed, they act not only like readers, but like novelists, too. Like novelists, her heroines enable people to speak through them, they are arrangers and conduits of others' feelings. Anne Elliot in *Persuasion* (1818) dislikes, for instance, that the Musgroves speak to each other through her, dislikes 'being treated with too much confidence by all parties, and being too much in the secret complaints of each house'. Like novelists, the heroines have to retreat to their study, to reflect, as it were, on their material, as if they were both writing and reading the material that the novel has presented them with. This is Anne Elliot's first instinct at the end of *Persuasion*, when she has won Wentworth: 'Anne went home to think over all that she had heard.' All of Austen's heroines retreat to a room of their own, often prompted by the intimacy of a letter (which functions a little like the written contract that allows female subjectivity). Like novelists, her heroines have the capacity of memory, while the rest of the characters have only 'pasts'. It is the heroines who must learn about these pasts, who must enquire into the past. When they are gregarious, these heroines have the novelist's genius for negative capability, the capacity to find justice in the other side, to act a role. Emma catches herself doing this in an argument with Mr Knightley: 'to her great amusement, [she] perceived that she was taking the other side of the question from her real opinion, and making use of Mrs Weston's arguments against herself.'

Mansfield Park makes perhaps the strongest case for the novel, and for the heroine's novelist-like powers. When the household at Mansfield Park decides to stage a play in the house (it is Kotzebue's *Das Kind der Liebe*, translated by Mrs Inchbald as *Lovers' Vows*), Fanny Price objects to the impropriety, in particular to the prospect of the ladies of the house acting in compromising roles with the gentlemen of the house. Fanny's objection, which appears to be supported by Austen and by the thrust of the entire novel, seems priggish, and has occasioned much comment, because Austen and her family used happily to stage, as children, amateur dramatics. But Austen's objection might be that the play does not act like a novel. Recall that Fanny's first response to the idea is to withdraw with the text of the play and read it like a novel. Though Austen does not say so, there is a sense in which the play is improper because, by forcing people to act in highly charged emotional situations, it might precipitate actual emotional situations, off stage, that should remain latent. In other words, the stage artificially speeds up dilemmas and relationships. Things ought to go at a novel's pace (and *Mansfield Park* is a lengthy, spacious novel) and not at the pace of two melodramatic hours on stage. Though we don't know it yet, Fanny is right. The play, which intimately throws together Henry Crawford and Maria Bertram (who is already engaged to her foolish neighbour, Rushworth), accelerates their flirtation: later in the book, Henry elopes with Maria, now married to the unfortunate Rushworth.

Austen's fiction is either celebrated or attacked for being conservative; but it is, of course, a strenuous argument on behalf of the deserving poor – deserving not because of gentility but because of goodness. Austen's ideal world, glimpsed in the puff of harmony that is exhaled at the end of her novels when the heroine gets her husband, would be an ethical meritocracy, in which the best dowry the heroine can bring to her match is her goodness. These best virtues are earned, not bestowed, and are

internal. Austen's heroines are heroic because of their inwardness. Think of Anne Elliot at the end of *Persuasion*. She thinks
that Captain Wentworth 'must love her', and she goes around
the room, looking at her father and sister and Lady Russell, and
feels inclined 'to pity every one, as being less happy than
herself. . . Her happiness was from within.' Now Anne is in
love, and is pitying those who are not, just as Levin does in
Anna Karenina when he secures Kitty. But Austen's argument is
stronger than that. Tolstoy describes Levin's happiness as a
temporary advantage: he is in love, it is a gorgeous spasm of
early love, it will pass. It is a sublime hallucination, really. But
the whole of *Persuasion* – indeed, the whole of Austen's oeuvre
– suggests that Anne will always be happier than those around
her. Anne's horrible father and sister might, conceivably, fall in
love, but Anne will still be happier than they will be. And why?
Because her happiness is 'from within' and the others do not
exist 'within'. They are 'out'. She is a heroine.

It is consciousness that makes one happy; consciousness is
intelligence, and consciousness is inwardness. Even when the
agitation of consciousness is not happy, it is always welcome, it
is always good – and *a* good. Elizabeth Bennet likes to 'indulge
in all the delight of unpleasant recollections'. I suspect that Jane
Austen, so private, so enigmatic and contradictory, went
through life as if she were the possessor of a clandestine
happiness. Like her heroines, she saw things more clearly than
other people and therefore pitied their cloudiness.

The All and the If: God and metaphor in Melville

When it comes to language, all writers want to be billionaires. All long to possess so many words that using them is a fat charity. To be utterly free in language, to be absolute commander of what you do not own – this is the greatest desire of any writer. Even the deliberate paupers of style – Hemingway, Pavese, late Beckett – have their smothered longings for riches, and make their reductions seem like bankruptcy after wealth rather than fraud before it: Pavese translated *Moby-Dick* into Italian. Realists may protest that it is life, not words, that draws them as writers: yet language at rush hour is like a busy city. Language is infinite, but it is also a system, and so it tempts us with the fantasy that it is closed, like a currency or an orchestra. What writer does not dream of touching every word in the lexicon once?

In *Moby-Dick*, Herman Melville nearly touched every word once, or so it seems. Language is pressed and consoled in that book with Shakespearean agility. No other nineteenth-century novelist writing in English lived in the city of words that Melville lived in; they were suburbanites by comparison. No other novelist of that age could swim in the poetry of 'the warmly cool, clear, ringing, perfumed, overflowing, redundant days . . .' And so, despite the usual biographical lamentations, despite our knowledge that *Moby-Dick* went largely unappreciated, that in 1876 only two copies of the novel were bought in the United States; that in 1887 it went out of print with a total sale of 3,180 copies; that these and other neglects narrowed Melville into bitterness and savage daily obedience as a New York customs inspector – despite this, one says lucky Melville, not poor Melville. For in writing *Moby-Dick,* Melville wrote the novel that is every writer's dream of freedom. It is as if he painted a patch of sky for the imprisoned.

In most of the available biographies, Melville emerges as a very thick shadow. Partly this is because biographers obscure Melville with detail. Hershel Parker, Melville's best and most thorough chronicler, is absolutely superstitious about facts, and throws them about like salt, apparently hoping that they will drive out the devil of interpretation. All the moments in Melville's early life which might bear a little pressure – his increasing scepticism towards his inherited religion, his joyous discovery of radical metaphysics (an adventure that can be plotted as easily as Melville's first sea-voyage), his growing infatuation with metaphor, an obsession which bursts into the love-affair of *Moby-Dick* – are rubbed back into the mild pastels of 'information'. Parker quotes from almost every published contemporary review of Melville's novels – he fills twelve pages with reviews of *Mardi,* Melville's failed third novel – but almost neglects to describe, let alone interpret, the novels themselves. But his biography is at least a fine family chronicle, in which Melville moves and suffers. Parker sees that families wallow in detail – in letters, homes, arrangements, travel. For the Melvill family (as they spelt their name at the time of Herman's birth, in 1819), money was the bulking detail. Herman's parents, of Scots and Dutch origin, were the children of wealth, privilege, and Revolutionary courage. But Alan Melvill, Herman's father, was a deluxe Mr Micawber, apparently importing French dry goods but actually threshing his way through the family inheritance. It is reckoned that, in all, he borrowed $20,000 from his father and from his parents-in-law. In June 1830 he borrowed $2,500 from his father; a month later, another $1,000; in November $500 'to discharge some urgent debts'. Nobody knows what this money satisfied. But when he died, abruptly, in 1832 (he seems to have suffered some kind of mental collapse), he left the family deep in debt. Melville was twelve. He was removed from school and sent to work in a bank at $150 a year.

This was a bleak apprenticeship-to-nothing. Melville was a year and a half at the bank, and after the bank came work in his brother's store as a clerk, schoolteaching, and his decision, at the age of twenty, to join a whaling ship. In Polynesia, Melville jumped ship and spent time with a tribe of cannibals. His first novel, *Typee* (1846), is an autobiographical account of his adventures, and was taken as such by contemporary readers. Melville's unsympathetic view of the activity of Christian missionaries in Polynesia guaranteed hostile reviews from certain papers and journals associated with the Churches. He was, said one review, 'one of Christianity's most ungrateful sons'. A fuse had been lit: such critics would flash at all future examples of religious scepticism in Melville's writing. But the book was an international success. Largely because of the unconventional sexual escapades described by a willing Melville, the young writer became what Parker calls 'a contemporary sex symbol'.

It is in his oddly suave account of Melville's religious development that Parker's biography fails most tremendously. Although Parker deals the occasional detail about Melville's churchgoing (or lack of it: Melville was a fitful attender) or about the stern Calvinism of his mother, Maria Melville, it is not until very late in his story that he considers Melville's difficult relationship to his inherited faith, a relationship which is the absent, sunless centre of all his greatest fiction, poetry and letters. His comments here and there do not suggest a very deep understanding of Melville's blockages. 'Original Sin had not become an outmoded theological conceit in Maria Melville's house, and till his death her second son [Herman] had to resort to that concept, at times, to make sense of the world.' But Melville could not make sense of the world – and partly because the idea of Original Sin had broken his world. In the period just before writing *Moby-Dick*, Melville burrowed in Montaigne's *Essays* and in Pierre Bayle's great, and deeply sceptical, seventeenth-century *Historical and Critical Dictionary*, a book that systematically undermines every rational basis for religious belief, and which concludes that our belief must be re-founded on blind unreason. These authors were useful, breezes Parker, 'for their wordly-wise skepticism, which braced him against the superficial pieties demanded by his time' – which is altogether too worldly-wise an interpretation. Melville, the author who cried out again and again in bitter complaint that 'Silence is the only Voice of our God', did not need to be braced against the pieties of his age, and they demanded nothing from him; he needed to be braced against the flickering horror of his refusal to believe, and then braced against the sour clarity of his refusal entirely to unbelieve.

Melville was born into the Calvinism of the Dutch Reformed Church. At his baptism, his parents were asked if they understood that all children are 'conceived and born in sin, and therefore are subject to all miseries, yea to condemnation itself, yet that they are sanctified in Christ, and therefore as members of his Church ought to be baptised'. It was a theology that stressed a quality of helplessness: we are predestined by God's free grace to be chosen, or not chosen, into the elect, but nothing we can do in the way of 'good works' on earth will make any difference. We can be hired or sacked, but it is no good scheming for promotion. In a typically glittering metaphor, Melville writes in *Pierre* (1852), the disastrous novel that followed *Moby-Dick,* that if our actions are 'foreordained . . . we are Russian serfs to Fate'. Pierre is described as someone who is captured by 'that most true Christian doctrine of the utter nothingness of good works', and is therefore inconsolable when tragedy overwhelms him. For he can do nothing to alter his fate. Melville's writing is entirely shadowed by Calvinism, in the way that Nabokov's ape, when given a sheet of paper, drew the bars of his cage. 'But we that write & print', he joked to Evert Duyckinck in 1850, 'have all our books predestinated – & for me, I shall write such things as the Great Publisher of Mankind ordained ages before he published "The World" – this planet, I mean.' Hawthorne best described Melville's struggle with belief. In 1856, Melville was briefly in England, to visit Hawthorne in Liverpool. The two sat on the beach at Southport, and continued the unequal marriage of the last six years – Hawthorne silent and tidy, Melville messy with metaphysics. At this time, wrote Hawthorne, Melville said that he had 'pretty much made up his mind to be annihilated'. He added: 'It is strange how he persists . . . in wandering to and fro over these deserts, as dismal and monotonous as the sandhills amid which we were sitting. He can neither believe, nor be comfortable in his unbelief; and he is too honest and courageous not to try to do one or the other.'

2

Melville, in his relation to belief, was like the last guest who cannot leave the party; he was always returning to see if he had left his hat and gloves. And yet he did not want to be at the party, either. It is just that he had nowhere else to be, and would rather be with people than be alone. He was tormented by God's inscrutable silence. Moby-Dick himself, who is both God and Devil, flaunts his unhelpful silence as God does to Job: 'Canst thou draw out leviathan with a hook?' In the chapter 'The Tail', Ishmael admits that if he cannot really comprehend the whale's rear, then he can hardly see his face: 'Thou shalt see my back parts, my tail, he seems to say, but my face shall not be seen', an appropriation of the verse in Exodus in which God tells Moses that 'thou shalt see my back parts: but my face shall not be seen.' Likewise, Melville was gripped by the torment of the Pyramids and their emptiness. In 1857, while travelling through Egypt, he visited the Pyramids. In his journal, he writes again and again as if, by repetition, to rid himself of the memory of it: 'It was in these pyramids that was conceived the idea of Jehovah.' In *Moby-Dick*, we are reminded by Melville of the 'pyramidical silence' of the whale. In *Pierre*, he will not leave alone this torment and fingers it like a wounded rosary, which is partly why the book is so impacted. It is in *Pierre* that he writes: 'Silence is the only Voice of our God . . . how can a man get a Voice out of Silence?' He jibes at God: 'doth not Scripture intimate, that He holdeth all of us in the hollow of His hand? – a Hollow, truly!' Perhaps, he proposes, all our searches are like this:

> By vast pains we mine into the pyramids; by horrible gropings we come to the central room; with joy we espy the sarcophagus; but we lift the lid – and no body is there! – appallingly vacant as vast is the soul of a man!

More than this, Melville saw that the world did not look like God's world, and that we fail as God's children, because His standards are cruelly impossible. He has Plotinus Plinlimmon say this in the sermon called 'Chronometricals and Horologicals' in *Pierre*. God keeps one kind of time, says Plinlimmon, and man keeps another, though man is always conscious that he ought to be living his life according to God's time. The difficulty is that, if we really did live in the world according to God's time, we would be thought mad: for this is just what Jesus did. Jesus carried 'Heaven's time in Jerusalem', but the Jews 'carried Jerusalem time', and killed him for his strangeness. Therefore, concludes Plinlimmon, though 'the earthly wisdom of man be heavenly folly to God; so also, conversely, is the heavenly wisdom of God an earthly folly.' And who has not been struck, continues the sermon, by 'a sort of infidel idea, that whatever other world God may be Lord of, he is not the Lord of this; for else the world would seem to give the lie to Him; so utterly repugnant seem its ways to the instinctively known ways of Heaven.'

We can get a sense of the violent bevel on which Melville's faith quivered – half on and half off – if we compare him to two Christians who were writing thoughts exactly like Melville's character Plotinus Plinlimmon at this moment in the middle of the nineteenth century. In Denmark, Kierkegaard strengthened Christianity (as he saw it) by reminding us, like Plinlimmon, that Christianity is a 'folly' for humans, that, as he put it in his *Journals*, 'one must be quite literally a lunatic to become a Christian'. And in England, at almost exactly the same time, Cardinal Newman looked at the world, and, in his *Apologia Pro Vita Sua*, almost agreed with Melville:

> I look out of myself into the world of men, and there I see a sight which fills me with unspeakable distress. The world seems simply to give the lie to that great truth, of which my whole being is so full . . . I look into this living busy world, and see no reflexion of its Creator. This is, to me, one of those great difficulties of this absolute primary truth, to which I referred just now. Were it not for this voice, speaking so clearly in my conscience and my heart, I should be an atheist, or a pantheist, or a polytheist when I looked into the world.

Both Kierkegaard and Newman suffered like Melville, and suffered eloquently, feeling the lack of what Newman beautifully calls 'the tokens so faint and broken of a superintending design'. But both could hear the voice of God, however thick its accent. They were full of it. For Melville however, it was 'Silence'. In his trip to Egypt and to Jerusalem in 1857, God is an 'idea', a malign 'conception' that cannot be unconceived. But God is never a voice.

So Melville slapped at God. He could not help playing the infidel: he is one of the most delvingly sacrilegious writers who has ever existed. For him, metaphysics could not stop like a day-trip at some calm watering-place. Dialectic was always an elastic solitude stretching into the desert. In his letters to Hawthorne – a writer he self-describingly praised as one who 'says No! in thunder', for 'all men who say *yes* lie' – he churns himself into atheistical taunting, using Hawthorne's reticence as a stand-in for God's. Nobody can bear truth, he says again and again. He whirls around, magnificently, in 'atmospheric skepticisms'. Why is it, he asks in a letter written in April 1851, while he was in the middle of writing *Moby-Dick*, that 'in the last stages of metaphysics a fellow always falls to *swearing* so? I could rip for an hour.' (Parker's white comment: 'he could "rip" for an hour; but he did not' — this, about a letter in which Melville has already been ripping for an hour.) Most people, he tells Hawthorne, 'fear God, and *at bottom dislike* Him . . . because they rather distrust His heart, and fancy Him all brain like a watch.' Then he adds an elevated sneer: 'You perceive I employ a capital initial in the pronoun referring to the Deity; don't you think there is a slight dash of flunkeyism in that usage?' He slapped at God; but in some way, he could not do without the idea of being slapped by God in return.

3

Between 1847 and 1850, Melville majestically discovered three things: metaphor, metaphysics, and Shakespeare. These were the years in which he grew into the labour of writing *Moby-Dick* (which was written between February 1850 and the summer of 1851). *Mardi* (1849), his third novel but the first in which he indulged in philosophical 'ripping', had been poorly received. Quickly, disdainfully, he turned out two hotcakes for money, *Redburn* (1849) and *White-Jacket* (1850). Intellectually, his mind was abroad. His reading, which had been eager but arbitrary, now took on a systematic wildness. In 1847 and 1848, he bought or borrowed an edition of Shakespeare, a volume of Montaigne, and a volume of Rabelais. In February 1848 he acquired Coleridge's *Biographia Literaria*. In March, he read Sir Thomas Browne (clearly, after Shakespeare, his chief influence) and Seneca; in June, Dante. In 1849 he bought Pierre Bayle's heretical *Historical and Critical Dictionary*. In the same year, he noted in his new edition of Milton that Milton had wandered in his religious belief: 'I doubt not that darker doubts crossed Milton's soul, than ever disturbed Voltair [*sic*]. And he was more of what is called an Infidel.' But it was Shakespeare who furrowed his soul. He could not believe, he wrote to Evert Duyckinck in February 1849, that he had lived so long without properly reading Shakespeare, who now seemed to him like Jesus: 'Ah, he's full of sermons-on-the-mount, and gentle, aye, almost as Jesus. I take such men to be inspired. I fancy that this moment Shakspeare [*sic*] in heaven ranks with Gabriel Raphael and Michael. And if another Messiah ever comes twill be in Shakespere's [*sic*] person.' He found himself drawn to the dark characters in Shakespeare, to Lear, Iago, Timon, the Fools. Through them Shakespeare 'craftily says, or sometimes insinuates the things which we feel to be so terrifically true, that it were all but madness for any good man, in his own proper character, to utter or even hint of them!' In his copy, he marks moments of madness.

In the summer of 1850, he met Hawthorne for the first time. His letters begin to sway somewhat maniacally. He assures Hawthorne that 'I am not mad, most noble Festus!' In another: 'This is rather a crazy letter in some respects, I apprehend.' It is simply that he is growing: 'Lord, when shall we be done growing?' he asks. Between 1849 and 1852, he is in a creative temper, flinging around words and ideas. In these letters he turns over, obsessively, the silence of God, and the sense that to speak truthfully in America demands a fit of secrecy. 'Truth is ridiculous to men.' Above all, while he is busy seeing a world stripped of God's presence, he is busy theologizing literature. God has disappeared and returns as literature. If the Messiah comes again, it will be as Shakespeare. But the Messiah has come again, and he is called Melville. It is Melville who, in *Moby-Dick*, will follow 'Shakespeare and other masters of the great Art of Telling the Truth'. Here in America, Shakespeares are being born, Christ-like creatures who will be crucified for telling the truth. 'Though I wrote the Gospels in this century, I should die in the gutter', writes Melville in June 1851. Five months later, in November, he is groaning, fretting, racing: 'Appreciation! Recognition! Is Jove appreciated?' In the same letter, he whistles, Whitman-like: 'I feel that the Godhead is broken up like the bread at the supper, and that we are the pieces.' Literature is the new Church, and *Moby-Dick* its Bible. He is building what he calls (in that novel) 'Noah Webster's ark', a dictionary-ship, a bible-boat.

We hear, in these letters, the hymning, the fattened hysteria of *Moby-Dick*, its leaping exultations. But we also hear the self-pity and self-absorption, the will-to-punishment and self-destruction that make *Pierre* so intensely unlikeable a book. In that novel, allegory points only to itself, and is thus a continual self-advertisement. The entire book is an allegory supposed to remind us that such a book cannot really exist in America. *Pierre* is a kind of Calvinist self-mutilation at the literary, rather than the theological level. It is as if Melville says, in this book: 'Well, if good works really do get you nowhere theologically, here is a good work – this book – that will get me nowhere, because no one will acknowledge it as a good work.' *Pierre* reads as if Melville, anticipating that no one would appreciate his novel, deliberately ruined it (he writes in it that the best writers can never 'unravel their own intricacies' but instead can only offer 'imperfect, unanticipated, and disappointing sequels'). Here writing becomes an unthanked charity.

During the time that Melville wrote *Moby-Dick*, he underwent a kind of hysteria of metaphor, an insanity of metaphor. It was Melville's love of metaphor that drew him ever further into 'Infidel-ideas'. Metaphor bred metaphysics for Melville. His metaphors have a life of their own; it is not only Melville that is 'growing' but also his language. Melville is the most naturally metaphorical of writers, and one of the very greatest. He saw the inside of the whale's mouth covered with 'a glistening white membrane, glossy as bridal satins'; at sea, the spouting jet of the whale made him look like 'a portly burgher smoking his pipe of a warm afternoon'. He drew on the example of late sixteenth- and early seventeenth-century poetry and prose as naturally as if he were of that age and not a nineteenth-century American. He saw how metaphor domesticates and localizes (the whale as a burgher) even as it enlarges. For once we use metaphor, as Sir Thomas Browne put it in his *Religio Medici* (1642), 'there is all Africa and her prodigies in us.'

Soaked in theology, Melville was alert to the Puritan habit of seeing the world allegorically, that is, metaphorically. The world was a place of signs and wonders which could always yield up its meaning, like secret ink. Melville did a certain amount of this sign-gazing himself. Writing to Evert Duyckinck in August 1850, he mentioned that he was writing on an old heirloom, a desk of his uncle's. 'Upon dragging it out to day light, I found that it was covered with the marks of fowls . . . eggs had been laid in it − think of that! − Is it not typical of those other eggs that authors may be said to lay in their desks . . .'

More usually, Melville had a way of following metaphor, and seeing where it led him. He wrote to Duyckinck, offering *Mardi* for his library, in the hope that it 'may possibly − by some miracle, that is − flower like the aloe, a hundred years hence − or not flower at all, which is more likely by far, for some aloes never flower.' A year later, writing to Hawthorne, he used an image which has become celebrated:

> I am like one of those seeds taken out of the Egyptian Pyramids, which, after being three thousand years a seed and nothing but a seed, being planted in English soil, it developed itself, grew to greenness, and then fell to mould. So I. Until I was twenty-five, I had no development at all. From my twenty-fifth year I date my life.

Both similes force Melville into dialectic. For, having embarked on them, he must follow their wandering, reverse logic. Thus he writes that his book is like an aloe, that it may flower in a hundred years; but then he is compelled − *compelled by the metaphor he inhabits* − to add that some aloes never flower, and since he has mentioned the flowering of the aloe, he must also mention the aloe's failure to flower. The second simile is more striking, because Melville made this comparison at the very height of his creative fever, while writing *Moby-Dick*. At this pinnacle, he foresees falling into literary decline (as, of course, he did, in real life). Why? Is it because Melville was eerily self-prescient? No, it is because, having likened himself to one of the seeds from the Pyramids, he must follow his own metaphor, and record that these seeds 'grew to greenness, and then fell to mould'. Melville does not really mean to offer a dark prophecy about his development; the thrust of his letter is that he is like one of the Pyramid seeds because he was dormant for so many years, and then suddenly flowered. But the simile he has chosen is a handshake with likeness; and it is a handshake that will not let him go. He *must* mention 'mould' because his metaphor forces him to.

Of course, no one is *actually* forced by metaphor, except a madman. But Melville's writing certainly displays an unusual devotion to the logic of metaphor, which is the logic of parallelism. Of all writers (Shakespeare and Keats resemble him in this) he understood the independent, generative life that comes from likening something to something else. His work is deeply aware that as soon as you liken x to y, x has changed, and is now x+y, which has its own, parallel life. This is why Melville's similes sometimes seem to be bizarrely elaborated, and to continue over sentences and sentences. Like Gogol, who was quite as God-intoxicated as Melville, quite as unstable, who also employs immensely long and detailed metaphors, and whose fiction is similarly tilted towards the allegorical, Melville reads as if he simply cannot tear himself away from the rival life, the alienated majesty, that metaphor offers. If the whale resembles a portly burgher out for a stroll, then Melville feels himself committed to add that the whale's water-jet is the man's pipe: this is how he thinks. Metaphor, in this sense, becomes the very essence of fiction-making, because when a writer commits himself to the independent life of metaphor, he is acknowledging the fictional reality of an imagined alternative. For this is what metaphor is: a fictional alternative, a likeness, an other life. Metaphor is the whole of the imaginative fictional process in one move. Keats spoke of how language 'yeasts and works itself up' – *works itself*. This was everything to Melville. Pondering Goethe's advice that one must 'Live in the all, and then you will be happy', he writes: 'This "all" feeling, though, there is some truth in it. You must often have felt it, lying on the grass on a warm summer's day. Your legs seem to send out shoots into the earth. Your hair feels like leaves upon your head. This is the *all* feeling.' What Melville is crediting here is our power to create new life, a life that exists independently from us. And we do this through metaphor. You live 'in the all', when you feel metaphorical, when you feel that your hair is not your hair but has become leaves, your legs not your legs but growing shoots. And once they are growing, who can stop them?

4

The theological implications of Melville's ravishment by metaphor are immense. Metaphor carries something over, it changes thought. In his letters and in his fiction, Melville thinks through metaphor, uses it to sway his thought. He ends one letter to Hawthorne by saying that he began his letter in a small way, yet 'here I have landed in Africa'. Recall Sir Thomas Browne's 'there is all Africa and her prodigies in us': metaphor transports him, and is then called upon to give image to that very transportation. In his note on Milton's 'wanderings in religious belief', Melville wrote that 'he who thinks for himself can never remain of the same mind' – Melville wanders, via metaphor, out of 'the same mind' into a different mind, out of sameness into likeness or difference.

The love of metaphor literally leads Melville astray theologically. His 'wandering' love of language breaks up his God, and he encourages this; his love of language bribes him, turns him against that rival, the Original Author. This can be seen again and again in the work. In Judea, in 1857, Melville is put into a cold trance by the rockiness of the landscape. 'Is the desolation of the land the result of the fatal embrace of the Deity?' he asks himself. The land must have produced the religion, he feels: 'As the sight of haunted Haddon Hall suggested to Mrs Radcliffe her curdling romances, so I have little doubt, the diabolical landscapes [*sic*] great part of Judea must have suggested to the Jewish people, their terrific theology.' What is terrific is the vulgar blasphemy of the metaphor. Ann Radcliffe wrote Gothic romances. Yet it is because Melville cannot resist the impulse of likeness that he is drawn into comparing the whole of biblical theology to a mere Gothic romance, and ends up implying, thanks to his simile, that Jewish monotheism was just a creative prompting from the landscape, a creative idea for a book – The Book.

Wandering, and the wandering of metaphor, is the subject of Plotinus Plinlimmon's sermon in *Pierre*. In that sermon, Melville likens God to Greenwich Mean Time. God, says Melville, is the universal meridian. We, his creations, are like the chronometers in ships. These chronometers give the time at Greenwich, even when a ship is in the Azores. That is how we are supposed to be, says Melville, carrying God's time throughout the world, even if it contradicts the mere local time. Yet this is impossible, continues Melville. If a man is in China, he should live by local Chinese time, not by Greenwich time. A man who lived according to Greenwich time in China would be mad. But this is exactly what God impossibly asks us to do. He asks us to live as if we were in heaven, and not on earth. This lovely five-page passage combines all of Melville's characteristic tendencies. It is a complaint against God, of considerable philosophical power. It is a metaphor at once homely and grand, which Melville establishes and then commits himself to, elaborating both its allegorical logic and its independent life over many paragraphs, so that the metaphor becomes the vehicle of blasphemous complaint. Once the metaphor is in place, Melville must follow its violent implications to the end. And it is a metaphor about metaphor, for it is an allegory about wandering, about straying. Melville's complaint against God is precisely that, like ships, we tend to stray from God's co-ordinates, and cannot help doing so. To wander is natural – and here, he says, is a wandering metaphor to prove it.

Moby-Dick represents the triumph of this atheism of metaphor. Or perhaps, this polytheism of metaphor. For it is a book in which allegory explodes into a thousand metaphors; a book in which the Puritan habit of reading signs and seeing stable meanings behind them is mocked by an almost grotesque abundance of metaphor. In this book meaning is mashed up like a pudding. The Godhead is indeed broken into pieces. Truth is kaleidoscopically affronted. The whale is likened to everything under the sun, and everything under the moon, too – a portly burgher, an Ottoman, a book, a language, a script, a nation, the Sphinx, the Pyramids. The whale is also Satan and God. The whale is 'inscrutable'. It is so full of meanings that it threatens to have no meanings at all, which is the fear Ishmael confesses to in the celebrated chapter 'The Whiteness of the Whale'. Critics who persist in seeing in Melville an American Gnostic do so because the whale is a demiurge, a bad god (the Gnostic premise was that we are ruled by a bad god). But what, Melville asks, if the whale means nothing at all? What if, at the very heart of the sarcophagus, there is absolutely nothing?

5

By late summer 1851, it was over. This great novel was done. Melville had asked the question: how does an American writer make tragedy worthy of Shakespeare's without setting the story in the remote past? He answered it by making his novel an historical novel whose epoch is the whale – thousands of years old. As Sir Walter Scott filled his novels with the dust of medieval France or Scotland, with clothes, dates, battles, so Melville filled his book with the clothes, dates and battles of the whale. The whale is a country and an age.

How easily it might not have worked! The power is all verbal. Without the language the metaphysics would just be grain. Although one remembers the rhapsodies of poetry, one forgets how precise, how grounded is the language, with what vernacular swing it moves. (Melville founded American vernacular prose equally with Twain: to know this, compare the rhythms of Bellow's *The Adventures of Augie March* with the rhythms of *Moby-Dick*.) Melville Americanizes Shakespeare, gives it tilt. Where Shakespeare has Antony like a dolphin, showing its back above the element it lived in, Melville has a democracy of porpoises, tossing their backs to heaven 'like caps in a Fourth of July crowd'. Queequeg, the cannibal, can go anywhere: 'Transported to the Indies, his live blood would not spoil like bottled ale.' Not for nothing does Ishmael pray to 'the great democratic God'. Again and again one is thrilled by the teeter of metaphor, watching it almost fail, and then take like a skin graft. There is a mad persistence to this metaphorizing, a fiery pedantry. There is the noise the whale makes, 'an enormous wallowing sound as of fifty elephants stirring in their litter'; the harpooners turning their harpoons in the very quick of the beast, and yet delicately, 'as if cautiously seeking to feel after some gold watch that the whale might have swallowed'. There is Pip, the little Negro boy, who falls into the water 'like a traveler's trunk . . . Bobbing up and down in the sea, Pip's ebon head showed like a head of cloves.' There is Ahab's soul, 'a centipede, that moves upon a hundred legs'. And at last, the final chase, the whale sliding like metaphor itself through its fluid of meanings: 'on each bright side, the whale shed off enticings'.

This carnival comes to a chill rest in the chapter called 'The Whiteness of the Whale'. Here Ishmael asks if it is the whiteness of the whale that torments. For whiteness may signify many things (sacredness, purity, superiority) or it may signify nothing. Whiteness 'stabs us from behind with the thought of annihilation . . . whiteness is not so much a colour as the visible absence of color, and at the same time the concrete of all colors . . . a colorless, all-color of atheism from which we shrink . . .' Here, in whiteness, is the end of allegory, and therefore the end of metaphor, and therefore the end of language. It is silence, God's

Silence, and it sits in the book like some unnamed sea, ready to suck down all who come upon it. *Moby-Dick* is the great dream of mastery over language. But it also represents a terrible struggle with language. For if the terror of the whale, the terror of God, is his inscrutability, then it is language that has made him so. It is Melville's abundance of language that is constantly filling everything with meaning, and emptying it out too. Language breaks up God, releases us from the one meaning of the predestinating God, but merely makes that God differently inscrutable by flooding it with thousands of different meanings. I think that language and metaphor were a great torture as well as a great joy to Melville. Melville saw – and *Moby-Dick* is the enactment of this vision – that language helps to explain God and to conceal God in equal measure, and that these two functions annul each other. Thus language does not help us explain or describe God. Quite the contrary, it registers simply our inability to describe God; it holds our torment. Yet language is all there is, and thus Melville follows it as Ahab follows the whale, to the very end.

Theologically, metaphor acts like language. It insists on relationship, but to compare one thing with another is also to suggest non-relationship, for nothing *is* ever like anything else. Metaphor always carries the danger of being a wandering away *from* relationship. Thus metaphor, which so promises to illuminate and enlarge, also registers our ultimate inability to compare things. Metaphor, like language, holds our torment, and this explains the peculiar doggedness, almost madness, of Melville's obsession with metaphor. Melville is always using metaphor to solve a problem which metaphor itself only complicates. Melville's metaphors resemble the medieval preference for describing God by His attributes, for describing Him indirectly. But when you have done this, you have not really known Him, and perhaps you have only aggravated the difficulty by bombarding Him with approximations. The very project is futile, and also heretical, because as soon as you liken God to something else, you bring God into the sea of metaphor, on equal status with everything else. You dare the infidel idea that *God is only a metaphor.* No, language is a voice that does not help us get any nearer to the silence of God; it is its own voice.

Melville may have become another Messiah in writing *Moby-Dick*; master of meaning, Melville is the real 'great democratic God' to which Ishmael is pledged and by whom he is predestined. But to be a literary God is not to get closer to an actual God, and Melville, who could not entirely release the monitor of God from his life, surely, bitterly knew this. He certainly knew that language is one of the veils of theology, not one of the clarities: 'As soon as you say *Me*, a *God*, a *Nature*, so soon you jump off from your stool and hang from the beam,' he wrote to Hawthorne. 'Yes, that word is the hangman. Take God out of the dictionary, & you would have Him in the street.'

No more than anyone else did Melville manage to get God into the street. He went tidally, between belief and unbelief. Melville has Ishmael argue that life is always a ceaseless tide:

> There is no steady unretracing progress in this life: we do not advance through fixed gradations, and at the last one pause: – through infancy's unconscious spell, boyhood's thoughtless faith, adolescence, doubt . . . then scepticism, then disbelief, resting at last in manhood's pondering repose of If. But once gone through, we trace the round again: and are infants, boys, and men, and Ifs eternally. Where lies the final harbor, whence we unmoor no more?

Theologically, Melville lived his life in an eternal If, which his love of metaphor only encouraged. Linguistically, in the gorgeous play of metaphor, he lived his life in an eternal All – which was at the same time an eternal If, because it could not console, could not banish the If, and in fact only deepened it. The entity Melville most loved, language, separated him from the entity he most desired, God. A god of a thousand meanings may be as absent as the God of one meaning. Ahab's

46

monomaniacal hunt of the whale is not so far from Ishmael's multiple tolerance of it. Any true life is a blasphemously exhaustive hunt, and Melville lived a true life. Poor Melville, lucky Melville!

Half-Against Flaubert

I

It is hard not to resent Flaubert for making fictional prose stylish – for making style a problem for the first time in fiction. After Flaubert, style is always mirrored, always self-conscious, always a trapped decision. Style became religious with Flaubert, at the same moment that religion became a kind of literary style, a poetry, with Ernest Renan. Flaubert himself admired Rabelais, Cervantes and Molière as if they were beasts of mere instinct: 'they are great . . . because they have no techniques.' Such writers 'achieve their effects, regardless of Art', he wrote to Louise Colet in 1853. But Flaubert could not be free as these writers were: 'One achieves style only by atrocious labour, a fanatic and dedicated stubbornness.' He was imprisoned in scruple, and he imprisoned his successors in scruple. He is the novelist from whom the Modern, with all its narrow freedoms, flows.

Style, no doubt, had always been a battle for novelists, but Flaubert turned it into a perpetual defeat. Indeed, fiction itself was felt as a kind of defeat by Flaubert, it became a vessel defined by what it could not hold. His letters speak again and again of squeezed hours at his mother's house at Croisset, of how little he has written, of the monstrous difficulty of writing a sentence. It is at first surprising that this new consciousness of limit was born in the apparently limitless heyday of the novel, at the moment when the novel began to have a sense of how it should be conducting itself – the moment of European 'realism'. Flaubert was beholden to realism but also detested it. He was torn into two sensibilities, he wrote to his lover, Louise Colet: 'In me, when it comes to literature, there are two quite distinct creatures: one who is very *taken* with being a *loud-mouth*, with lyricism, with soaring like an eagle with all sonorities of phrase and loftinesses of idea; the other who digs and delves into the truth as far as he can, who loves to represent the little detail as powerfully as the other kind, who would like to make you feel almost *materially* the objects he describes.' Yet the romantic was stronger than the realist in Flaubert. His first major literary effort was the wildly lyrical *The Temptation of St Antony*, a book he partially abandoned in 1849 after reading it aloud (over four days) to his friends Maxime Du Camp and Louis Bouilhet. They told him, in effect, that it was a lush failure, that he must thin his wardrobe of luxuries, discipline his style, and choose a nice bourgeois subject: he chose Emma Bovary's provincial adulteries. (*Madame Bovary* appeared in 1857.) But he returned again and again to his beloved *Temptation*, eventually publishing it in 1874. In that curious failure of a novel, St Antony is tempted by sumptuous sensuality (the Queen of Sheba in flowing robes), by visions of power offered by the Devil, and by heresy. The book, which is written out in the form of play, is silkily, weightlessly fantastical. Yet Flaubert's letters reveal that this book was the marriage of his life, and all the others merely affairs.

It is too simple to say that Flaubert romanticized realism. Yet clearly his obsession with the sentence represents an attempt to turn prose into lines of consecutive verse, 'to impart to prose the rhythm of verse (leaving it still prose and very prosy'), as he put it in 1853. Certainly, Flaubert's self-consciousness in this regard represents the collision of realism and romanticism, of the ordinary and the exotic, rather as strange forms of etiquette emerge when an old epoch falls into economic distress. The novel was triumphant at the middle of the century, and there is a sense in which Melville, Flaubert and Gogol, all of them writing roughly contemporaneously, were poets who wanted to make the novel a genre that could consume all others and then perform all their functions at once – a stomach of genres, digesting satire, poetry, epic, the historical novel, realism, and fable. (*Moby-Dick, Dead Souls* and *Madame Bovary* are all prose-poems of a kind, and were all called this on publication.) Flaubert was forever restless, telling his correspondents that he would write a fairy-tale, or a fantasy, or an historical epic, or his celebrated dictionary of stupidities; his gargantuan reading seems an ingestive response to this borderless hunger.

But under Flaubert the novel's great expansion was actually an expansion into limit. Flaubert was marched by his little army of ambitions into a war of literary possibilities, only to be overwhelmed by sheer option. The novel discovered all that it could do, all that it then had to do, and collapsed out of fatigue into *style*, into the one thing any writer must do – not immediately, of course, not for a century, not until the *nouveau roman*, whose leading representative, Nathalie Sarraute, rightly asked in 1965: 'How can it be doubted that Flaubert is the precursor?' Likewise, Alain Robbe-Grillet, in his manifesto, *Pour un nouveau roman*, called Balzacian realism the enemy, and pronounced Flaubert the writer who changed the old order: 'But then, with Flaubert, everything begins to vacillate. A hundred years later, the whole system is no more than a memory.' When the novel became madly ambitious to be everything, it began to chastise itself for failing to do everything; taking everything as its only measure, it became afflicted with a sense of its failure, and began to throw off those ambitions, like a plane dumping fuel, until only one was left: its very essence, style itself. Until Flaubert, the novel had been mithridated in its own unself-consciousness, as an alcoholic thoughtlessly medicalizes himself; Flaubert took away its sweet, ignorant poisons, and it began to die impressively.

Style was a trapped decision for Flaubert, as it is for all his successors, because he, and we, are always in a relationship with style; indifference to style is no longer possible, and is converted into dilemma. Today, those writers who write 'plainly', who leave style alone, must trudge along the plains looking at the mountains they have chosen not to climb. And then, of course, the plainest writers now become stylists too, of renunciation. Flaubert gave birth to Nabokov on one side, and to Hemingway on the other. In short, Flaubert made the novel a painterly activity, and perhaps in so doing he destined the novel to the danger of irrelevance. He aspired to write 'a book about nothing, a book with no external attachment . . . The most beautiful books are those with the least matter', he wrote in 1852; and in the same letter he wrote that 'from the point of view of Art, there is no such thing as a subject, style being solely in itself an absolute way of seeing things.'

From the present day, when novels 'about nothing' abound, Flaubert's words seem ominous. For 'an absolute way of seeing things' becomes too easily an obsession with the *way* of seeing; the important things disappear. Thus it is that Georges Perec's tedious book *Things: A Story of the Sixties*, which attempts heavily to log the impedimenta of a decade (the clothes, fabrics, styles), is actually a novel that sees negligible things, but that prides itself on its way of seeing things. And the way of seeing things turns out again and again to be only *seeing* – the visual. From Flaubert comes that fetishizing of the visual for which Nabokov is always praised and which is actually his deepest limitation. Flaubert is a great writer, and his talent for visual detail is a joy, one of the deep textures of his writing, whether it is the smoke of a moving railway engine, 'stretched out in a horizontal line, like a gigantic ostrich feather whose tip kept blowing away', or this lovely tableau from *Sentimental Education*: 'The proprietor and his wife were having supper with the waiter in the corner by the kitchen; and Regimbart, with his hat on, was sharing their meal, and indeed getting in the way of the waiter, who was forced to turn slightly to one side at every mouthful.'

This is beautiful, with that gently ridiculous comedy that Flaubert sometimes produces. Yet the danger of Flaubert's heavily visual details is that they flatter the visual over the unseen, the external over the interior (and Flaubert is not really a great novelist of interiority), that writing becomes primarily, and in some cases only, a way of making us feel 'almost *materially* the objects [it] describes'. Furthermore, in addition to the tyranny of the visual, comes the tyranny of the detail. Paul Valéry, who did not care for Flaubert's fiction, commented sourly in a notebook of 1924: 'Another vice of this style – there's always room for one more detail.' Flaubert gave birth to the orthodoxy that the finest style of writing is a procession of strung details, a necklace of sensualities. We see this in Updike and above all in Nabokov, who, in his story 'First Love', describes a man whose head is twisted rather as Regimbart's was in the café in *Sentimental Education:* 'On the promenade near the casino, an elderly flower-girl, with carbon eyebrows and a painted smile, nimbly slipped the plump torus of a carnation into the buttonhole of an intercepted stroller whose left jowl accentuated its royal fold as he glanced down sideways at the coy insertion of the flower.' This description sounds more like a logic-puzzle than a sentence, a kind of anagram of detail appealing for decoding. In Nabokov especially, the anxiety with which Flaubert surrounds detail – the awful chosenness of it – becomes a kind of terror, an inability to draw away from detail; and a concomitant paralysis, a static cult of the local; a frieze. Updike's ridiculous 'the miraculous knit of his jockey shorts' is a logical perversion of Flaubertian style.

The failings of contemporary writers reveal certain weaknesses in Flaubert's greatness, as an ugly baby forces our reappraisal of its attractive parents. Flaubert, for better or worse, established for us our idea of realism: a pressure of detail, a poised, deliberate chosenness. In Flaubert, the monstrous chosenness of detail is revealed through reticence. The pressure of the prose is the pressure of the thought that preceded it but which does not lie on the page. The great descriptions in Flaubert – the great ball at La Vaubyessard in *Madame Bovary*, or the agricultural show in the same novel, or the Parisian barricades of 1848 in *Sentimental Education* – are surrounded by the ghost of avoidance, by everything that was rejected to produce this style, by the careful hiatus, by the intelligent starvation. It is the idea of paint, of depiction rather than thought or commentary: the very speck of the real. Contemporary writing – Robert Stone is an obvious example – takes Flaubert's controlled visual sweep, shaves off some of its richness, and merely cinematizes it. How would a town square in Italy or Brazil be described nowadays? I will parody the style: 'In the north-east corner, a woman threw out her bucket of water, the contents of which briefly yellowed the large, red slabs of the town square. On the other side, a priest, who had been reading the excitable morning paper, looked up and smiled, apparently to himself. His paper rustled in the small, hot breeze like fire. A piano could be heard; Miss Dupont was giving her first lesson of the day.' This kind of thing, or something like it, is the staple not only of realism, but of magic realism and of thriller-writing. And there is good reason, because precise, observed detail is the food of any decent fiction. But Flaubert surely institutionalized this way of writing, canonized it into orthodoxy. Flaubert made it into a style: 'A breeze from the window ruffled the cloth on the table, and down in the square the peasant women's big bonnets lifted up, fluttering like white butterflies' wings.' (*Madame Bovary.*)

In particular, Flaubert licensed the idea that writing does not comment on itself. It presents and withdraws, like a good footman. Flaubert is famous for his desire for impersonality. He wanted the author to look down from above. 'When will all the facts be written from the point of view of a superior farce, that's to say, as the good God sees them, from on high?' he asked Louise Colet in 1852. From this flows Stephen Crane and Ernest Hemingway, the ideal of highly stylized reporting. Indeed, in some respects, Flaubert's descriptions of revolutionary urban violence in *Sentimental Education* might be said to have influenced war-writing and the way novelists write about war. 'Frédéric felt something soft under his foot; it was the hand of a sergeant in a grey overcoat who was lying face down in the gutter.' When Roque fires into a crowd of prisoners and shoots someone, Flaubert marshals that cold discipline we think of as a twentieth-century invention: 'There was a tremendous howl, then nothing. Something white remained on the edge of the grating.' His prose, like a good doctor, does not get emotionally involved; it refuses to follow the anarchy of its subject-matter – and thus, in one respect, *denies* its own subject-matter, acts *as if the subject is not there*. One recalls Flaubert's dream of writing a book about nothing, that would contain 'the least matter'. Flaubert is able to achieve his two contradictory ambitions, to write on the one hand fiction that is densely detailed, densely involved with matter, and on the other hand fiction without matter, because his style refuses the pull of matter, asserts itself over matter. His prose will not register emotionally what it depicts visually. Again, there are excellent literary reasons for Flaubert's strictness in this regard, and in his letters he gives them: the avoidance of sentimentality is the chief advantage. But the legacy of Flaubert's rigour of denial is, nowadays, too often a dumbness, an unthoughtful, undemonstrative literature preening itself on its inability (rather than its unwillingness) to feel, broken into units of hard sensation, and merely swiping at life.

From Flaubert, then, come the two main strands of contemporary writing: the aestheticism of style, or books 'about nothing' (the *nouveau roman*, the avant-garde, and so on); and the silence of fact, or books simply strung on detail, or on nuggets of hard, empirical observation (which can mean a wide range of fiction, from the more worked writing of Hemingway and Perec to the plainness of Carver and Robert Stone). Philosophically, the legacy can be put thus: on the one hand Flaubert is the father of aestheticism and symbolism; and on the other, he is the father of literary positivism. Flaubert reveals that these two kinds of writing have something in common: neither can ever be innocent about the primacy of style, and thus both are a form of aestheticism. Flaubert invented hard aestheticism and soft aestheticism, as it were. And furthermore, lest one seem too hard on Flaubert, it should be said that he is Joyce's father, that writer who supremely unites these two streams, and who plunged into the heart of the human yet with the most rarefied and most beautifully aesthetic of styles.

2

Flaubert insisted that fiction should not judge. Like Chekhov, he felt that the writer should resist conclusion, should only ask the right questions. 'Stupidity consists in wanting to reach conclusions. We are a thread, and we want to know the whole design.' A novel, he wrote, is to be 'without love or hate for any of the characters'. His dream of impersonality was in part a desire to withdraw from judgment: 'one must accept everything, resigned to not concluding.' Yet Flaubert did in fact judge, and he did conclude – of course, being 'resigned to not concluding' is a form of conclusion, is a resignation. He was bearishly fatalistic: 'I deny individual freedom.' One sees in Flaubert the mid-nineteenth-century aestheticizing of religious attitudes which also afflicted Ernest Renan and Matthew Arnold. 'What attracts me above all else is religion', he wrote in 1857. 'I mean all religions, no one more than another. Each dogma in particular is repulsive to me, but I consider the feeling that invented them as the most natural and poetic of humanity.' He wrote often of 'aesthetic mysticism'. 'To my mind, the true poet is a priest.' His life was a monkish sequestration: 'Great achievements always require fanaticism. Fanaticism is religion . . . In Art as well, it is Art-fanaticism which is the artistic feeling.'

Yet although Flaubert aestheticized religion, he retained the old judgmental habits of Christianity, the renunciatory disgust, the penance of being alive. Flaubert is distinctly medieval. 'A man is no more than a flea', he complained in August 1853. 'How nothingness encroaches on us!' After a visit to the dentist, in December 1846, he exclaimed: 'during our lives we are merely corruption and putrefaction, in succession and alternation.' Seven days later, once again to Louise Colet, he elaborated: 'What can it be that made me so old as I left my cradle, gave me such a distaste for happiness before I had even tasted it? Everything to do with life is repellent to me . . . I have within me, deep down, a radical, intimate, bitter, incessant *vexation* which stops me enjoying everything and fills my heart to bursting.' However, because Flaubert was not a religious believer, religious judgment had long since lost all grandeur for him, and had become metaphysically null. Judgment lost its holy prestige and became a kind of secular mid-nineteenth-century whining – irritation, boredom, disgust, a perpetual 'vexation' at the 'ridiculousness' of humanity. Compared to religious judgment, this judgment exists in a demoted metaphysical space. It is almost a kind of bourgeois pettiness, and Flaubert, who abhorred the bourgeois but who recognized his own bourgeois traits, probably sensed the littleness of his complaint, its non-tragic nature. Flaubert, one suspects, was bored by his boredom, disgusted at his disgust, aroused by his monkishness. He could not help evacuating religious judgment of the religious.

So it is not really that Flaubert withdraws from his books to become God as such, for God does not exist. No, he withdraws only to the *place* God would occupy, if He existed. This strange, vacated metaphysics is reflected in the fiction. The insistent thrust of his fiction is towards nullification. Flaubert looks upon his fictional world like an angry God who no longer exists. He lays waste to his people; he would rather they did not exist. Henry James, who admired Flaubert, rightly complained that Frédéric, the hero of *Sentimental Education*, is an uninteresting blank, and that the novel is thus something of an 'empty epic'. The only burning question of *Sentimental Education* is whether Frédéric is going to have sex with his various lovers. Perhaps Flaubert wanted to create a character so foolishly vain and empty that he would wander through Paris during the 1848 revolution and nullify the excitements around him. He does, but then the novel also nullifies them, and rather nullifies itself, despite its many, many ravishments. If Frédéric is something of a dud, St Antony, as Valéry complained, 'hardly exists'. Temptations swirl around him, but they seem largely an opportunity for Flaubert to aerate his style. The psychology of desire interests Flaubert not at all. Emma Bovary is a beautiful creation, yet one feels that the truest, most vivid Flaubertian character is Homais, the vain and pompous chemist in that novel, a character straight out of Molière. Flaubert's characters seem like mistakes; his disgust is felt on every page. *Madame Bovary* ends on a note of disgust at the continuance, the persistence of these mistakes: 'He [Homais] has just been awarded the Legion of Honour' is its famous, sour last sentence. Flaubert complained that it was a great effort to write *Madame Bovary*, because 'I find them [the characters] deeply repulsive.' Realism was a kind of penance. During the early, youthful writing of *The Temptation*, he had felt full and voluptuous. But now, 'I have to spend every minute living under the *skins* of people that I cannot stand. For six months I have been making love platonically and at the moment I am most catholically exalted at the sound of church-bells . . .' One notes his italicization of 'skins'; he feels realism as a religious mortification, a lashing of his own skin in order that he might inhabit that of others.

A comparison might usefully be made with Chekhov. Although Chekhov agreed with Flaubert that literature should not draw obvious conclusions, the writers differ in revealing ways. Flaubert did in fact draw conclusions, resignedly; and so did Chekhov, but rebelliously. In contrast to Flaubert's disgust at his characters, or even to Flaubert's advice that one should neither love nor hate them, Chekhov told Tatiana Shchepkina-Kupernik: 'Love your characters – but not aloud!' Thus it is that we feel that Flaubert's characters are doomed, while Chekhov's are only imprisoned. This is best seen in the way both writers use a technique which might be called alternation – the alternation of high and low, of the serious and comic, the sublime and the ridiculous. Alternation is the large principle of both writers: while Paris importantly burns, Frédéric thinks trivially only about sex; when poor Gusev dies in Chekhov's story of the same name, he is wrapped in sailcloth, and looks like a radish, broad at the top and narrow at the bottom. It is also the local stylistic principle of both writers. A famous example occurs in *Madame Bovary,* when Rodolphe seduces Emma in the town hall. The couple sit at the window and watch the doltish agricultural show below. An especially pompous prefect's deputy is addressing the villagers about agricultural techniques, while upstairs, the cynical Rodolphe is filling Emma's susceptible ear with high-minded words about 'fate' and 'love' and 'beauty'. The passions, says Rodolphe, who means not a word of it, are 'the source of all heroism and enthusiasm, poetry, music, everything'. Meanwhile, the speech downstairs has got onto flax, cabbage, and manure. Flaubert intercuts these two speeches, running them like lines of alternating verse:

'And I've stayed with you, because I couldn't tear myself away, though I've tried a hundred times.'
'Manure!'

This is a much-admired scene, yet it seems vicious, the ironies suffocating and deterministic, the technique somewhat crudely insistent. What would seem an accidental alternation in Chekhov – the two lovers have happened to find themselves at the foolish fair – seems a deliberate juxtaposition in Flaubert. He tells us, in effect, that both spectacles, both speeches, are idiotic, that Emma will never escape this idiocy: both her prison and her escape are stupid. Chekhov's great story, 'The Lady With the Dog', is instructive by comparison. In *Madame Bovary*, a woman foolishly begins an affair in high hopes of escape, and finds herself doomed. In Chekhov's story, the structural 'alternation' proceeds in exactly the opposite direction: a man cynically begins an affair with no hope except for a dalliance, is surprised by its power, and finds himself imprisoned. He and his lover plot to escape from their imprisonment. In Chekhov, alternation is not used to nullify, as Flaubert uses it, but to intensify the desire for escape. Very beautifully, alternation allows Chekhov to show his characters both the prison and the key to that prison in the same moment. For instance, in 'The Lady With the Dog', the adulterers meet at the theatre, and snatch a kiss on the stairs to the circle. From above, in a detail that Nabokov admired, two schoolboys watch them, while smoking cigarettes. The schoolboys have an arbitrary, careless presence that Flaubert would not have allowed. But more than that, they are both prison and release. They represent the watchful society that oppresses the adulterers and makes their affair so impossible; yet they are only schoolboys, without real judgment, and in some ways they represent a world beyond concern. Similarly in 'The Russian Master', the provincial teacher feels suffocated by the kind of small-town littleness that Flaubert drew so finely in *Madame Bovary*. The teacher is haunted by a single recrimination uttered by a colleague: 'Have you never read Lessing?' As Flaubert alternates Emma's romances with Homais's pompos-ities, Chekhov uses the sentence about Lessing as an alternating refrain in the story. But where Homais is nothing more than Emma's prison-warder, and one who outlives both her and Charles Bovary to end the novel in obtuse prosperity, Lessing is both prison and key to the teacher. The question oppresses the teacher, yet Lessing, the German philosopher, represents an escape, a world of reading and knowledge that exists beyond the small town.

There is a sense in which Chekhov – without of course meaning to, and in a very different aesthetic and political context – 'solved' all the desperate literary dilemmas that consumed Flaubert. If, as Stephen Heath puts it in his brilliant book about Flaubert, 'it is with [Flaubert] that literature becomes *essentially* problematic', then it was with Chekhov that it became again essentially unproblematic (in the aesthetic sense that Heath intends). If realism was a stylistic agony for Flaubert, it was a moral necessity for Chekhov; if Flaubert retained and aestheticized religious judgment, Chekhov paganized life; if Flaubert disliked his characters from afar, Chekhov loved his from afar; if Flaubert's people are all mistakes, Chekhov's, even the fools, are always forgiven; if Flaubert turned style into a monkish fetish, Chekhov made of it a worldly devotion. Where Flaubert judges his characters' fantasies, Chekhov indulges them. Yet in the last hundred pages of *Madame Bovary*, as all readers have surely encountered, something beautifully Chekhovian begins to happen. The novelist who found realism such a penance begins, as it were, to be aroused by his own mortification. The hairshirt prickles suggestively. St Gustave is tempted – tempted into love. Emma begins to live, she pulls away from Flaubert's earlier disapproval. Flaubert seems to forgive her for the tawdry escapism of her dreams, and begins to sympathize with her. Something heroic stirs in the folds of her scanty soul. The novel, eerily, finds a momentum of its own, as if it had created itself. It is utterly mysterious, this transformation, and only shows what a great writer Flaubert, despite his failures, really was. It is certainly a kind of 'aesthetic mysticism', worthy of our entirely unmystical reverence.

Gogol's Realism

Nikolai Gogol is a satirist standing on one leg. He said one thing and did quite another. On the one hand, he is the earnest Christian who argued, in an essay in 1836, for satire's traditional moral divide-and-rule. Literature teaches us what is good and bad, he wrote, by showing 'the ridiculous side of customs and vices and the highly touching qualities of human virtues and lofty sentiments'. This Gogol appeared to see literature as a kind of holy owl, ready to pounce on the verminous, and then fly up into the heavenly heights. Although he only published one volume of his great novel, *Dead Souls* (1842), he intended a moral armada of three volumes based on Dante's *Divine Comedy*, in which the characters would be punished for their sins in volume two, and would then fall on their knees and repent in volume three. This Gogol is the fanatical Christian who, always didactic, became insufferably sermonic in the 1840s, as the grotesque health of his Orthodox Christianity began to devour him. Under the fierce government of a sinister priest, Father Konstantinovsky, this Gogol renounced literature and food, incinerated the manuscript of the second part of *Dead Souls* and, in 1852, starved to death.

On the other hand, there is the satirist who is always falling over in laughter, who is never a convincing Christian, whose fanaticism seems parodic. This Gogol, despite his own pro-nouncements about literature's moral task, seems essentially incapable of creating decent, saintly, or even normal characters. He is far more at home with fools than with holy fools. This

Gogol is a monopolist of the negative; it is as if there were no time for the Good to make its tongue-tied appearance in his fiction. In his writing, no space is made for 'human virtues and lofty sentiments'. The occasional flurries of Russian nationalism and sacred lecturing in his fiction seem ironically intended. This is the writer who is diabolically mobile, who hoped that his fiction was 'taken from the life which turns around each person'. He is, at best, a negative idealist. Both Gogols needed each other, one suspects. The fanatical Gogol, we are told, destroyed Part 2 of *Dead Souls* because fiction was an unworthy activity for a saint. But is it not possible that the writerly Gogol, who had devoted twelve years to this manuscript, saw that a fiction of religious exhortation was no fiction at all, and not worth having?

Gogol was born in the Ukraine, in 1809. His family was not quite gentry, and when a new law threatened to deprive all non-gentry of land and holdings, Gogol's grandfather falsified family documents so as to give the Gogols a quick promotion. Rank, and the stripes of social identity, would be Gogol's constant preoccupation as a writer. He arrived in St Petersburg at the age of nineteen, determined to thrive, and was immediately unhappy. His early stories capitalized on a vogue for his exotic and romantic homeland. They are full of patriotic songs, foolish bravery, Ukrainian food. Most are nostalgic and ultimately comforting – oats for the moping, émigré animal. In several, a devil makes a supernatural raid on events, and is repulsed with the help of Christ. Even if one lends Gogol the benefit of the doubt, and credits him with the simultaneous worship and parody of Ukrainian muscularity, these writings seem at best recreational.

But they made Gogol famous in his early twenties, and gained him a reputation as a somewhat fluorescent historian of Russian nationalism. Eager to make something of this celebrity, Gogol manipulated himself into a professorship. The young writer without a university degree was appointed, in 1834, Professor of World History at St Petersburg University. Few, perhaps, could fill this Hegelian sedan; Gogol quickly slipped out of it. The dual personality was the actual professor. Gogol's strong instinct towards idealism and moralistic pedagogy had impelled him to seek students. He dreamed of a platform from which he might reform Russia's youth, and preach goodness and wholesome nationalism. But Gogol the writer and prankster, always subversively on the move, quickly emerged. His first few lectures were intellectually impressionistic – great historical canvases dripping with gore – but were well received. Then he simply stopped attending his own lectures, or appeared with a bandaged chin, apparently gagged by toothache. Since Gogol believed that geography should be taught without the distraction of maps, and that historical dates were portable, the year and a half he lasted at the university seems itself a triumph of elasticity.

Like his characters, Gogol was a defensive fantasist. He threw lies around himself like hoops, and danced within them. He was an actor, a liar, a peacock, a salesman of treasures. Friends reported that he was amusing to travel with because he had a great dislike of showing his passport or yielding his name. He liked aliases (Gogel, Gonel, and so on). He irritated others by playing card games he had invented and then changing the rules during play. He became rather selfishly involved with undercooked macaroni cheese, a dish he made again and again for guests. He dressed delicately, sometimes wearing a tall, yeasty, poetical hat: in his fiction, he always notes clothes with jubilation. A landowner in *Dead Souls* wears a bathrobe that is so worn it shines like leather. In 'The Nose', a woman has 'a pale yellow hat as light as a pastry'; in 'Nevsky Prospect', the sleeves of a woman's dress are surreally seen as resembling 'two airborne balloons, so that the lady would suddenly rise into the air if that man were not holding her'. Gogol, whose fiction is itself a sky of airborne objects and airy aspirations – it is fitting that Chagall illustrated *Dead Souls* in 1924 – himself seems to fly upwards. He is hard to hold down. Biography does not yield an explanation, for example, of why Gogol, having established his playful reputation for flying oddities, left St Petersburg in 1835, and began the solemn, wandering reclusion (Baden Baden, Paris, Rome, Jerusalem) of the rest of his life; nor why his bold sense of comedy curdled into the religious hectoring of his later years.

Gogol's greatest work – *The Government Inspector*, 'The Nose', 'The Overcoat', 'Diary of a Madman' and *Dead Souls* – is speedy, unsolemn, moving (in both senses). It is a reminder that fiction may, at times, be happily entrepreneurial. In such cases, the writer has a single flashing idea, and hotly syndicates it in scene after scene. Gogol knew this, and garaged the plot of *Dead Souls* like a domestic invention, warning correspondents not to breathe a word about it. In 'The Nose', a man wakes up to find that he has lost his nose, and spends several anguished days searching for it. In 'The Diary of a Madman', a man thinks he is the King of Spain, and that dogs are talking to one another. Above all, both Gogol's play, *The Government Inspector*, and *Dead Souls*, expand, in picaresque fashion, from a single trick or lie: in the former, the trick of arriving in town and posing as a government official, and in the latter, the trick of arriving in a small town and buying dead serfs (or 'souls') from the town's landowners.

Characters in Gogol lie to each other, and Gogol himself seems to be lying to us, at one moment pessimistically comic and at the next rhapsodically earnest. Gogol's fiction is streaked, here and there, with a somewhat hysterical didacticism. *Dead Souls* bursts into occasional hymn to Mother Russia. In 'The Overcoat', Gogol makes a lachrymose appeal for his hero, the poor solitary clerk: 'Many a time in his life he shuddered to see how much inhumanity there is in man, how much savage coarseness is concealed in refined, cultivated manners . . .' But Gogol seems to parody, at these moments, his own solemnity. What kind of truth does he tell? Did he depict an actual Russia of slothful landowners and pluming noblemen? Or is he a dark surrealist, something closer to Kafka or Mayakovsky? Gogol's work nourishes contradiction. His sentences run away with, and from, reality. On the one hand, his characters are madmen or devils, and so the fictional world would seem to be a fantasy, 'reality' constantly inflamed by characters who fan it to the reader. Noses disappear and ghosts flit. Yet on the other hand, Gogol's superb details, while feverish, are flushed with the actual. On the second page of *Dead Souls*, we see Chichikov's arrival in a nameless town, and are drawn to his two servants, who are carrying his belongings into an inn. First the trunk is taken in, and then 'they carried in a small chest of mahogany with marquetry of Karelian birch, a pair of shoe trees, and a roasted chicken wrapped up in blue paper.' A writer who notices that roasted chicken in blue paper has a very full reality-account. Throughout the work, we are offered realities that are coarsely human: a woman whose hands, offered to Chichikov for an introductory kiss, smell as if they 'had been washed in pickle-brine'; Ivan, an idle servant, lying on his back and spitting at the ceiling, 'hitting the same spot quite successfully'; the tailor in 'The Overcoat', who is seen sitting barefoot, the big toenail of one foot 'thick and strong as tortoise-shell'; Pliushkin, the miserly landowner in *Dead Souls*, who keeps, at the entrance to his house, one pair of oversize boots for the use of all his servants.

The argument over Gogol began in the 1830s and continues. Gogol is Russian literature's great custody battle. For most of his contemporaries, he was a radical realist, an inspired plagiarist who simply copied down what the country gave him. In his work could be found a relentlessly accurate analysis of corrupt bureaucracy, the evil of serfdom, the bitterness of poverty. 'The Overcoat' was seen as a great, humane argument on behalf of the 'little man'. In *Dead Souls*, it was thought, Gogol showed the final corruption of an indefensible, and tenuously persistent, institution. (The serfs were emancipated in 1861.) Vivid decisions were made about Gogol because they were stormed by politics. In Gogol's time, Russian intellectual life was split between 'Slavophiles' and 'Westernizers' – crudely, nationalists and internationalists, conservatives and radicals. Gogol, who supported serfdom, might be seen as belonging, insofar as he belonged anywhere, to the first group, along with Tolstoy (complicatedly) and Dostoevsky; such people as Alexander Herzen, Vissarion Belinsky and Ivan Turgenev belonged to the second. Yet despite Gogol's avowed politics (conservative, nationalist, Christian) he was, for the Westernizers, and indeed for most of his readers at this time, a great radical, a social realist. Herzen praised *Dead Souls* as 'a practical course for studying Russia', and Belinsky was so concerned to emphasize the novel's seriousness of realism that he claimed, absurdly, that it did not have a funny word in it. This earnestness was brushed aside in the first decades of this century, by writers who claimed Gogol as a proto-modernist, a surrealist, a linguistic game-player whose structures were not parented by real life. And this revisionism was itself erased by a swipe of ideology in 1934: from that moment until the early 1980s, the official Soviet doctrine became a version of nineteenth-century radical opinion. Gogol was a realist, a critic of tsarist iniquities. The Soviet reading, like that of the Westernizers, stripped Gogol of his comedy and surrealism. Gogol's readers have oscillated between Gogol's own axes: realist and preacher for the Westernizers and the Soviets; surrealist and fantasist for twentieth-century modernists such as Andrei Bely and Vladimir Nabokov.

Since Nabokov's little book on Gogol appeared in the 1940s, a certain kind of Anglo-American reading of Gogol has been dominant. It borrows from Nabokov, who described Gogol as primarily a verbal athlete, a writer much more interested in the sentence than in anything approaching 'reality', and adds to it the postmodern assumption that complicated texts are systems of signification that refer largely to themselves. Richard Pevear, who with Larissa Volokhonsky has translated both *Dead Souls* and most of Gogol's stories, joins these lines in his introduction to *The Collected Tales*. For him, and for most contemporary scholars, Gogol is a deconstructionist *avant la lettre*, a writer so enamoured of the riddling word that he shows reality to be nothing more than a set of verbal fictions. The world disappears into the 'airy nothing' of the word. Gogol's thousand-eyed sentences are about nothing real; actually, they are about themselves. The fiction is a subtle solipsist. He approvingly quotes Andrei Sinyavsky, who writes that Gogol's prose 'has its context and even, if you wish, its subject in itself,' and is 'in a pure sense *about nothing*'. The St Petersburg of these tales is less the actual historical city than 'a closed fiction', writes Pevear, and his tales reveal social rank to be 'a deception, a pure fiction'. The word 'fiction', when applied to reality by contemporary theory, means more than something simply invented; it means a text, a text identical with the text under discussion. Sure enough, Pevear finally suggests that Gogol exposes rank to be nothing more than 'an instance of the groundlessness of reality itself'.

Because of the Soviet tyranny, it has become almost impossible to discuss Gogol as a realist, as if this category of thought were a room in which such horrible events had occurred that it cannot be reentered. But the fumigations of postmodernism – in which Sinyavsky's idea that Gogol's prose is 'about nothing' is merely the absurd negative to Herzen's absurd positive – have their own, new sterility. Why should the fictionality of the real be the only opposition to the realism of fiction? An exaggerated scepticism the only opposition to an exaggerated fidelity? In ridding Gogol's work of an extrinsic political message, there is no need to rid it of an intrinsic human communication. In fact, 'realism' is beautifully flexible and longeval, and has always contained within it, as a single note contains its harmonics, its potential mixtures. Realism produces surrealism; it funds its own defaulters. Gogol reinvents realism; he is both an inflamed realist and a precise fantasist.

Far from being the fantasist of 'nothing', Gogol's work often strives to teach fantasy the lesson of the real. Take, for instance, Gogol's almost Austenesque interest in society and social rank. His stories abound in snobs and greasers. 'The Diary of a Madman' is touching partly because the madman, in his paranoia and insanity, dreams of something which perfectly sane people also dream of: social promotion. 'What makes me a titular councillor, and why on earth am I a titular councillor? Maybe I'm some sort of count or general and only seem to be a titular councillor?' That this man believes himself to be the King of Spain, and the local barber to be spreading Mohammedanism throughout the world, does not deprive his social dreaming of its social reality. Indeed, in this tale, Gogol reveals paranoia to be a kind of society sickness, a form of gossip imagined by a gossip, and turned against him; paranoia is a cocktail party in which all the drinks are poisoned. Likewise, the great story 'The Nose', whose frigid ludism anticipates 'The Metamorphosis', never leaves society. Gogol makes it clear that Kovalev, the unfortunate who awakes to find himself noseless, is the victim of a rather ordinary mishap: his barber steadies Kovalev's head by holding his nose when he gives him his daily shave. It might be the barber's theft. Kovalev is socially anxious. He has been a collegiate assessor for only two years, 'and therefore could not forget it for a moment'. Covering his razed face with a handkerchief, he runs outside in search of his nose. Suddenly, he catches sight of it. His nose has turned into a man, a state councillor (to judge by his uniform). He follows his nose into a cathedral, and accosts him. But the state councillor is snobbish, and tells Kovalev that he should know his place. He refuses to speak to him. Kovalev weeps. We realize, suddenly, that Kovalev's nose does not 'know its place' and has got above itself – literally. Thus, in a strange and beautiful way, Gogol's story is not at all anti-realistic; quite the opposite, it is a dogged literalization of a fantastic social reality. It takes seriously the idea that Kovalev's nose is socially ambitious; that Kovalev has been looking down his nose at other people, has had his nose in the air.

If 'The Nose' were only this, it would be a great story. But in the cathedral Kovalev has a tiny jolt, thrown off casually by Gogol, in one of those humane whispers with which his work is crowded. Kovalev, handkerchief to his face, sees some old peasant women 'with bandaged faces and two openings for the eyes, at whom he had laughed so much before . . .' The bandaged Kovalev realizes his kinship with the bandaged peasants. He surely realizes, at this moment, that despite the fantastic loss of his nose, reality is not mad, or 'groundless', but painfully *real*. And by the same token, Gogol's fiction reminds us not that society and social rank don't exist, but that it is literally mad to treat this kind of society as the whole of life (recall that Kovalev 'could not forget for a moment' his social rank). Gogol was not really a postmodernist, so much as a nineteenth-century Romantic, in flight from society's oppressive reality.

And because reality exists so fiercely for his characters, they in turn exist fiercely for us. Gogol's people are fantasists, their inner lives are often entirely fictional, but the world is real to them, and it is this awful reality which has turned them into fantasists. Perhaps the loveliest moment in his writing occurs in 'The Overcoat', when Akaky Akakievich, the poor unmarried clerk, decides that he will buy a fine new coat. He decides to save. And Gogol tells us that even the idea of the coat consoles him: 'From then on it was as if his very existence became somehow fuller, as if he were married.' Akaky Akakievich is sustained by a fantasy whose sustenance makes it a reality for him well before he actually buys the coat. Like most of Gogol's characters, he is an internal expansionist. (One sees how much Chekhov, whose characters also thinly yearn, learned from Gogol.)

It is *Dead Souls*, that grave frolic, that most overwhelmingly qualifies, and indeed, contradicts, the contemporary conviction that Gogol is an anti-realist. For *Dead Souls* is in some ways about the education of fantasy by real life. Chichikov, the devil-hero, is defeated by life. The book is allegorically layered. It is a parody of the picaresque novel, in which a traveller, catapulted by a sling of episodes, is in welcome motion. It is also, in some respects, a parody of the novel of social advancement, for in buying dead serfs, Chichikov is acquiring property, making himself a man of means – a man for whom the ends are the means, and which justify any means. And *Dead Souls* is also an allegory of Orthodox Christianity, a novel which tells us, though always obliquely, never pedagogically (as it would have done had the second and third parts been written), that the soul is not burst by death's sting but flies out of the grasp of the devil. In *Dead Souls* we are never truly dead.

That Gogol manages this parable gently, suffusedly, without hectoring, is probably a happy accident of the calendar. He wrote much of the novel in Rome, in the late 1830s. By 1841, a year before its publication, he was already in something of a religious teeter. He hinted, in letters, at his potential involvement in Christ's Second Coming. In 1841, he wrote to a friend in the coped, biblical Russian he now used for such communications: 'But hearken, now you must heed my word, for my word is doubly powerful over you, and woe unto anyone who does not heed my word.' He read his correspondents their spiritual Miranda rights, showering them with enforcements and entitlements. Two years after the publication of *Dead Souls*, he infuriated his friend, the writer Sergei Aksakov, by ordering him to read a chapter a day of Thomas à Kempis's *The Imitation of Christ*, preferably in the evening. (Aksakov replied that he had read Thomas à Kempis before Gogol was born.) A small passage near the end of *Dead Souls* gives an idea of what the second volume might have become, when Gogol exudes the authorial hope that 'in Chichikov . . . the passion that leads him on is not part of him, and in his cold existence there lies hidden that which will one day make man fall on his knees in the dust before the wisdom of the heavens.' But this is a rarity. Fortunately, most of *Dead Souls* seems to have been written in something of a profane lull, before the saintly madness.

Gogol's fictional devils got more real as he aged. In his early stories, the devil is just a dirty ghost, frankly supernatural, and somewhat intermittently present. Chichikov, by contrast, is the devil in harness. He is absolutely real, and as professional as an accountant. He arrives at a small town. He is in moral camouflage. He quickly ingratiates himself with the town's notables, and embarks on his plan. It was common for landowners to buy serfs from each other. They paid taxes to the government on their serfs. Moderate prosperity might mean the possession of two hundred serfs (Gogol's father owned this number), of whom a few would probably have recently died. It is these dead serfs which attract Chichikov. He proposes, to several landowners, that he buy these dead names at a bargain rate. The dead serfs are still named as if alive on the owner's list, because a new census has not yet erased them, and the owner will have to pay taxes on these names. Chichikov, in buying the names, relieves the owner of a tax burden, and gathers his own list of apparently live serfs. Thus credentialed as a gentleman and property-owner, he will use this false wealth to secure a mortgage. But Chichikov is not really interested in social advancement, and Gogol makes this quickly clear. No, Chichikov's motives are an abyss, and the reader's logical inference is that he is Satan, come to acquire men's souls for the army of death. Life, however, intrudes, and gloriously. One of Chichikov's interlocutors realizes his game, and threatens to have him beaten. Another, Sobakevich, suggests that Chichikov is not offering enough for these names. After all, he says, no one made better bricks than Milushkin, and Mikheev was the finest carriage-builder imaginable, and Stepan was a remarkable carpenter. Chichikov should pay better money for these men, says Sobakevich. But they are dead!, complains Chichikov, and Gogol relishes the ironies of a scene in which a Russian landowner who never cared much for his serfs when they were alive becomes protective on their behalf only when they are dead.

Yet they are not dead. They live in their names. When Chichikov peruses these lists, he is struck by the nicknames of the dead: John-the-Wheel, No-Respect-for-the-Pig-Trough, Grigorii Try-to-get-there-but-you-won't. Even on paper they signify something. And as Chichikov studies his new possessions, they rise off the paper and wave their lives before his eyes. Chichikov cannot help imagining the carpenter and the carriage-maker, their appetites and tardiness, their drunkenness and labours: 'it seemed as if these muzhiks had been alive only yesterday. As he gazed long at the names, Chichikov's spirit was touched and, with a sigh, he uttered: "Good heavens, how many of you are crowded in here!"' Once the dead rise, we know that Chichikov-the-devil is doomed. In secular terms, life has stirred, reasserted itself. He has learned Kovalev's lesson, that we are all bandaged in the same reality. And in religious, or allegorical terms, the devil has been slain by the Word, for these serfs are only words on a scrap of paper, yet how these words smoke! In this novel, miraculously, the two sides of Gogol's personality are briefly reconciled: the realist and the fantasist; the flying satirist, with his wild imagery, and the Christian moralist, who locates his redemptive powers in the very Host of his own mischievous prose.

In 1835, travelling from the Crimea to Moscow, Gogol and a friend, Paschenko, played a trick that Gogol had heard about from Pushkin. Gogol sent Paschenko on ahead of him, to announce in the next town the imminence of a government inspector, who was travelling incognito. They were, of course, given royal passage. This was the seed of his play, *The Government Inspector*. The postmodernist theorist might remark that Gogol took a literary tale from Pushkin, acted it out, and then returned it to literature in his own play. Literature giveth and literature taketh away, and there is nothing outside this cycle. But Gogol duped whole towns in 1835 not because Russia was a fictional world, but because it was a fiction-believing world. This fiction-believing world appears in *Dead Souls*; Chichikov propels himself on gusts of others' belief. It is thus a realistic novel. Or put it this way: Gogol wrote about a world which credited the great reality of his fiction by acting in an unreal, Gogolian fashion.

And it is a world that still exists in Russia. Three years ago I found myself on a collective farm near Ryazaan, about six hours from Moscow. A relative of mine was working for a Western financial foundation, helping Russians to privatize their farms. A group of us were crowded in an old woman's hut. It was dark;

the woman sat in the corner and silently sewed a burlap sack. Moon-like icons, tilting from the rough walls, suggested themselves. The farm's Chief Agronomist was not there; he was in hospital, sleeping off his alcoholism. The heads of the families had been told that the greater their number of dependants, the larger would be their government grant. People had been trying to claim dead family members as live ones. There was a brief discussion, and then the financial representatives plugged a laptop computer into the chalky wall, and made their swift, electronic census of the available 'souls'. At that moment, my relative and I turned to one another, and said, simultaneously: 'But this is exactly like . . . !'

What Chekhov Meant by Life

What did Chekhov mean by 'life'? I wondered this while uncomfortably watching a Broadway production of *A Doll's House*. Mild, slippery Chekhov once told Stanislavsky, with soft surprise as if it were something too obvious to say: 'But listen, Ibsen is no playwright! . . . Ibsen just doesn't know life. In life it simply isn't like that.' No, in life it simply isn't like that, even while sitting in a theatre. It was summer. Outside, the Broadway traffic sounded like an army that is getting close but which never arrives. The fantastic heat was sensual, the air-conditioners dripping their sap, their backsides thrust out of the window like Alisoun who does the same in Chaucer. Everything was the usual noisy obscurity. Yet inside, here was Ibsen ordering life into three trim acts, and a cooled audience obediently laughing and tutting at the right moments, and thinking about drinks at the interval – the one moment of Chekhovian life being that, in the lobby, the barman could be heard putting out glasses, tuning up his little cocktail orchestra. The clinking was disturbing Ibsen's simpler tune.

A Doll's House tells the story of a woman's subjection to, and eventual escape from, her husband. Ibsen is not wholly clumsy; he does not make Nora's husband, Torvald, monstrous so much as uncomprehending. And yet he cannot resist telling us how foolishly uncomprehending is Torvald. Nora deceives her husband in order to protect him; he discovers the deception and is furious. Towards the end of the play, Nora tells him that she is leaving him because she has never been more than his toy.

Torvald 'forgives' her for her deception. Nora cries because Torvald cannot understand. 'Why are you crying?' asks Torvald. 'Is it because I have forgiven you for your deception?' At this moment, the audience snickered knowingly. Poor, foolish Torvald, who thinks he can make things all right by forgiving his wife! Ibsen wants no part of Torvald's foolishness to escape us. Surely Chekhov's objection to Ibsen was founded in the feeling that Ibsen is like a man who laughs at his own jokes. He relishes the *dramatic* 'ironies' of the situation; indeed, he can think only in dramatic ironies, like someone who can write only on one kind of wide-margin paper. Ibsen's people are too comprehensible. We comprehend them as we comprehend fictional entities. He is always tying the moral shoelaces of his characters, making everything neat, presentable, knowable. The secrets of his characters are knowable secrets, not the true privacies of Chekhov's people. They are the bourgeois secrets: a former lover, a broken contract, a blackmailer, a debt, an unwanted relative.

But Chekhov's idea of 'life' is a bashful, milky complication, not a solving of things. We can get a good understanding of this from the notebook he kept. This notebook was, in effect, the mattress in which he stuffed his stolen money. It is full of enigmas in which nothing adds up, full of strange squints, comic observations, and promptings for new stories.

Instead of sheets – dirty tablecloths.

The dog walked in the street and was ashamed of its crooked legs.

They were mineral water bottles with preserved cherries in them.

In the bill preserved by the hotel-keeper was, among other things: 'Bugs – fifteen kopecks.'

He picked his teeth and put the toothpick back into the glass.

A private room in a restaurant. A rich man, tying his napkin round his neck, touching the sturgeon with his fork: 'At least I'll have a snack before I die' – and he has been saying this for a long time, daily.

If you wish women to love you, be original; I know a man who used to wear felt boots summer and winter, and women fell in love with him.

What is noticeable is that Chekhov thinks of detail, even visual detail, as a story, and thinks of story as an enigma. He was not interested in noticing that the roofs of a town look like armadillo shells, or that he was confused about God, or that the Russian people represented the world-spirit on a troika. He was drawn neither to the statically poetic nor to the statically philosophical. Detail is hardly ever a stable entity in Chekhov's work; it is a reticent event. He found the world to be as deeply evasive as he was himself – life as a tree of separate hanging stories, of dangling privacies. For him a story did not merely begin in enigma, but ended in enigma too. He had a character in 'Concerning Love' complain that 'decent Russians like ourselves have a passion for problems that have never been solved.' Chekhov had such a passion for problems, but only if solution might stay unrequited. The writer Ivan Bunin said that Chekhov loved to read out random oddities from the newspapers: 'Babkin, a Samara merchant, left all his money for a memorial to Hegel!' The attraction of such tales, one suspects, was that a newspaper imagines that it has explained a story when all it has done is told one. Bunin supplied a true anecdote about a deacon who ate all the caviare at a funeral party; Chekhov used this at the beginning of 'In the Ravine'. His writing, which is strewn with unsolved details, is a kind of newspaper of the intimate fantastic. In this respect, his stories are like tales of crime in which nobody is a criminal.

There is no introspection in Chekhov's notebook. Everything has the same hard, found, random quality. We can infer as much of Chekhov's personality from one entry as from all of them together. A friend said that he 'lacked gaiety, and his fine, intelligent eyes always looked at everything from a distance.' From the various memoirs by relatives and friends, we can imagine a man who always seemed a little older than himself, and older than anyone he met, as if he were living more than one life. He would not make himself transparent: he was approachable but unknowable. He had an arbitrary smile, and a comic's ability to make strange things seem inevitable. When an actor asked him to explain what kind of writer Trigorin is, in *The Seagull*, he replied: 'But he wears checkered trousers.' He had a horror of being the centre of attention. He delivered his judgments in a tone of weary generosity, as if they were so obvious that he had simply missed someone else saying them earlier. He was deeply charming; seasonally, a different woman fell in love with him. On this picture has been built the Anglo-American vision of Chekhov, in which the writer resembles the perfect literary Englishman – a writer of the religion of no religion, of instincts rather than convictions, a governor of ordinary provinces whose inhabitants may be unhappy or yearning for change, but who eventually learn to calm down and live by the local laws. D. S. Mirsky, the Russian critic who lived in England, argued that Chekhov was popular in England because of his 'unusually complete rejection of what we may call the heroic values'. But this idea of Chekhov as the nurse of the prosaic is far from the truth, and Chekhov's writing, which is odd, brutal, despairing and unhappily comic, gives no excuse for it.

The fullest biography to appear in English, by Donald Rayfield, clouds the soft Anglo-American idea of Chekhov, which is a good thing. In this account Chekhov is still charming, tactful, and decent. He is still the man who bought new books for the library of his hometown, who dispensed free medicine and became a hospital inspector near his farm at Melikhovo. But we also see that Chekhov's life was a long flight into his work. He ran from human connections. There is something cruel, even repulsive in a man who was so sensitive to pain, about the way Chekhov encouraged women to fall in love with him, and then, month by month, cancelled their ardour. He would reply scantily or not at all to their letters. His most productive writing years, between 1892 and 1900, were spent on his Melikhovo estate, about fifty miles south of Moscow, where he lived with his dutiful sister, Masha, and his parents. Here he tried to ration unnecessary involvement with people. Chekhov had the temperament of a philanderer. Sexually, he preferred brothels or swift liaisons. (This picture overpowers with superior evidence V. S. Pritchett's benign suggestion that Chekhov lacked sexual appetite.)

His one loyalty was to his family, for whom he became the breadwinner while at medical school in Moscow. He was born in Taganrog, in southern Russia, in 1860. His father, Pavel, may be seen as the original of all Chekhov's great portraits of hypocrites. Pavel was a grocer, but he failed at everything he touched except religious devotion. In between flogging his children – he was exceptionally cruel – he became kapellmeister of the cathedral choir, where his love of the liturgy made services interminable. In church, 'Pavel never compromised over his favourite quality, splendour.' He was horribly pious. There is the story of Pavel finding a rat in a barrel of olive oil in his shop. 'He was too honest to say nothing, too mean to pour the oil away, too lazy to boil and re-filter it. He chose consecration: Father Pokrovsky conducted a service in the shop.'

Chekhov would become a writer who did not believe in God, hated physical cruelty, fought every sign of 'splendour' on the page, and filled his fiction with hypocrites. The ghost of Pavel can be found everywhere in Chekhov, in the complacent Dr Ragin in 'Ward 6', who lectures his abused patients at the local asylum about Marcus Aurelius and the importance of stoicism, and in the fatuous priest in 'In the Ravine' who, at dinner, comforts a woman who has just lost her baby while pointing at her with 'a fork with a pickled mushroom on the end of it . . .' Yet the son did not abandon the father. Once the Chekhovs had moved to Moscow, Anton calmly assumed the sustenance of his whole family. He checked his dissolute elder brothers with that strange, sourceless maturity of his, which sometimes gives him the air of being the sole possessor of a clandestine happiness. There are eight rules by which 'well-bred people' live, he told his brother Nikolai in a long letter. You restrain yourself sexually; you do not brag. 'The truly gifted are always in the shadows, in the crowd, far from exhibitions.' Until Donald Rayfield gained access to previously censored archives, the last line of this letter has always been soothed into English as: 'You have to relinquish your pride: you are not a little boy anymore.' But the actual version runs: 'You must drop your fucking conceit . . .' It is good to tear our idea of Chekhovian perfection with these little hernias. We should see the lapses, the mundanities, the coarseness, the sexual honesty which Russian censors and English worshippers removed. Chekhov is still philo-Semitic and a supporter of women's rights. But every so often his letters fall, show a little bulge of prejudice – 'Yids' appear from time to time, and women are verbally patted.

The Chekhov family lived off Anton's literary earnings. These were small at first. Chekhov wrote hackishly for six years – comic stubs, sketches, cartoons and colourings for newspapers. (His mature work, of course, has a briskness, and sometimes a slapping, educative motion reminiscent of the form of a cartoon or sketch.) His meeting with Alexei Suvorin, the owner of the newspaper *Novoye Vremya*, was the foundation of his greatest writing. Suvorin had had his eye on Chekhov's writing. From 1887 until 1900, he was Chekhov's patron and deepest correspondent. He was also the writer's opposite, thus Chekhov had to function like Suvorin's kidney, extracting the business-man's poisons – his anti-Semitism (they quarrelled over the Dreyfus affair when Chekhov announced himself a Dreyfusard), his artistic conservatism, his wariness of the slightest political radicalism. Suvorin was reviled by most enlightened thinkers, and Chekhov's alliance with him was often scorned. But then

Chekhov also became friendly with Gorki, and his fiction was sometimes simultaneously claimed by both right and left: the pantomime horse of politics fighting inside itself for front and back legs, and then collapsing on stage.

'The Steppe' (1888) was the first story to appear in a 'thick journal': Chekhov was a renowned writer for the rest of his life. He was only twenty-eight, and the story has its hesitations, such as a weakness for lurid theatrical gargoyles (Moses and Solomon, the Jewish traders) which seem Dickensian but which are obviously lifted from Gogol. But much of the beauty of mature Chekhov is here; it is just an early footprint made by a lighter man. In particular, the bashful pace of the writing, which moves at the aimless, random speed of the imagination. We follow a little boy, Yegorushka, who is going to a new school, and who has hitched a ride with two men – a wool trader called Kuzmichov, and a priest called Father Christopher. As they leave the boy's home village, at the start of the journey, they pass the cemetery in which his father and his grandmother are buried. Chekhov's description drifts.

> From behind the wall cheerful white crosses and tombstones peeped out, nestling in the foliage of cherry trees and seen as white patches from a distance. At blossom time, Yegorushka remembered, the white patches mingled with the cherry blooms in a sea of white, and when the cherries had ripened the white tombs and crosses were crimson-spotted, as if with blood. Under the cherries behind the wall the boy's father and his grandmother Zinaida slept day and night. When Grandmother had died she had been put in a long, narrow coffin, and five-copeck pieces had been placed on her eyes, which would not stay shut. Before dying she had been alive, and she had brought him soft poppy-seed bun rings from the market, but now she just slept and slept.

Woolf and Joyce admired Chekhov, and, faced with little Yegorushka's drifting thought, one sees why. (Just as, watching the didactic *A Doll's House*, one sees why George Bernard Shaw admired Ibsen.) For this is a form of stream-of-consciousness, more natural and less showy than Anna Karenina's mania at the end of Tolstoy's novel. 'Before dying, she had been alive . . . but now she just slept and slept.' This is not only how a small boy thinks, but how all of us think about the dead, privately: *Before dying, she had been alive.* It is one of those obviously pointless banalities of thought, an accidental banality which, being an accident, is not banal, is never banal. But something deeper about Chekhov's art is revealed a page later, when Yegorushka cries because he misses his mother, and Father Christopher comforts him. 'Never mind son,' the priest says. 'Call on God. Lomonosov once travelled just like this with the fishermen, and he became famous throughout Europe. Learning conjoined with faith yields fruit pleasing to God. What does the prayer say? "For the glory of the Creator, for our parents' comfort, for the benefit of church and country." That's the way of it.' Of course, Father Christopher is offering no comfort at all; he is self-involved. His solace has no dramatic point, in the Ibsen sense. He is speaking his mind, literally. He speaks in the same apparently arbitrary manner as the boy thinks. This use of stream-of-consciousness would, in later years, become the basis of Chekhov's innovation in stagecraft; it is also his innovation in fiction. Chekhov sees the similarities between what we say to ourselves and what we say to others: both are failed privacies. Both are lost secrets, the former lost somewhere between our minds and our souls, the latter lost somewhere between each other. Naturally, this kind of mental speech, whether turned inward or outward, has the arbitrary quality of memory or dream. It *is* memory or dream. And this is why it seems comic, because watching a Chekhov character is like watching a lover wake up in bed, half-awake and half-dreaming, saying something odd and private which means nothing to us because it refers to the preceding dream. In life, at such moments, we sometimes laugh and say: 'You're not making any sense, you know.' Chekhov's characters live in these two states.

Sometimes, his characters turn their thought outwards, and speak it; sometimes their thought remains inward, and Chekhov describes it for us – and very often these two ribbons of revelation are indistinguishable from one another, as in Yegorushka's remembrance of his grandmother. 'The Bishop', a late story which Chekhov completed in 1902, two years before he died, is a good example of this new fluency in storytelling. A dying cleric starts to think about his childhood . . . and suddenly, he is adrift. He remembers 'Father Simeon, who was very short and thin, but who had a terribly tall son (a theological student) . . . Once his son lost his temper with the cook and called her "Ass of Jehudiel", which made Father Simeon go very quiet, for he was only too ashamed of not being able to remember where this particular ass was mentioned in the Bible.' Such richness, such healthy secularism of detail! Yet the great novelty of Chekhov is not in discovering or inventing such details and anecdotes, for we can find details as good in Tolstoy and Leskov. It is in their placement, their sudden flowering, their lack of apparent point, as if Chekhov's characters were coming across something unwanted, certainly unexpected. The thought seems to be thinking the characters. It is the movement of free consciousness in literature for perhaps the first time: neither Austen nor Sterne, neither Gogol nor Tolstoy allow their characters quite this relationship to memory.

The great pleasure of seeing Chekhov develop as a writer, from 'The Steppe' to 'The Lady With the Dog' eleven years later, is to see the way he discovers and enlarges this idea of apparently arbitrary detail. For it is not merely Chekhov's characters who think in sudden lunges and bites of detail. It becomes the very principle of Chekhov's prose style. Nabokov once complained about Chekhov's 'medley of dreadful prosaisms, ready-made epithets, repetitions'. Nabokov was certainly wrong. Chekhov's metaphors, nature-scenes and visual details are often finer than Nabokov's (and invariably finer than Tolstoy's) because they have an unexpectedness that seems to break away from literature. He sees the world not as a writer

might see it but as one of his characters might. This is the case
even when he is telling a story as 'Chekhov', apparently from
outside a character's head. 'From somewhere far off came the
mournful, indistinct cry of a bittern, sounding just like a cow
locked up in a shed.' This is not an obviously poetic likeness; it
is how a villager might think of a bittern's cry. 'A cuckoo
seemed to be adding up someone's age, kept losing count and
starting again.' A girl about to burst into tears, 'her face oddly
strained as if her mouth were full of water'. (The key there is the
word 'oddly'. Oddly to whom? To the other characters in the
room, one of whom is Chekhov: he is no longer a writer.) The
noise, in a poor village, of 'an expensive-sounding accordion'.

More completely than any writer before him Chekhov
became his characters. A great story like 'Gusev' is impossible
without this identification. It is set on a boat returning to
Russia. In the sick-bay, a stupid peasant called Gusev is dying.
The other patients make fun of his primitive imagination – he
thinks that the winds are chained up somewhere like dogs to a
wall, and that it is stormy because they have been let loose. As
Gusev lies in the ship, he recalls his home village, and we see
that his imagination is not primitive. Soon, he dies, and is buried
at sea, wrapped in a sail. 'Sewn up in the sailcloth,' writes
Chekhov, 'he looked like a carrot or radish: broad at the head
and narrow at the feet.' As he falls into the sea, clouds are
massing. Chekhov writes that one cloud looks like a triumphal
arch, another like a lion, a third like a pair of scissors. Suddenly
we realize that Chekhov sees the world as Gusev does. If Gusev
is foolish then so is Chekhov! Why is it more foolish to think of
the wind as a chained dog as Gusev does, than to think of a
cloud as a lion or a corpse as a radish, as Chekhov does?
Chekhov's very narration disappears into Gusev's.

Stupendously, Chekhov's fullest biographer has little time for
Chekhov's writing. It appears to obstruct the siege of biographical 'fact'. Donald Rayfield tells us in his preface that Chekhov's
works are discussed 'inasmuch as they emerge from his life and
as they affect it, but less as material for critical analysis.

Biography is not criticism.' Of course, this separation of life and work, as a butcher might use separate knives for raw meat and for cooked, is primitive. Biography is criticism, especially in the case of Chekhov, who so often evaded life to strengthen his work. Undoubtedly, Rayfield offers a newly full idea of Chekhov's life – he is more brutal, more cruel, more ordinary, more lonely. But his book is only greyly rich: a massive diary of travel and letters and meetings. About the writer, he tells us almost nothing, and in several places disarms facts of their literary context. On the whole, it would be better if he never mentioned Chekhov's work, because his brief comments seem merely mandatory. 'Gusev', he tells us, 'is an awesome portrayal of nature's indifference to death . . . Chekhov's post-Sakhalin phase had begun.' 'Ward 6' is 'a bleak allegory of the human condition. There is no love interest.' Of 'The Student' (Chekhov's own favourite), he comments: 'This is "late Chekhov", where . . . all is evoked, not stated.' And so on. Most of the stories are brushed off in a line or two. He forces stories into biographical cells, distorting many of them. At other times, he takes comments by Chekhov and skins them of the literary. For example, in January 1901, Chekhov was in Rome with his friend, M. M. Kovalevsky. Chekhov, according to Rayfield, was ill and depressed. He had three years to live. Offered as evidence of Chekhov's state of mind is his response to a penitential procession that he saw with Kovalevsky at St Peter's. Rayfield comments: 'Anton's mood grew grim: he told Kovalevsky he was writing nothing long, because he would soon die. [He] watched a penitential procession in St Peter's. Asked how he would describe it, he replied, "A stupid procession dragged past." ' But Kovalevsky's memoir (most recently reprinted in Andrei Turkov's book, *Anton Chekhov and His Times*, which was published in Moscow in 1990) makes clear that Chekhov's was a literary response. Kovalevsky discusses Chekhov's dismissal in the light of his 'avoidance of any kind of unnecessary detail' as a writer. When they had watched the procession go by, Kovalevsky suggested that, 'for a belletrist', what they had seen was 'not without a certain attraction'. 'Not the slightest,' replied Chekhov. 'The modern novelist would be obliged to satisfy himself with the phrase: "A silly procession dragged on." ' The literary context is not only truer and more interesting than the wrongly biographical reading; it tells us more about the 'biographical' Chekhov.

In 1890, Chekhov made a long journey to Sakhalin, a prison island off the coast of Siberia. Chekhov saw Russia's human leavings on Sakhalin, a kind of living death-camp. Near the end of the book-length report he published in 1895, Chekhov describes seeing a murderer being given ninety lashes. Then this Chekhovian detail – a whining military medical assistant who asks a favour. 'Your worship, please let me see how they punish a prisoner.' There were times, wrote Chekhov, when 'I felt that I saw before me the extreme limits of man's degradation . . .' Chekhov believed in the importance of good schools and medicine. But Sakhalin heated his meliorism. At Melikhovo, the estate he bought in 1892, he helped to build a new school, gave freely of his medical expertise. His greatest stories became darker, more absolving. Prisons are everywhere in them: even the lovers in 'The Lady With the Dog', published in 1899 while Chekhov was first involved with his future wife, Olga Knipper, feel trapped in a cage, 'and it was impossible to escape from it, just as though you were in a lunatic asylum or a convict chain-gang!' The bleak 'Gusev' (1890) was seeded when Chekhov saw two men die on board the ship bringing him back from Sakhalin. 'Ward 6' (1892) is set in an asylum. A complacent doctor, who has ignored the sufferings of his patients, finds that his own mind is lapsing. He in turn is thrown into the asylum. From the window, he can see the town prison: 'There's reality for you!' thinks the doctor. He dies in the asylum, and as he leaves consciousness he goes on a mental safari, and Chekhov awards him one of those gorgeous lunges, one of those random aerations or white apertures that are so distinctive a feature of his work: 'A herd of deer, extraordinarily beautiful and graceful, which he had been reading about on the previous day, raced past him; then a peasant woman stretched out a hand to him with a registered letter . . .' These stories have a rather frantic humanism: Chekhov wrote to Suvorin in 1898 that the writer's task was to 'stand up for the guilty if they have already been condemned and punished'. This was a year after he made his first public stand, on behalf of Dreyfus.

What did Chekhov believe in? In his essay on the writer, the philosopher Lev Shestov suggested (approvingly) that Chekhov had 'no ideal, not even the ideal of ordinary life'. His work, he said, murmurs a quiet 'I don't know' to every problem. Certain Soviet critics decided that Chekhov's 'hopeless' characters were not prophetic enough about the imminent revolution – too pessimistic about Russia's future. But because Chekhov's stories confound philosophy they do not necessarily lack it. Susan Sontag is surely right when she suggests that Chekhov's writing is a dream of freedom – 'an absolute freedom,' wrote Chekhov, 'the freedom from violence and lies.' And freedom is not merely political or material in his work. It is a neutral saturate, like air or light. How often he describes a village, and then, at the village's edge – 'the open fields'! The narrator of 'Man In a Case' remembers the freedom of being a child when his parents went out, 'and we would run around the garden for an hour or so, revelling in perfect freedom.' And because Chekhov is truthful, because he is not a Tolstoy who will shuffle his characters towards the light of the Godhead, or a Gorki who will lead his characters to instinctive socialism, he must admit that freedom is not always attractive to us, and that it frightens us. Perhaps freedom is only the freedom not to exist? 'Oh how nice not to exist,' cries Chebutykin in *Three Sisters*. Often we notice that his characters long to escape into a freedom whose vastness depends on its nonexistence. Moscow is not just an impossibility for the three sisters. It does not exist, because their desire for it has made it disappear. Perhaps the gap between yearning for a new life – the most familiar gesture of Chekhov's characters, and one the writer saw firsthand amongst his own family – and yearning for no life, is small. But whatever happens to Chekhov's characters, however they yearn, they have one freedom that flows from his literary genius: they act like free consciousnesses, and not as owned literary characters. This is not a negligible freedom. For the great achievement of Chekhov's beautifully accidental style, his mimicking of the stream of the mind, is that it allows forgetfulness into fiction. Buried deep in themselves, people forget themselves while thinking, and go on mental journeys. Of course, they do not exactly forget to be themselves. They forget to act *as purposeful fictional characters*. They mislay their scripts. They stop being actors, Ibsen's envoys.

Chekhov's characters forget to be Chekhov's characters. We see this most beautifully in one of his earliest stories, 'The Kiss', written when he was twenty-seven. A virginal soldier kisses a woman for the first time in his life. He hoards the memory of it, and bursts to tell his fellow soldiers about his experience. Yet when he does tell them, he is disappointed because his story takes only a short minute to tell, yet 'he had imagined it would take until morning'. One notices that many of Chekhov's characters are disappointed by the stories they tell, and somewhat jealous of other people's stories. But to be disappointed by one's own story is an extraordinarily subtle freedom in literature, for it implies a character's freedom to be disappointed not only by his own story but, by extension, by the story Chekhov has given him. Thus he wriggles out of Chekhov's story into the bottomless freedom of disappointment. He is always trying to make his own story out of the story Chekhov has given him, and even this freedom of disappointment will be disappointing. (That this freedom is awarded and managed by the author is of course a trivial paradox: how else could it arise?) And yet it *is* a freedom. We see this so finely in 'The Kiss'. The soldier forgets that he is in Chekhov's story because he has become so involved in his own. His own story is bottomless, and yearns to last all night; Chekhov's story 'takes only a minute to tell'. In Chekhov's world, our inner lives run at their own speed. They are laxly calendared. They live in their own gentle almanac, and in his stories the free inner life bumps against the outer life like two different time-systems, like the Julian calendar against the Gregorian. This was what Chekhov meant by 'life'. This was his revolution.

Virginia Woolf's Mysticism

I

There is a story that the young Virginia Woolf and others visited Rodin's studio in 1904. The sculptor told the party that they could touch anything except the figures still under sheets. When Woolf began to unwrap one of the sculptures, Rodin slapped her. The story is probably apocryphal; but like the grave of an unknown soldier, we can have it as the emblem of an invisible struggle. Woolf's literary struggle was to uncover figures, in a way that they had never before been denuded. She unwrapped consciousness. To do this, she would have to disobey the generation that stood behind her, its slapping hand outstretched like Rodin's. Woolf's best biographer, Hermione Lee, tells the anecdote in a chapter titled 'Madness': Woolf was on the edge of an attack of mental instability. But there is also what Henry James called the madness of art.

The modernist Virginia Woolf, the writer betrothed to a creeping project, is the Woolf who matters. 'Bloomsbury', the big floral distraction, has obscured her. For she was much more serious, and more seriously literary, than her celebrated friends and relatives, who look nowadays like mere threads of 'promise'. The academy has stinted the achievement of Woolf's writing by offering a general amnesty to all of it, however unsuccessful; or simply by converting literary questions into political ones. Thus *The Waves* becomes an example of 'postcolonial carnivalesque', according to Jane Marcus. But postcolonialism, even modern feminism, would have happened without Woolf; whereas her fiction would not. The writer – single, snobbish, new, rare – can be found in her great essays, in her diaries, with their combination of sharp wail and steady literary appetite, and in her best novels, *Mrs. Dalloway, To the Lighthouse* and *The Waves*.

Much about Woolf's childhood can be learned from a ninety-page memoir called 'A Sketch of the Past'. Woolf wrote it in 1939 and 1940, just before she took her life. In it, she looked again at the origins of her literary rebellion, which she found in the impress of her parents, and in the thick air of the family home, at Hyde Park Gate in West London. Virginia Stephen was born in 1882, into the very riot of Victorianism. She wrote that she and her sister, Vanessa, represented 1910 and her parents 1860. All her writing would offer an insubordination to the sure captaincy of the Victorians. They were represented by her mother, Julia Stephen, whom Virginia complicatedly loved, and her father, Leslie Stephen, whom she complicatedly hated. Julia Stephen, a Victorian idealization of the wife and mother, was unselfish, an emotional wetnurse to her husband, devoted to good works outside the home. When Virginia started writing book reviews in 1905, she felt the ghost of her mother (who had died in 1895) warning her to be femininely decorous, and to soothe male reputations. Woolf, characteristically, wrote at this time that 'My real delight in reviewing is to say nasty things.' Leslie Stephen became Mr Ramsay in *To the Lighthouse,* the needy monolith surrounded by the poor pebbles of his battered family. He was one of those Victorians who seem like portable zeitgeists. He was one of the most important agnostics of his generation, a literary critic, a Cambridge rationalist, the author of *The History of English Thought in the Eighteenth Century*. Stephen had a grinding, puritanical mind. 'He would ask what was the cube root of such and such a number; for he always worked out mathematical problems on railway tickets,' wrote Woolf in 'A Sketch of the Past'. Woolf selects one sharp memory which gives us a picture of difficult pleasure. She remembers him stooping from his intellectual labours to mend his little daughter's sailboat, and snorting in embarrassment: 'Absurd! – what fun it is doing this.'

In *To the Lighthouse*, Mr Ramsay is seen struggling to get beyond letter Q in the intellectual alphabet. It is one of Woolf's most beautiful similes: 'It was a splendid mind. For if thought is like the keyboard of a piano, divided into so many notes, or like the alphabet . . . then his splendid mind had no sort of difficulty in running over those letters one by one, firmly and accurately, until it had reached, say, the letter Q. He reached Q. Very few people in the whole of England ever reach Q . . . But after Q? What comes next?' Leslie Stephen acted like a genius but he thought like a merely gifted man. His tantrums, his loud groaning about the difficulty of mental activity, his domestic helplessness, his virile activity (a twenty-mile walk was nothing), the intellectual fez he wore on his head – does it not look, to us, a little like the self-conscious opposite of a dunce's cap? – the foaming beard; all this was sanctioned by the age. It is how 'great men' acted. But Stephen once confessed to his daughter, with his admirable honesty, that he had only 'a good second-class mind', and Woolf wrote: 'He had I think no feeling for pictures; no ear for music; no sense of the sound of words.' Unwittingly, her father trained her in hostility, taught her how to float away from him in his own shallow waters. The way she summed up his limitations would be the way she pounced on the limitations of a whole class of people. Repeatedly, one comes across these portraits in her diaries. Her father was the model 'insider'. He was an institution, which could be abbreviated to 'Eton-Cambridge', places from which she was excluded. Such people were what she called 'Romans' (whereas she was Greek). They kept the Empire spinning, politically and intellectually. They were necessary, she wrote, 'like Roman roads'. But in her father, she found 'not a subtle mind; not an imaginative mind; not a suggestive mind. But a strong mind; a healthy out of door, moor striding mind; an impatient, limited mind; a conventional mind entirely accepting his own standard of what is honest.' (Stephen's truest contemporary is that supple but flat insider, Noel Annan, who wrote his biography.)

Leslie Stephen can be caricatured, though Woolf never did this. Yet the education he gave his daughter was deep. Virginia Stephen did not go out of the house to school. Her childhood was violently isolated, and spent in the shadow of her father, who expected that Virginia would 'become an author in time'. Virginia ran through the battery of his books. He read, of course, to the collected family – the thirty-two Waverley novels of Scott, Carlyle's *The French Revolution*, Jane Austen, and the English poets. But Woolf's own reading, under her father's tutelage, constituted her real education. It was like a less heated version of John Stuart Mill's upbringing. She read Greek – Plato, of course – with Walter Pater's sister. Leslie Stephen gave her history and biography. During 1897, when she was fifteen, he chose for her Pepys's *Diary*, Arnold's *History of Rome*, Campbell's *Life of Coleridge*, Macaulay's *History*, Carlyle's *Reminiscences,* and *Essays in Ecclesiastical Biography* by James Stephen, her grandfather. We see Woolf developing that deep, secretive relationship with language that often characterizes the solitary child. 'I have spotted the best lines in the play,' she wrote to her brother, Thoby, who was at Cambridge. 'Now if that doesn't send a shiver down your spine . . . you are no true Shakespearean!' And more plaintively, again to Thoby: 'I dont get anyone to argue with me now, and feel the want. I have to delve from books, painfully and alone, what you get every evening sitting over your fire and smoking your pipe with Strachey etc.'

Woolf's background, like a patronymic, was something that marked her publicly. She lived for twenty-two years in her father's house, and escaped only when he died in 1904. This was her first escape – out of Hyde Park Gate, and into Bloomsbury, where she lived with her brothers and sister, in Gordon Square. Her second escape was into literary journalism. Here, most commentators are not attentive enough. For Woolf, I think, became a great critic, not simply a 'great reviewer'. The *Collected*

Essays, which are still being edited, is the most substantial body of criticism in English this century. They belong in the tradition of Johnson, Coleridge, Arnold, and Henry James. This is the tradition of poet-critics, until the modern era, when novelists like Woolf and James join it. That is, her essays and reviews are a writer's criticism, written in the language of art, which is the language of metaphor. The writer-critic, or poet-critic, has a competitive proximity to the writers she discusses. That competition is registered verbally. The writer-critic is always showing a little plumage to the writer under discussion. If the writer-critic appears to generalize about literature, that is because literature is what she does, and one is always generalizing about oneself.

Of course, all of Woolf's work is a kind of tattoo peeled off the English poets and rubbed onto her sentences; all of it is poetically metaphorical. But these early experiences encouraged the tendency toward metaphor found in all her fictional work. In her criticism, the language of metaphor becomes a way of speaking to fiction in its own accent, the only way of respecting fiction's ultimate indescribability. Metaphor is how the critic avoids bullying fiction with adult simplicities. For it is a language of forceful hesitation. Its force lies in the vigour and originality of Woolf's metaphors; its hesitation lies in its admission that, in criticism, the language of pure summation does not exist. Criticism can never offer a successful summation, because it shares its subject's language. One is always thinking through books, not about them. Woolf's father had written 'successfully' *about* books, with a vigorous alienation from his subjects. Leslie Stephen's essays chew through books to the cardboard, grimly intent on the same universal mastication, whether the subject is Pope or the history of the Popes. Therein lay his limitations, and Woolf could surely see this, even if, as a young woman, she could only articulate this limitation as the apprehension that her father's essays were not 'literary' enough. Woolf, by contrast, is 'literary', which is to say metaphorical.

She approaches fiction gently, seemingly anxious not to overwhelm it with strong comprehension.

All criticism is itself metaphorical in movement, because it deals in likeness. It asks: what is art *like?* What does it resemble? How can it best be described, or redescribed? If the artwork describes itself, then criticism's purpose is to redescribe the artwork in its own, different language. But literature and literary criticism share the same language. In this, literary criticism is completely different from art and music and their criticisms. This is probably what James meant when he spoke of the critic's 'immense vicariousness'. To describe literature critically is to describe it again, but as it were for the first time. It is to describe it as if literature were music or art, and as if one could sing or paint criticism. *Again, but for the first time*: the critic shares the language of her subject, but then changes every word, makes it her own tilted subjection. All critics do this, but the writer-critic, wanting to be both faithful critic and original writer, does it acutely, in a flurry of trapped loyalties. The writer–critic's relationship to the writer she reviews may be likened to hearing, in the next room, a sibling playing something on the piano that you yourself know well, but have not yet played yourself.

The language of metaphor is the language of this secret sharing, of approximation, of likeness, and of competition. For, as a critic, Woolf was always in competition with what she was reviewing, and her language's proximity constitutes a luxurious squabble. Again and again, her metaphors are used to deliver a judgment which marks both her nearness to her subjects – her ability to use an artistic language – and her separateness. Forster, she writes, is too fidgety as a novelist, always stepping in to talk about his characters: 'he is like a light sleeper who is always being woken by something in the room.' (Proust, in similar metaphorical mood, likens the writing of his novel to 'a long, sunken fatigue'; and V.S. Pritchett complains, in an essay, that Ford Madox Ford was too awake: 'he never sank into the determined stupor out of which greater novelists work.' Proust, Woolf and Pritchett all use metaphor to hurry into truth their paradox – of an artist having to will himself into artistic sleep.) Dickens, she felt, rather vulgarly made excitement by inventing new, disposable characters: 'Dickens makes his books blaze up not by tightening the plot or sharpening the wit, but by throwing another handful of people upon the fire.' George Moore, she felt, was too literary a novelist: 'Literature has wound itself about him like a veil, forbidding the free use of his limbs.' Many of her essays were written for the *Times Literary Supplement,* whose contributions were, until recently, unsigned. But this anonymity was ideal: surely Woolf knew that her prose had to sign itself. So her essays, both in texture and in content, were self-advertisements. Between 1917 and 1925, she produced her delicate manifestos, which insisted on the break that her generation, the Georgians, must make with the Edwardians. Her generation, as she defined it, meant Lawrence, Joyce, Forster, Eliot. The Edwardians meant Shaw, Galsworthy, Wells, Arnold Bennett. In 'Modern Novels' (1919), 'On Re-Reading Novels', 'Mr Bennett and Mrs Brown' (1923) and 'Character in Fiction' (1924), she argued that character was at the centre of great fiction, and that character had changed 'on or about December 1910'. This was a literary change. Character, to the Edwardians, was everything that could be described; to her generation it was everything that could not be described. The Edwardians blunted character, she felt, by stubbing it into things – clothes, politics, income, houses, relatives. She wanted to sharpen character into the invisible.

First of all, said Woolf, what was 'reality'? To the Edwardians, reality was a furniture sale, everything that could be seen, tagged, and marked. But Woolf wanted to break from what she called this materialism, and to look for darker corridors. Reality is 'a luminous halo, a semi-transparent envelope surrounding us from the beginning of consciousness to the end'. It was 'consciousness', and its relation to the 'luminous halo', that was the exquisite distress of Woolf's literary generation. But this new awareness was not a mere evaporation into the aesthetic. Again and again, Woolf insists on her word, 'life'. It was because she felt that life had escaped from Arnold Bennett's novels that she punished them so: 'perhaps without life nothing else is worth while.' She chafed at the vagueness of the word, yet its vagueness was its spur. It was the fate of modernist writing to be merely an advance in failure, because 'life' is so resistant to being broken into words. 'Tolerate the spasmodic, the obscure, the fragmentary, the failure', she implored her sceptical readers. 'We are trembling on the verge of one of the great ages of English literature.' 'I think', she wrote in her *Diary*, of *The Waves*, 'this is the greatest opportunity I have yet been able to give myself: therefore the most complete failure.'

And certainly, Woolf failed from time to time: the current amnesty, which blows triumph over everything she wrote, just imprisons her in hot air. It should be possible to demonstrate that all the novels have weak passages, and to discuss the inevitable chanciness of her use of interior monologue, without attracting the charge of being a 'masculine' reader. *Mrs. Dalloway* is not, in the end, as suggestive as it wants to be (Woolf seemed herself to sense this); *The Waves,* though a great book whose last twenty pages are a pure example of secular mystical writing, is too often tediously involved in its own procedures (almost every character has something to say about the difficulty of language); *Between the Acts* seems unfinished. But when Woolf fails it is generally when she is being Victorian, not when she is being Georgian, or modernist. In *Mrs. Dalloway*, for instance, she compares twilight in London to a woman changing her clothes for the evening, 'but London would have none of it, and rushed her bayonets into the sky, pinioned her, constrained her to partnership in her revelry.' In *To the Lighthouse* she compares spring to 'a virgin fierce in her chastity, scornful in her purity'. In *The Waves*, she likens the sea to 'a girl couched on her green-sea mattress . . . with water-globed jewels that sent lances of opal-tinted light falling and flashing in the uncertain air like the flanks of a dolphin leaping, or the flash of a falling blade'. Rebecca West thought that *The Waves* was 'pre-Raphaelite kitsch', which is not true. But certainly, in all these cases a cliché of Victorian poetry – twilight, spring, and the sea all compared to woman – seeps from Woolf's childhood into her prose and luridly stains its pristinities.

When Woolf's prose succeeds, there is no other twentieth-century English novelist who seems so native, so germinally alive, in her language. She wrote of 'words with roots'. She, who loved first and most dearly the Elizabethans and Carolinians – like Melville, she revered Sir Thomas Browne – historicizes language. She jams herself into the wheels of the clock of English prose; she stops the motion, and then, installed, starts it again, absorbing all the historical vibrations. Her prose makes one think of Diderot's bequeathing his library to Catherine of Russia: she gives us, in her prose, the room of her entire accumulated historical reading. Her rarity is that she has one ear open to metaphor, and the other ear open to adjectives and adverbs. (Melville, again, has this Shakespearean double-ness.) She sees that words, when chosen with an overpowering concentration, begin to turn into abstractions, in the way anything does if it is stared at for long enough: she embarrasses words into confessing their abstract pigments: words begin to seem like colours in her hands. We see this in the fiction and in the superb one-line brush-strokes in the *Diary*. Especially, perhaps, in the *Diary*, where she runs adjectives after each other without the cushion of commas. She looks at the Sussex landscape: 'A heavy flagging windy cloudy day with breadths of sun . . . Lovely are the curves of the grey clouds sweeping; and the long barns lying.' Or this, in *The Waves*: 'Colour returns. The day waves yellow with all its crops.' (This is a great sentence, and simply needs to be repeated again and again.) From *To the Lighthouse*: 'The arrow-like stillness of fine weather . . . Tortoise-shell butterflies burst from the chrysalis and pattered their life out on the window-pane.' And in her *Diary*, she watches people, and throws adjectives at them: 'steamy grubby inarticulate Rex Whistler'. Or Mrs Keppel, a great society hostess: 'a swarthy thick set raddled direct . . . old

97

grasper'. She combines words so paradoxically: 'a nimble secondrate man' (this of a professor of English literature). Of Stephen Spender: 'a loose jointed mind – misty, clouded, suffusive. Nothing has outline. Very sensitive, tremulous, receptive & striding.' Of Edith Sitwell: 'All is very tapering & pointed, the nose running on like a mole.' Of Bunny Garnett: 'that rusty surly slow old dog with his amorous ways and primitive mind'. And then, amidst so much uncertainty and fragility, one finds this little ecstasy, which lights up everything else: 'Dear me, how lovely some parts of The Lighthouse are! Soft & pliable, & I think deep, & never a word wrong for a page at a time.'

2

But Woolf disliked being complimented for her sentences, and wrote that we must go to novelists 'for chapters, not for sentences'. And in truth her achievement is not measured in sentences; and not measured in chapters either. Her break with the Edwardians lies in the way she writes about consciousness. It is here, especially in the flowing form of *To the Lighthouse*, that she did something astonishing. Most readers know Woolf, in the caricature, as a writer who allows her characters to ramble internally, moving randomly, it seems, from thinking about death or memory at one moment to a bowl of fruit at the next. Well, the caricature goes, this was the Bloomsbury way, the soft metaphysics of the upper classes. The caricature has a name for it: stream-of-consciousness. But Woolf's development of stream-of-consciousness is much more interesting than that. It allows absent-mindedness into fiction for the first time. A character is allowed to drift out of relevance, to wander into a randomness which may be at odds with the structure of the novel as a whole. What does it mean for a character to become irrelevant to a novel? It frees characters from the fiction which grips them; it lets characters forget, as it were, that they are thicketed in a novel. Undoubtedly, Woolf learned some of this from Sterne, and perhaps from Austen. More immediately, she learned it from Chekhov, about whom she wrote in 1917, in 1918, and in 1919. She admired the way, in that writer, 'the emphasis is laid upon such unexpected places that at first it seems as if there were no emphasis at all.'

There is an obvious difference between the fiction she wrote before and after reading Chekhov. But she found her way slowly. In her first novel, *The Voyage Out* (1915), there is a moment which hangs on the verge of stream-of-consciousness. Clarissa Dalloway (who reappears ten years later in *Mrs. Dalloway*) is going to sleep. She is reading Pascal, and thinking drowsily about her husband. What would become a current of thought in Woolf's later books, is here stopped, and converted into a dream. She falls asleep, and her dream, which is a fantastic vision of huge Greek letters, wakes her up. At which point she reminds herself that she has been dreaming. The chapter ends, and everything is closed off neatly. In what it allows, this passage is hardly different from the beginning of chapter 16 (vol. 1) of *Mansfield Park*, in which Fanny Price, highly agitated, also goes to sleep while thinking to herself. Austen writes: 'She fell asleep before she could answer the question, and found it as puzzling when she awoke the next morning.' In both passages, sleep ends internal thought. Random thought, at this stage in Woolf's career, can only exist as drowsiness or as dream. It is not yet day-dreaming. In this first novel, if you forget yourself, you must fall asleep. In her best novels, you stay awake and forget yourself.

Everything gathers in *To the Lighthouse*, Woolf's greatest novel, which she wrote in a high spasm of activity between 1925 and 1927. Mr Ramsay, the philosopher, and Mrs Ramsay, are on holiday, with their children. James, the youngest, wants to take a boat to the lighthouse. There are houseguests: Charles Tansley, an atheist philosopher and former pupil of Ramsay's; Augustus Carmichael, a lazy old poet who sits all day in a deck-chair, purring lovely phrases; and Lily Briscoe, who sits on the lawn painting, painting her 'attempt at something'. Woolf dances between these consciousnesses, so that it seems to be a novel in which everything happens at the same time. Clearly, all these people *are* thinking at the same time, as people do in real life, and the writer's struggle is to outwit narrative-sequence, whereby one is forced to follow the thread of one mind and then the next. Narrative sequence, at bottom, is nothing other than the materiality of words, which forces us to order phrases in sequence, rather than on top of each other. A painter, like Lily Briscoe, can actually mix paints, but a writer cannot do this. The closest a writer can come to this is in the yoking of metaphor, whereby one thing is pushed against another, and a flashing simultaneity is achieved. Thus we see how Woolf's inveterately metaphorical instinct, at the level of language, in part encouraged her discovery of metaphorical narrative techniques. Metaphor is the way to explode sequence.

But even with metaphor, a novelist cannot literally combine five consciousnesses. Yet if you allow your characters to forget that they *are* consciousnesses, you allow the reader to forget this too. And when you do this, you allow the reader to forget that fictional consciousness, with its severe descriptive limitations, exists at all. Something else comes into being: the unconscious. This is what Woolf does with Mrs Ramsay, three times in the book. The first moment of forgetting is the quietest and the most magnificent, and occurs twenty pages into the novel. For twenty pages, more or less, we see things through Mrs Ramsay's drifting thoughts. She thinks about how much her son wants to go to the lighthouse; she is cross with Tansley for saying that the weather will not be good enough for the boat-trip; she thinks a little about Tansley, and about all her husband's camp-followers – earnest frigid young men who like to discuss university prizes and who has 'a first-rate mind'.

And then a gigantic new climate begins in English fiction. Mrs Ramsay looks out of the window at the lawn, and sees Augustus Carmichael; and then sees Lily Briscoe painting, and decides that Lily is not really a serious artist. And then Mrs

Ramsay remembers that she 'was supposed to be keeping her head as much in the same position as possible for Lily's picture'. In other words, Mrs Ramsay has forgotten, and has only just remembered, that she is at the centre of Lily's painting. And she has forgotten that she is at the centre of the twenty pages we have just read. Yet Mrs Ramsay's forgetting that she is at the centre of the painting, and at the centre of the first twenty pages, has itself taken twenty pages to read! Her forgetting that she is at the centre has been at *our* centre, has been at the centre of what we have just read. We have experienced this forgetfulness with her. We have travelled with her, and in this way out of her. It is as if the novel forgets itself, forgets that Mrs Ramsay is a character. She has been at the centre of the novel all along and we have hardly noticed it, because we have inhabited her own invisibility. Our realization of this gives a strange new meaning to Mrs Ramsay's keeping her head still, or 'in the same position'. For, although her head might, externally, have been quite still, or in the same position, *inside her head* nothing has been still, nothing has been 'in the same position', indeed, Mrs Ramsay is incapable of keeping her thought in the same position. She has been, in the deepest sense, absent-minded.

When, in real life, we are asked by a friend what we are thinking about, we often say 'Nothing.' Mrs Ramsay would say the same; Woolf informs us later on that Mrs Ramsay hated to be reminded that she had been seen by anyone 'sitting thinking'. Yet Woolf's delicate method shows us that we are never thinking about nothing, that we are always thinking about something, that it is impossible for us not to think, even if the thought is merely the process of forgetting something. She lets her readers not only read this but almost enact it for themselves. It is a perilous process, and some readers decide that it is just a maze of pretty trivia. But it is real; undoubtedly, it brings us closer to what Woolf called 'life'. In her novels, thought radiates outward, as a medieval town radiates outward – from a beautifully neglected centre.

3

But Woolf, who did not properly read Freud until the last few years of her life, was more than a historian of the mind's creases or a novelist of the unconscious; and more than the bold native of English prose. What so moves us in her great novels, and moves us when we picture her at work in her garden hut in Sussex − Bernard in *The Waves* refers to the 'incessant unmethodical pacing' of artistic work − is the constant effort to find a meaning behind 'life'. Was this hidden meaning only aesthetic? Famously, she once wrote that 'behind the cotton wool is hidden a pattern; that we − I mean all human beings − are connected with this . . . that the whole world is a work of art.' This is the formally agnostic side of Woolf that trusted in art, as Pater did, to do somewhat hazily the work of religion. The hope was that such art would best explain the mysteries of things by, precisely, failing to explain them. In place of confident Victorian preaching was the proper stutter of art; in place of system was tangle; in place of solution was compound. Art's failure was its success. The more obscure the 'pattern' behind reality, the more real its obscurity. Woolf's celebrated 'moments of being', in this view, were indescribable clouds which only art could attempt to describe, because art was the true moment of being. Art and reality became one in their mystery. Art, in this sense, acts like ritual rather than doctrine: it cannot define truth, but it nicely ornaments what cannot be known. 'I'm certain that the only meanings that are worth anything in a work of art are those that the artist himself knows nothing about', Woolf wrote. She disliked the 'mysticism' in *A Passage To India*, because she felt that Forster was an artist who did not trust enough in art alone, who 'despises his art and thinks he must be something more'. Forster was too much of a mystic, or Cambridge Platonist. Thus Woolf the aesthete.

But what of Woolf the religionist? Woolf the Forsterian or Platonist? For there is some evidence that Woolf, without of course despising her art, looked for 'something more', and that she felt that this 'something more' lay beyond or outside art. She felt herself to be 'mystical'. At times she seems to have been looking not so much for the aesthetic pattern behind reality, as for a further metaphysical pattern behind the aesthetic pattern. What this further pattern, so amply recessed, looked like, she could not say. Whether it was also aesthetic, she did not know. She could never describe it. But she suspected that she did not make it herself: it was real, it was revealed, it was given to her. We know this, because she tells us that she sensed this deeper reality in her moments of mental instability. Woolf broke down, mentally, in 1897, in 1904, and most severely in 1913, when she nearly killed herself. In 1926, while finishing *To the Lighthouse*, she again became ill. She would have periods of feverish intensity and insight, followed by weeks of clogged depression. These bouts were terrible. Hermione Lee quotes this self-record: 'Oh its beginning its coming – the horror – physically like a painful wave about the heart – tossing me up. I'm unhappy unhappy! Down – God, I wish I were dead . . . Wave crashes. I wish I were dead! I've only a few years to live I hope. I cant face this horror any more.'

But once this had passed, Woolf felt that her depression had been 'interesting'. She saw through to some kind of 'truth' while ill. 'I believe these illnesses are in my case – how shall I express it? – partly mystical.' Most significantly, she told Forster that her illness had 'done instead of religion'. She wrote that in periods of intensity, she heard a third voice – not hers, not Leonard's, but another's. Scattered in her writings are moments of mystical feeling. Bernard, at the end of *The Waves*, does not give a Paterian account of the primacy of art, or the ultimate aesthetic pattern of all things (the usual reading), but rather, he undergoes a breakdown which is described in spiritual terms. In September 1926, she wrote of 'the mystical side of this solitude; how it is not oneself but something in the universe that one's left with.' She continues: 'One sees a fin passing far out.' Five years later, in February 1931, amid the flushed *triste* of having finished *The Waves*, she writes: 'I have netted that fin in the waste of waters which appeared to me over the marshes out of my window at Rodmell when I was coming to an end of *To the Lighthouse*.' Now it is difficult to know whether this is a report or an approximation. Did she *see* a fin in 1926, a mystical bulk; or was the idea of a fin merely her image of precisely what she *could not see* but only imagine? Was this a mystical sighting of an actuality, or a lunge at the idea of such? (Verbally, perhaps, it is not accidental that 'fin' is 'end', and is the kernel at the heart of 'finitude' and 'infinitude'.) Repeatedly, she complains of the difficulty of describing this reality. But it was a reality: 'If I could catch the feeling, I would: the feeling of the singing of the real world, as one is driven by loneliness and silence from the habitable world.'

This idea, of a real world behind the habitable world, reminds us of the Victorian Platonism in which Woolf was raised. But Woolf's version is both a fruit of, and a pit shied at, this Platonism. Woolf's father was an agnostic and a rationalist. Victorian Platonism put the good in place of God. This good was an invisible order behind the world of appearances. It could be reached, says Plato in *The Republic*, but only by philosophical thought. Inheriting this tradition, Woolf changes the code: like her father, she did not believe in God. Like the Platonist, she intuited a real world behind the apparent world. But it is not the form of the Good. It is intrinsic, indescribable. And most importantly, it cannot be reached through philosophical reasoning, but only lunged at every so often by that faculty that Plato somewhat despised: the imagination.

So Woolf saw beyond art, and not only in moments of mental brokenness, but in the very midst of that art. Her greatest fiction is moved by the faith that to have visions is to see beyond aesthetic vision. At the end of *The Waves*, Bernard casts off 'this veil of being', and asks: 'What does this central shadow hold? Something? Nothing? I do not know.' Importantly, he feels that he has pierced a silent world without need of language or art, 'a new world . . . without shelter of phrases'. At the end of *To the Lighthouse*, Lily Briscoe sits at her easel, painting 'her attempt at something'. Her attempt at something is more than the attempt to paint a picture. The picture is irrelevant. She reflects that her painting will be hung in an attic or even destroyed. Lily wants, writes Woolf, 'the thing itself before it has been made anything'. Lily's attempt is to grasp time, to restore a moment of the present as it ages before her. This is explicitly not just an aesthetic exertion. That would be tautological: it is art which has gathered this moment, so it would be weak to say that the meaning of this moment is only art. No, what is so moving in this novel is the spreading apprehension that the very vagueness of that invisible 'something' that we are all seeking beyond the senses makes it mystical, pushes it beyond the reach of aesthetic form. The indefinability of the 'something' is what goads Woolf's art into art; but the indefinability is also what exhausts that art. It encourages the very quest it cannot satisfy. This contradictory belief, that truth can be looked for but cannot be looked at, and that art is the greatest way of giving form to this contradiction, is what moves us so intensely. At her best, Woolf is not an 'impressionist', because she has a metaphysician's interest in impressions. Her work is full of the sense that art is an 'incessant unmethodical pacing' around meaning rather than towards it, and that this continuous circling is art's straightest metaphysical path. It is all art can do, and it is everything art can do. And fin-like, the meaning moves on, partially palpable, always hiding its larger invisibilities.

Thomas Mann: The master of not quite

I

Too often, Thomas Mann is credited with everything except being a novelist, rather as Goethe is credited with everything except being a poet. This is partly because such writers are their own Eckermanns, always offering the shoulder of criticism to the emotions of their own art. In such writers the prosaic is a kind of lyricism in disguise. Has not Mann's novelistic lyricism become invisible? He is accused of 'superessayism' (by Nabokov and others). He is read in ideational uniform, as if his work were the inevitable treaty to the war of nineteenth-century German philosophy, a document badged with heavy, mournful subheadings: 'Nature', 'Spirit', 'Aesthetics', 'Time', 'Death'. Even those sympathetic to the novelistic textures of Mann are likely to argue – as Richard Blackmur did – that Mann's novels are full of parody because the great contemporary writers are incapable of creating whole characters and unwilling to resort to type.

Mann was comprehensively anxious about the quality of the novelistic in his work. He feared that there was too much *Kritik* and not enough *Plastik* in it. Unlike a natural genius, he felt, his way was a burgherly crawl, and he was defensive of its jowelly merits: 'the modern approach, minuteness, accumulation of details, lack of genius, intellectuality, allied with tenacity, work, endurance of will, can successfully go in for ambitious tasks.' His novel *Doctor Faustus*, he lamented, is 'joylessly earnest, not artistically happy'. There is a pathos to the image of Mann 'reading with a pencil', as he put it, consuming hundreds of books as preparation for his novels, patiently cleaning his errors, slowly building the contraption of truth. There he sits in Munich or in Zurich, in his study, whose implacably closing door was acutely remembered by his children, his beloved cigar with its slow ash the very emblem of gradualism, his unlovely face exactly adequate to the deliberate task in hand, his moustache like a bourgeois underlining, like an emphasis – and there he writes his great fiction, slowly, thoroughly, but also thoroughly anxiously, fiction about which someone once said to him, at a reading: 'What I admire about your work is that I always feel that it is the best you could possibly have done.' In his *Reflections of a Non-Political Man*, Thomas Mann said that this comment made him happier than almost any other.

'Only thoroughness can be truly entertaining,' writes Mann at the beginning of *The Magic Mountain,* and that thoroughness is held against him by some, or is not credited as entertainment by others who do not hold it against him. But thoroughness is exactly what is most novelistic about Mann, it is the key to both his grandeur and his considerable delicacy as a novelist; it is the fine entertainment of his work. Its thoroughness, its length and almost repetitive quizzicality, allow us to feel that we are living within a cosmos of ideas, that ideas are heavily mobile rather than busily static. The thoroughness of Mann's fiction is not business or busyness, but labour – and therefore not bourgeois exactly, despite Mann's own claims. This labour is aesthetic and metaphysical. The writer, in his thoroughness, discovers our abysses, he breaks through to sadness, to death, he does not turn away.

This anti-bourgeois principle of thoroughness is surreptitiously announced in Mann's first novel, *Buddenbrooks.* In this story of three generations of a family, several failed artists appear. One of them, Christian, is especially failed. He has not done much with his life, except sit in London theatres and take the Bohemian air. He carries a cane which 'had the bust of a nun for a handle' and came from 'over there' (London). He is sickly.

When he tells stories they are always too long, and slightly feverish. His sister, Toni, complains that 'he goes so unnaturally into detail . . . He looks at things in such a strange way.' His brother, Thomas, who is striving to be the perfect bourgeois, agrees: 'it is just the way people speak in a fever.' But much earlier in the novel, that word 'strange' has been linked with death. When Johann Buddenbrook, the original patriarch died, his last word was 'Strange!', and Mann writes that 'the family looked in each other's eyes and saw there something strange. It was the idea of death that had entered . . .' Christian's strangeness is that he sees death, and not only because he is sickly and useless, but because he has some distant quality of the artist – he 'goes so unnaturally into detail'. He is thorough, in a way. He opposes the bourgeois world, whose motto might be the repeated cry of Christian's mother, the Frau Consul, who likes to close arguments with: '*Assez!*' One sees here how thorough Mann is about thoroughness, and how novelistic, allowing that word 'strange' to revisit the narrative after years and pages away. Similarly, Mann leans novelistically, not allegorically, on the idea that Christian might be an artist, ensuring that although Christian may have a small aspect of the artistic, he is not made a representative of anything, because his illness and failure are his own. He lacks the healthiness of the author's spokesman; and indeed, Mann's fiction lacks the healthiness of easy allegory. It too goes 'unnaturally into detail' and in admitting death into its form, it risks becoming its own patient. Mann's fiction is, in both senses, patient.

But this thoroughness is not just metaphysical labour. It has a childlike quality, the artist's persistent simplicity, and simple persistence. The child is always unsatisfied with the pristine, and is a playful inquisitor. So hidebound is Mann's reputation – his first English translator called him 'Dr Mann' until Mann's death – that 'childlike' seems an impossible charge. But in fact his fiction is full of children. In *Buddenbrooks,* both little Toni and little Hanno are beautifully seen in their childishness, and neither is allowed to enter adulthood: Toni never really grows up, and Hanno dies as an adolescent. Christian, in the same novel, is the only adult who does not condescend to Hanno, and the only one who understands how thrilled the little boy is to receive a toy theatre for Christmas. Aschenbach, in *Death in Venice*, is seeking many things, but one of them is little Tadzio's innocence. His adulthood is consumed by this quest. Felix Krull is a wicked child, and Adrian Leverkühn, the diabolic composer in *Doctor Faustus*, is an inspired and dangerous child, who plays games with what he calls 'the world'. And what does the knowing, pompous, freedom-loving, thoroughly adult Settembrini call Hans Castorp, the hero of *The Magic Mountain*? 'One of life's problem children.'

Mann, too, is one of life's problem children, and like Hans, he was always educating himself, and making his novels the report of that education. The child examines, and is then examined: that is the banal dialectic of childhood, which is the profound dialectic of Mann's fiction. Mann's childlikeness is seen in the simple life of much of his fiction, its relish for novel detail. Much of this detail is childishly comical. In this he is akin to Tolstoy and Chekhov, about whom he wrote appreciative essays. One thinks of Frau Stöhr in *The Magic Mountain,* who boasts of being able to make twenty-eight different sauces for fish; or the dentist in *Buddenbrooks* who keeps a parrot called Josephus which tells patients to sit down and wait; or the ridiculous Herr von Gleichen-Russwurm in *Doctor Faustus,* who is memorable only for being 'Schiller's great-grandson'.

More deeply, Mann sees that a childish separation from the world is both the health and sickness of the artist. Simplicity is always nervous in Mann. His novels offer, again and again, images of separation that connect childishness, sickness, and the artist. Mann sees the great, necessary, selfish convalescence that is the patient's and the artist's labour. The artist must learn to 'wait and be patient', as the child and the sick person are similarly consoled. The artist must *be* a patient. These motifs appear everywhere in his work. In *Buddenbrooks*, in a very beautiful passage, Toni, now a young woman, meets Morten

Schwarzkopf, a radical young man. The two are at the beach, and Morten, the young radical, refuses to join Toni's glamorous and high-born friends. Instead, he 'sits on the rocks'. The phrase is taken up by the two, and appears later in the novel. Toni's brother, Thomas, the perfect burgher, is perfect only until he begins to question if he is a natural man, or is only really playing a role. He begins to think of the world as '*dehors*', or 'outside', and his grooming becomes decadently fastidious. The inhabitants of the sanatorium in *The Magic Mountain* think of the real world as 'the flatland' or 'the plains', 'with a gentle but clear trace of contempt'. One of the novel's repeated images is 'sitting out' or 'living horizontally', which refers to the regular rest-cure which the sanatorium's patients take. They wrap themselves in a rich camel-hair blanket, and sit on their 'splendid lounge-chairs' out on the terrace. Hans falls in love with 'living horizontally'. Here he does much of his reading. He calls these sessions 'playing king', which recalls a childhood game of his, in which he would imagine himself looking upon the world from above.

'Sitting on the rocks', '*dehors*', 'playing king': these are approximations of a radical separateness, which is the artist's necessary separation. Yet if the artist must *be* a patient, then the artist can become very sick – and not simply run the permanent high-fever of an artistic life, but actually become diseased. This is the danger of patience, a danger Mann would come to see acutely in the 'real world', with the rise of Nazism. But of course his fiction had anticipated this. He is always the novelist; his politics, as it were, were merely the slow-witted, belated readers of his novels. Hans, Settembrini and the sinister Herr Naphta are all, in a sense, 'playing king' on their Mount Olympus. They do not imagine that their wild discussions about freedom and religion, about time and torture, have consequences. *The Magic Mountain*'s vision of a civilization in sickness, about to burst into the First World War, suggests differently. *Doctor Faustus* is explicit, perhaps too explicit, in its allegorical message about the childish irresponsibility of the artist.

The necessity of artistic childlikeness and the danger of it, are held together in Mann's work. This is what allows him, in his essay 'Sufferings and Greatness of Richard Wagner', to write, on the one hand: 'Innocent may be the last adjective to apply to art; but the artist he is innocent.' And to write, on the other hand, in the same essay, this beautiful passage: 'To the artist new experiences of "truth" are new incentives to the game, new possibilities of expression, no more. He believes in them, he takes them seriously, just so far as he needs to in order to give them the fullest and profoundest expression. In all that he is very serious, serious even to tears – but yet *not quite* – and by consequence, not at all. His artistic seriousness is of an absolute nature, it is "dead-earnest playing".' Art is, in fact, 'playing king'; it is guilty innocence, innocent guilt.

2

It is through the dialectic that Thomas Mann's novels justify themselves as novels. In his work, the novelistic is the dialectic. Mann approaches the dialectic with great delicacy, a delicacy that is the result of an immense thoroughness, as the delicacy of tiredness is the result of hard work. Truth, or rather the idea of one overbearing truth, is exhausted into fragility by Mann. The ceaseless motion, back and forth, what Hegel called the 'labour of the negative', is shown to find its perfect form not in philosophy but in the novel. Literature has always prided itself on inventing the dialectic; it baptized it as 'negative capability'. But the novel, I think, offers an intensification, because the dialectic is implicit in the very idea of sympathy, which is peculiarly the novel's gentle calling. Free characters demand sympathy, and a sympathy that is extended only to obedient or likeable characters is not worth having. (Remember that Keats – whom Mann loved, and whose poetry appears in *Doctor Faustus* – was speaking of Shakespeare's novelist-like relationship to his free characters.) Real sympathy is the benign sentence handed down to those who do not deserve it. Each tests the other. Sympathy, then, is a strong image of the dialectic, whereby each side completes each other, and is constantly moving between each other. And we know that the novel is the real home of this sympathy precisely because it routinely demands from us a sympathy that we could not possibly want to extend, in real life, to real people – to murderers, bores, paedophiles. The novel is able to test, and enrich, our powers of sympathy in this way both because it is real and because it is not real. Because, in Mann's terms, it is absolutely serious and then *not quite* serious. It is true, and a game – a true game, but still not life. Which is why we can allow our ideas of things to remain unresolved in fiction as we rarely do in real life.

Though Mann never made an argument like this for the novel, he certainly made an argument for literature's solving irresolution, its sympathetic interminability. In his essay 'Goethe and Tolstoy', which he wrote in 1922, he suggested that the 'artistic principle' is 'reserve'. In music, he said, we recognize it as 'the painful pleasure of the prolonged note, the teasing melancholy of the not-yet . . .' And 'in the intellectual sphere we love it as irony: that irony that glances at both sides, which plays slyly and irresponsibly – yet not without benevolence – among opposites, and is in no great haste to take sides and come to decisions . . .' He continues that 'the real goal to reach is not decision, but harmony, accord. And harmony, in a matter of eternal contraries, may lie in infinity; yet that playful reserve called irony carries it within itself, as the sustained note carries the resolution.' One notes here that Mann speaks not of the novel, but only of 'the intellectual sphere'. Of course, his greatest novel, *The Magic Mountain*, which was to appear only two years later, makes the novel's own case for the novel. This is the great book of the sustained, Mahlerian note. (Mahler's music, with its descending seconds and long irresolutions, is the true brother of Mann's fiction, even though Mann did not especially enjoy it.)

It is in *The Magic Mountain* that Hans Castorp decides, very beautifully, that 'man is the master of contradictions', or (in another translation and even more beautifully) 'the lord of counterpositions'. The novel's very form is thus a confession, an apologia, as was 'Goethe and Tolstoy', for Mann's intellectual behaviour during the years of the First World War, when he put his prominent support behind Germany's war-effort. For during the war, Mann had sounded like a tyrant of one position – as had his brother, Heinrich, except that his brother was right. In an essay on Zola, written in 1915, Heinrich attacked those writers and intellectuals whose writings, and whose lack of political commitment to democracy and freedom, had encouraged Germany's tyrannical slide into war. Such writers – and Heinrich made private allusions in this essay to Thomas – had 'betrayed Mind, betrayed Man'. Writers like Thomas were 'intellectual time-servers'. The real artist did not, like Thomas, have a 'false profundity', a fastidious isolation from politics. The real artist, according to Heinrich Mann, 'recognizes spiritual quality only where some moral effect has been achieved'. Nietzsche, in Heinrich's view, had served only his spirit, not the spirit of Man.

Heinrich and Thomas were much closer politically than either suspected. Thomas, in 1910, in a notebook, had written that his own generation was influenced by 'Nietzsche militant', whereas the younger generation (the warmongers) were influenced by 'Nietzsche triumphant'. What separated them, and would always separate them long after they were reconciled, long after their politics were so similar that Heinrich could joke that Thomas was 'just a little more radical than I', was the very different ideas they held about art. Heinrich's loud, simplifying, cinematic novels were commandeered by politics, and Thomas had, as a younger man, attacked their 'farcical' nature, their 'crudity' and 'sentimentalism'. Thomas's enormous tract, *Reflections of a Non-Political Man,* which appeared in 1918, was a bullet aimed at Heinrich. It is at heart a defence of a certain kind of art, which does not sag when politics leans on it, which does not have a preconceived political idea of how to conduct itself.

Repeatedly, Thomas states that he refuses to surrender to system. He will remain the non-political man, 'the impossible man', to be mistaken, to be pessimistic. When he discusses the Reformation, he is also, one gathers, discussing what he wants from art, and from Germanness: 'an event and fact of the soul actually not capable of interpretation or criticism, like life . . . One can call this revolutionary or reactionary, rebellious or preserving, democratic or anti-democratic: it is all this at once.' This essentially Romantic view of the uninterpretable artwork is threatened by, and in turn opposes, Heinrich's simplicities, his bright certainties about large notions like Progress, Freedom, Democracy. Thomas scorns his brother as a Frenchified concept-machine, 'civilization's *littérateur*'.

Reflections of a Non-Political Man is a valid artistic cry made at an invalid political moment – and necessarily so of course, because Thomas refuses to be political, and refuses to see his refusal as itself political. (He would eventually come to the opposite conclusion, and argue that 'Nothing that is living can sidestep politics. Even a rejection of politics is political: it merely connives at the politics of evil.') The book is intensely political, written as if by a more decorous Céline. Mann blames the war on everyone else, arguing that Britain and France were the true warriors. Democracy, he writes, 'is foreign and poisonous to the German character'. Interestingly, however, his aesthetics are not very different from those that would produce *The Magic Mountain* and all his subsequent work. He argues that fiction is a passage through error; he praises Nietzsche for writing that 'the need for belief, for any sort of absolute yes and no, is a proof of weakness', and cherishes Goethe for his impatience with mere one-sided opinions. His sensitivity for the artistic dialectic was not impaired by his enthusiasm for the war; it was his politics that suffered even as he claimed he had none, and it was his politics, not his art, that would spend the next twenty years repairing themselves. His art, on the other hand, would atone for his politics. It would atone dialectically – which would mean, in the end, and supremely in *Doctor Faustus*, that it would have to atone for itself, for art.

3

The Magic Mountain represents the very defiance of system for which Mann was crying so loudly in *Reflections*. It is – to borrow Mann's phrase – *not quite* interpretable. It is an allegory that behaves like a novel, except when it is behaving allegorically. Its length, and its thoroughness, keep all its many ideas agitated. Like the *Inferno*, it lives several lives at once. It is a *Bildungsroman* and a parody of one, because Hans Castorp's education at the sanatorium is really an education in death, spent in Hades. It is an essay about time, but also a novel about time, because it enacts its own profound meditations on time. Can one narrate time? asks Mann. No, of course not, he replies. This would be like a note held for hours on end without resolution. But that is exactly what *The Magic Mountain* is.

Indeed, just in one remark about time, we can catch *The Magic Mountain* atoning for *Reflections*. Hans remarks at one point that time is 'a turning-point in a circle', it is never linear. This seems to refer to Hegel's idea that 'bad infinity' is linear, but that real infinity is dialectical, and circular. Hans explains that the days get longer during winter, and when we get to the longest day, on June 21st, the start of summer, the days are getting shorter. 'Like some practical joke,' says Hans, 'the start of winter is actually spring, and the start of summer is actually autumn.' Then why, asks Hans, do people celebrate the solstice, dancing and cheering at the longest day? 'Because they are now headed back down into the dark, maybe? . . . Is it melancholy mirth at the high-point? . . . Melancholy mirth and mirthful melancholy . . .' It is hard to read this and not think, as we are supposed to do surely, of the 'long summer' of 1914, before the start of war, of the elation which was actually despair, and the triumph that was actually defeat. But there are two other profound pendants hanging from this small meditation on time's circularity. One is formal. *The Magic Mountain* constantly reprises itself, constantly repeats, while simultaneously slightly altering every repetition, its massive themes. (Mann's thoroughness, again.) The entire life of the novel's community, at the sanatorium, is based on a circular, daily, repetitive routine, and the book mimics this routine. Thus when Hans discusses the circularity of time, he is discussing the novel's own procedures. The novel is, as it were, discussing its own circularity *while in the process of being circular* – for this is at least the twentieth moment that the novel has discussed time. Form and content are absolutely entwined in this book. Secondly, Mann's notion of time's circularity, so essential to the form and matter of *The Magic Mountain*, refutes the very premise of *Reflections*. In *Reflections*, Mann wrote that he had realized from the start of the war that it 'would be a turning-point in world history . . . that afterwards, everything would be different, that nothing could become the same as before.' It is impossible to read *The Magic Mountain* and believe such a thing; or rather, impossible while actually reading the novel, impossible while held in the serious game of '*not quite*'. In the world of this novel, the only turning-point is circular. There are no new departures, no new epochs, only the endless, foolish, circular regression to where we started from. The circle of the artistic dialectic has defeated the linearity of politics.

The Magic Mountain is an allegory about European civilization's sickness. But it is above all a *novel* about that sickness, full of a novel's sympathy for those who do not deserve it, and for ideas which do not deserve it. Thus Mann brilliantly represents Settembrini, who has Heinrich's liberal politics, with kindness, and represents Herr Naphta's religious fascism with fascinated wariness. To put it crudely, which is to deny what is novelistic in the book, Hans, like the reader, is revolved between these two positions, only to see that each contains the other, and that each does not merely contradict the other, but also contradicts itself. In the famous chapter 'Snow', Hans skis into a snow-drift, and gets lost by turning around in circles. He stops, and meditates. He feels himself between Settembrini and Naphta, between the licence of freedom and the sentence of religion, between ignoring death and being consumed by it, 'between mystical community and windy individualism'. But no, he decides that 'man is the master of contradictions, they occur through him, and so he is more noble than they . . . more noble than life, too noble for it . . . I will grant death no dominion over my thoughts.' Hans decides that the community to which he belongs should have 'silent regard for death' but should not have (as the sanatorium has, as Germany did) 'faithfulness to death . . . *For the sake of goodness and love, man shall grant death no dominion over his thoughts.*' It is a noble passage, and Mann is faithful simultaneously to the spirit of dialectic and to the spirit of the novelistic (for they are identical) when he adds, a page later, in his characteristic irony, that by Hans's bedtime, 'his dream was already beginning to fade'. There is no resolution, can be no resolution. What is intellectually appropriate is also humanly true in this case: our grandest self-statements are mere frail memoranda.

It is this human and novelistic power one wants to emphasize, only because the intellectual tides are too often discussed at the expense of the novelistic waters. The best means of examining the extraordinary novelistic form of *The Magic Mountain* is to look, very briefly, at Mann's use of one leitmotiv, that of the idea of 'living horizontally'. It is Settembrini who jocularly coins this expression near the beginning of the book, thereby enlarging the daily rest-cure into metaphor. The phrase is mocking, and refers both to a placid idleness, and also, perhaps, to the posture required for intellectual or artistic criticism. The world outside does not live horizontally. Two hundred pages later, the metaphor appears again. Hans and his group have wandered into town, and are visiting the local cemetery. Here are the graves of the sanatorium's patients, 'who had returned now for good and all to the horizontal form of existence'. The metaphor, repeated, has moved its meaning a little: it means death. A hundred pages later, Hans's uncle James Tienappel arrives for a short visit. He takes fright at the horrid, death-loving placidity, and flees. Hans suspects that when Uncle James returns to his bourgeois life, it will seem pointless. For he has seen death. Uncle James, he imagines, 'instead of heading off to his office after breakfast', will feel that he ought to 'take a short constitutional, then ritually wrap himself in blankets, and assume a horizontal position'. Now the phrase is reverting to one of its earlier meanings, that of the artistic or critical posture. Uncle James will return to his bourgeois life, hopes Hans, with an artistic sickliness. Finally, a hundred pages later, when Joachim, Hans's noble half-cousin, is dying, he becomes bedridden, and Mann writes: 'From then on Joachim assumed a permanent horizontal position.' The metaphor moves back and forth between its meanings, hovering somewhere between life and death, somewhere between art and sickness, somewhere between criticism and surrender, and somehow containing within itself both sets of opposed meanings. And each time the phrase appears, it has a true human pathos and power, not a theoretical one. Here the very form of the novel is itself the master of contradictions.

4

Thomas Mann, with characteristic thoroughness, did not stop prosecuting himself for his political errors in 1914–18. There is something exceptionally moving about his reconciliation with Heinrich, and the brothers' exile in California in the late 1930s and 1940s. California: surely this has a double pathos, for on the one hand only the most satirical and undignified centrifuge would have thrown Thomas Mann out to California; and on the other, the place's paradisal air, its pacific winds in a time of warring storms, its light during darkness, seem like a reward, not an exile, for Mann's great struggle. The extant photographs of Mann in Pacific Palisades are curious, because Mann is now old and august, and yet the photographs are light-filled like the photographs of childhood. Here are the Californian interiors, with the books Mann was able to salvage from Germany, and yet the light coming in through the windows makes the room seem outside, makes the carpet a lawn. It looks like play; it is 1942. Thomas delivered an address on Heinrich's seventieth birthday, delivered on 2 May 1941. As he had so often before, Mann once again systematically repudiated his earlier politics. 'The intellect today is unmistakably entering into a *moral* epoch, an epoch in which a new religious and moral distinction is being drawn between good and evil. That signifies a certain simplification and rejuvenation of intellect, in opposition to all manner of tired and sceptical sophistication.' He gladly becomes the concept-machine he once called his brother: 'Freedom, truth, right, humanity – intellect dares, once again, to pronounce these words . . . it must fight for them or itself perish.' Three years later, when Goebbels said 'we firmly believe the German nation has been designated for a great future, for itself but also for other people, and that it must prove itself in this war', Mann wrote in his diary: 'Roughly how I was writing 30 years ago.'

This was the *real* age of 'Nietzsche triumphant', not 1910, and Mann wrote a novel to prove it, whose devil-hero was partly based on Nietzsche: *Doctor Faustus*. The story of Adrian Leverkühn, the great composer who bargains with the devil, is perhaps too explicit. It lacks the metaphorical fertility of *The Magic Mountain*. Written during the war in a time of desperation, it wants to mean everything, and dries its meanings out in a waste of shame. The connection made between the twelve-tone system and fascism is occasionally strained, and yet much of the power of the allegory depends on it. Too often, perhaps, Serenus Zeitblom, the novel's narrator, tells us that Adrian is devilish, that music is Manichean and produces both its own goodness and its own badness: 'No one can follow my argument here who has not experienced as I have how close aestheticism and barbarism are to each other, or who has not felt how aestheticism prepares the way for barbarism in one's own soul.'

Doctor Faustus is as close as Mann's fiction ever came to the allegorical.

But it is a great book (how real Adrian is, how alive!) and in one respect *Doctor Faustus* is Mann's deepest artistic gesture. For in this book he atones for art, and in a buried way, for the dialectic of art. Early in the novel, Adrian strikes a chord, and says: 'A chord like this . . . has no key as such. It's all relationship, and the relations form a circle.' This is the first of many suggestions that music contains within it all the potentialities for good and for bad. Adrian invents a 'magic circle' in his music, which is his own sign to the devil. 'Music is ambiguity as a system', says Adrian, and the novel shows just the danger of that ambiguity. But Mann's work until this moment had been the very quintessence, the very movement of ambiguity. What, after all, is Adrian saying except that his chord is like time's circle in *The Magic Mountain*? Music is the master of contradictions, implies Mann. Yet *Doctor Faustus* tells the story of the corruption of this lovely circular dialectic, this sympathetic ambiguity. At any moment, suggests Mann, the ambiguity of art may be straightened out by a Master from Germany. The circle of the dialectic, the sustained note, crashes, in Adrian's hands, into the dissonance of the twelve-tone system.

These, Mann complained, were simplified times, and they demanded a new kind of commitment. *Doctor Faustus* is above all a novel of commitment. It asks whether Nietzsche's idea that 'any sort of absolute yes and no is a proof of weakness' is not dangerously ambiguous. Dialectically, it turns back on the dialectic, and accuses it of a liable ambivalence. It shows the vulnerabilities of irresolution, of pampered ambiguity, of the serious game that is *not quite* serious – 'and therefore not serious at all'. If art is 'not serious at all' then how might it withstand the most serious realities? Commitment, Heinrich's kind of commitment, was suddenly everything. Surely this was the reason why Mann called his novel a 'radical confession'. At the end of his career, he chastises the dialectic, and what moves us is that this is a self-questioning that is itself dialectical. The novel that wonders if *not quite* has become a danger, must itself be *not quite* – and therefore not quite the condemnation it seems to be. The circle moves again. In reproaching the dialectic, Mann affirms it. In questioning irresolution, he enacts it. And in so doing, he affirms the novelistic once again. This was 'the best he could possibly do'.

D.H. Lawrence's Occultism

Taking the clapper out of the bell makes no sense, but this is what we do too often with D.H. Lawrence. The writer who seemed to believe in dualisms – blindness over sight, blood over mind, pagan over modern, and so on – is broken into two like a stable door. Readers, critics and biographers insist on splitting Lawrence into writer or preacher, dogmatist or poet. On the one hand, there is the marvellous animist, the quick, vital writer of physical descriptions – the poet, say, who sees a kangaroo with its 'drooping Victorian shoulders', or a mosquito moving like 'a dull clot of air'. On the other, there is the preacher, the tiresome Lawrence of hoarse doctrine, the bully of blood, the friendless hammer who comes down again and again in the prose.

But Lawrence is one of the century's greatest religious writers, and it is impossible to canalize the tides of his writing. His descriptions are sermons, too; but his sermons are also descriptions. That is, when Lawrence writes about flowers or animals or people, his most gorgeous evocations have an insistent, repetitive didacticism whose impulse is the religious need to know; equally, however, when Lawrence sermonizes religiously about the need to die into a new life or the shadowy life beyond consciousness, he is not gesturing rhetorically but describing a reality that is as present as a flower or an animal. Lawrence is a mystic literalist. He is always a poet and always a preacher at the same time. He should not be opened into two. In his book *Apocalypse*, which was published posthumously in

1931, one of the pleasures he takes in the Book of Ezekiel and the Book of Revelation is the literalism of their half-pagan world of gods and flames and wheels and beasts. He enjoys that in this vision God is 'a great *actual* figure, the great dynamic god, neither spiritual nor moral, but cosmic and vital'. For Lawrence is not in fact a trader in dualities, despite appearances; he is devoted to oneness.

Of course, there are people who will not even allow him greatness as a writer, religious or otherwise. But he *is* a great writer, not simply by virtue of what he dares, but by virtue of what he achieves. 'Great' is silly: to oppose his critics, one should say that he is precise and not only rhapsodic, that he is a practical writer as well as a vatic one, that he has superb powers not only of visual metaphor and visual concretion but an almost *abstract* delight in adjectives and adverbs. This last combination is rare: Shakespeare and Keats have it. Take, for example, a phrase from his celebrated story, 'Odour of Chrysanthemums' (1911): a miner lies dead in a living room, stretched out in 'the naive dignity of death'. Or a moment in Lawrence's travel book about Italy, when he sees 'the eternal, negative radiance of the snows'. These kinds of phrases, rich in nouns and adjectives, are everywhere in Lawrence, and provide one of the reasons why readers find him clothy, heavy, perhaps a bit Germanic. Certainly they do not make anything immediately visible. But what they suggest is a delight in the way in which adjectives and nouns can be, precisely, anti-pictorial.

Lawrence savours the way in which language at its densest becomes its own medium, like night. At such moments one feels language's lack of transparency as a new kind of visibility; and this also enables one to see the old transparency as a new kind of obstruction. One sees this in something that became one of Lawrence's best-known prose habits, repetition. This sentence is representative: 'The flowers of autumn, big pink daisy-like flowers, and white ones, and many yellow flowers, were in profusion.' What one knows, immediately, is that this is not really repetition. To repeat is not to repeat but to change, and 'flowers' changes, takes on colours, as it proceeds through the sentence. (At the simplest level, the flowers are autumnal, then pink, then white, then yellow.) But repetition also affects the words that are not repeated: their singleness seems uncanny. The ordinary, almost casual, 'and white ones' seems remarkable in that sentence. These flowers are truly white *ones* – they are seen only once. The swift interruption, the singleness amidst repetition, captures the idea of seeing something once, in passing. Yet Lawrence is rarely given the proper kind of credit. Brenda Maddox, in her biography, *D.H. Lawrence: The Story of a Marriage*, writes rather grudgingly about this kind of delicacy of control as if it is not really control at all: 'Whether such passages echo the hypnotic refrains of the chapel hymns of his boyhood, the rocking of an anxious infant, or, as Lawrence maintained, the rhythmic thrust of the sexual act, they were deliberate.'

Hemingway has a reputation as a cold master of repetition, an icicle formed from the drip of style, while Lawrence is most often seen as a hothead who fell over himself, verbally. Yet Lawrence has far greater stylistic powers than Hemingway, and manages simultaneously to be both a purer and less mannered stylist. Here is Lawrence writing in 1916:

> And then the tussocks and tussocks of primroses are fully out, there is full morning everywhere on the banks and roadsides and streamsides, and around the olive roots, a morning of primroses underfoot, with an invisible threading of many violets, and then the lovely blue clusters of hepatica, really like pieces of blue sky showing through a clarity of primrose.

And here is Hemingway, writing in 1929:

> The fields were green and there were small green shoots on the vines, the trees along the road had small leaves and a small breeze came from the sea. I saw the town with the hill and the old castle above it in a cup in the hills with the mountains beyond, brown mountains with a little green on their slopes.

Both, as it happens, are writing about Italy. Both writers use one word three times ('green' for Hemingway, 'primroses' for Lawrence), and repeat two other words. Hemingway's passage is static. He is layering, using the coincidence of words to suggest a coincidence of colours, a pastoral monotony. But Lawrence's words work against their own repetition, to enact a sense of change and movement. Lawrence is describing the breaking of dawn, the changing of light. This is a verbal discovery. At each moment of higher light, the landscape is changing but remaining the same. What is being revealed is merely the fuller essence of the same landscape, as the light builds – 'a morning of primroses' culminates in 'a clarity of primrose,' as morning is finally born, and Lawrence realizes that the sky above his head is the same colour as the hepatica at his feet. The sentences move toward the light; we move into 'a clarity'. The language stays the same but alters, as light changes but remains the same; Lawrence merely lets us see a word from an improved angle. Repetition is difference. Hemingway, one feels, knows in advance just what his repetitions will be; Lawrence discovers, as he proceeds, that a word has changed its meaning as he has used it, and that he will need to use the same word because it now has a different meaning.

Lawrence is more refined than Hemingway, more of a true stylist, with a better ear; but he is also more natural than Hemingway. In this way, he is an intensely paradoxical writer. Just as he is a mystic literalist, so too he is a natural stylist. He knew this. He wrote to Edward Marsh about his poetry, thus: 'I have always tried to get an emotion out in its own course, without altering it.' And yet, he added: 'It needs the finest instinct imaginable, much finer than the skill of the craftsmen.' Lawrence's naturalness as a writer has to do with the way his voice is audible in his fiction. He is always there, hesitating, hectoring, colloquializing (how often in Lawrence that Notting-hamshire negative, 'Nay', appears), repeating, joking. Lawrence, said T.S. Eliot, was humourless. Actually, the appeal of his voice lies partly in its comedy. This is less obvious in the longer novels than in the stories, novellas, travel-writing and poems, writing which is given insufficient attention. Lawrence's enemies still deny his comedy, which was often self-deprecating. John Carey, who wants all writers to be nice (ideally, as decent as Arnold Bennett), wrote a book about the nastiness of various modern writers called *The Intellectuals and the Masses*. In it Lawrence is scolded for his 'fascism', his ecstasies of annihilation. Carey plucks a sentence from a letter written in 1915 to Ottoline Morrell. The war had ravaged Lawrence, psychically. Before it began he had felt that English life was on the edge of a resurrection. The slaughter in France removed his foundations. Lawrence was given, like Céline, to overstatement. 'It would be nice if the Lord sent another flood and drowned the world', he wrote to Lady Ottoline. This is the sum of Carey's quote. But Lawrence's letter continues, unseen by Carey's readers: 'Probably I should want to be Noah. I am not sure', which is funny, human, fallen.

Lawrence's comedy emerges, in his prose, as a briskness, a polemical dastardliness, a kind of trick. It is the verbal equivalent of cheating at cards: the writer slips something past the reader. And it is the social equivalent of cheating, for Lawrence's most characteristic humour is aimed at the English upper classes. The writer who wrote a poem called 'The Oxford Voice' shrewdly judged the mediocrity of many of his competitors. How swiftly the pretensions of the protagonist of his story 'The Man Who Loved Islands' (1927) are parcelled: 'He was not a great scholar: the usual public school equipment.' But Lawrence is most appealing when he is both satirical and apparently aware of his own absurdity. One recent biographer, Mark Kinkead-Weekes, reports that when Lawrence and Frieda arrived in Turin, in 1919, they stayed a night at the house of an industrialist called Sir Walter Becker. This was Lawrence's judgment, in a letter:

> The old knight and I had a sincere half-mocking argument, he for security and bank-balance and power, I for naked liberty. In the end, he rested safe on his bank-balance, I in

my nakedness. We hated each other – but with respect. But c'est lui qui mourra. He is going to die – moi non. He knows that, the impotent old wolf, so he is ready in one half to murder me. I don't want to murder him – merely leave him to his death.

This has charm, the kind of charm that one finds throughout the travel books, *Twilight in Italy* and *Sea and Sardinia*. And the writing has such crooked vitality: the vernacular bumping against the spoilt jaunty French, the slap of the phrases. What is most appealing about it is the quality of self-satire. It is hard not to feel that Lawrence finds himself as absurd as the old knight – that if Becker is an 'old wolf' then Lawrence is a young fox. The passage is comic because of the overstatement, as if 'naked liberty' could possibly be an adequate opposition for 'security and bank-balance and power . . .' Stylistically, the passage is comic because it is built on contradictions: the two hate each other, 'but with respect'; Lawrence tells us that he doesn't want to murder Becker, but he is verbally murdering him before our eyes. And then, the bristle of that phrase, 'impotent old wolf', foxily inserted in the sentence to look casual, yet drawing all the attention to itself . . .

The definitive three-volume Cambridge biography abounds in such moments. We see how self-conscious Lawrence was about class, and with what good reason. He was quick-tempered, warm-gutted, intensely lithe and vital, an inspired mimic. Everyone who met him, even those who disliked him, felt his vitality. David Garnett noticed his 'beautiful lively, blue eyes', and that he was 'very light in his movements'. He also noticed that his hair was the kind of colour, or non-colour, that only working-class men had. (It was reddish-fair.) When a young admirer called Ivy Low came to visit him one of Lawrence's first questions was whether he seemed working-class. He complained when she said yes. John Middleton Murry saw that when Lawrence went to a party given by H.G. Wells in 1914, it was with sickly determination that Lawrence insisted on going in evening dress. 'Now Lawrence,' wrote Murray, 'who looked his lithe and limber self in many kinds of attire, did not resemble himself at all when locked into a dress-suit . . . But something warned me . . . that this initiation into the dress-suit world was for him a serious ritual affair . . .'

It is Lawrence's unbuttonedness, his free eccentricities, that make his writing so remarkable. It is because he is not locked into any kind of dress-suit that the prose can wave its arms and ball its fists. Forster, so loyal to Lawrence, is constrained, and his writing, even at its finest, is more or less the kind of liberty that one expects to find within constraint. But Lawrence has a strange liberty; he is unaccountable. Christmas roses, 'the lovely buds like handfuls of snow'; 'the powerful, silver-pawed cypress tree'; 'In the silence, it seemed he could hear the panther-like dropping of infinite snow'; 'the flat unfinished world running with foam and noise and silvery light, and a few gulls swinging like a half-born thought'. What is beautiful is that the writing itself swings 'like a half-born thought'. It is immediate yet subtly abstract: how does one explain the panther-like snow?

Yet Lawrence is rooted, too. He was a practical man. Strangers – in England, Italy, Germany – were astounded to see him cooking, cleaning, gardening, and building. When he and Frieda moved to Hampstead in 1914, he knitted a loose cover for their sofa. He made hats for Frieda, and two sheepskin coats for the daughters of friends. 'While with us,' wrote one host, 'he cooked an omelette; furbished a hat of his wife; examined a Dutch cupboard my wife had recently bought, and said what its period was; came out into the garden and gave me hints on transplanting cabbages . . .' This practicality finds its way into the writing as a fine simplicity or homeliness of imagery – as when Katherine Farquhar, in the story 'The Border Line' (1924), realizes that her dead husband still possesses her, 'not just through one act . . . But as a cloud holds a shower . . . as the scent of a pine-tree when one stands beneath it.' Lawrence's simplicity produces one of the most beautiful passages in all his writing, and one of the most beautiful passages of speech in

English fiction. In his novella *St. Mawr* (1925), a Welsh stable-hand, Lewis, accompanies a rich American lady, Mrs Witt, on a horse-ride across southern England. Darkness has fallen and in the sky the couple can see shooting-stars. Mrs Witt has been teasing Lewis about his various rural superstitions, and in particular for his stubborn belief that a shooting-star represents some kind of cosmic signal. She asks him if he knows that a shooting-star is just a chemical spasm:

'Yes, Mam, I've been told. But stones don't come at us from the sky for nothing. Either it's like when a man tosses an apple to you out of his orchard as you go by. Or it's like when somebody shies a stone at you, to cut your head open. You'll never make me believe the sky is like an empty house with a slate falling from the roof. The world has its own life, the sky has a life of its own, and never is it like stones rolling down a rubbish heap and falling into a pond. Many things twitch and twitter within the sky, and many things happen beyond us. My own way of thinking is my own way.'

This is the novella that one biographer of Lawrence dismissed as 'a forest of abstractions, repeating words carelessly . . .'

Lawrence's great creative period stretches from 1912, when he met Frieda Weekley, to 1925, when he published *St. Mawr*. Much of the biographical material is familiar: the first, ecstatic trip to Italy in 1912, which produced *Twilight in Italy*; Frieda's unhappiness at being separated from her three children, and Lawrence's apparent indifference about this; the hot day in July 1913 when the two were married in London – a photograph shows the Lawrences and Murry and Katherine Mansfield standing in a London garden, with a line of plain washing hanging behind them like a white flag of truce or surrender; Lawrence's severed friendship with Bertrand Russell; the suppression of *The Rainbow* in 1915; the dim years (1916–1917) in Cornwall, when the Lawrences were being investigated by government authorities as possible German spies, and where he wrote most of *Women in Love*; the growing hatred of England, and the second departure to Italy in 1919, followed by the decision to leave England for good.

In her biography, Brenda Maddox slights Lawrence's unhappiness during the war years, noting that it was a little self-indulgent of the non-combatant Lawrence to complain while thousands of his compatriots fell in France. But Richard Aldington felt that Lawrence never recovered from the banning of *The Rainbow*, and Kinkead-Weekes follows him by placing this event at the centre of his narrative. The judge ruled that there was 'no justification whatever for the perpetration of such a book'. It was 'utter filth'. Methuen, the publishers, agreed. At *The Glasgow Herald*, a young reviewer, Catherine Carswell, who became one of Lawrence's most loyal friends, was sacked for writing a largely positive review. 'A monotonous wilderness of phallicism', wrote one reviewer. 'Such was England's official verdict on one of the great novels of the language', valedictorizes Mark Kinkead-Weekes. 'It would not be available in Britain again for another eleven years.'

Though Lawrence would not begin to look tubercular until the 1920s, it was during the war years that he grew the shrubby claw of beard that became his distinctive feature, and it was during this time that his vital, bastard twinkle disappeared. In bleak Cornwall, where he had a kind of breakdown, Lawrence became the shovel-faced reed of the later photographs, a stick of sick geometry. It was also in these years that Lawrence's 'doctrine' took on some of its unpleasantness, its glittering almost-fascism, its impatience with democracy (though Lawrence's impatience with Bertrand Russell's naïveté explains much of his swerve). Yet Lawrence's thought, for all of its undoubted irrationalism, is not much more offensive than Christianity, and has transparent similarities with early Christian mysticism. If one looks at *Twilight in Italy* and *Apocalypse*, for instance, one notes the Christian, trinitarian pattern of the thought, and the desire for a religious resting-place, a balance of opposites. One can take or leave the historical schema, the determination to see the

Renaissance as a gate in modern consciousness (though this is no more foolish than Eliot's dissociation of sensibility, or even Lukács's shift from the age of epic to the age of the novel).

Lawrence felt that since the Renaissance, modern man had oscillated between an over-assertion of the self (through the supremacy of the flesh) and a loss of the self (by dissolving the self into the greater self of Christ). Simply put, he longed to harmonize this discord, and to produce a stronger, purified selfhood that would blend the strength of self-assertion with the strength of self-abnegation. The new whole would be a kind of 'Holy Ghost', which 'relates the dual infinites into one whole': 'The Infinite is twofold, the Father and the Son, the Dark and the Light, the Senses and the Mind, the Soul and the Spirit, the self-and the not-self, the Eagle and the Dove, the Tiger and the Lamb.' But Lawrence felt that this new self was not visible; it would have to be found, and it could only be found by a kind of blindness, a dying into new consciousness. The Christian basis of the inversion is clear: the loss of self in order to find new self; the blindness that is true vision. The obsession with seeing, with darkness and light, may well have had its roots in the grim, coal-black inversion of life in the Nottinghamshire of Lawrence's childhood. After all, the life of the miner was a life of seeing in the darkness, and emerging (in winter, at least) from underground at nightfall. Lawrence's father, Arthur Lawrence, began work in the mines at the age of seven. Yet he knew the names of all the plants in the local area, and shared them with his son. So Arthur Lawrence was a very embodiment of the paradox of vision. From earliest days, he had been deprived of the visible world; yet he saw the world intently. Perhaps the entire colliery landscape seemed just such an inversion to Lawrence. In *Women in Love*, Gudrun tells Ursula that 'It is like a country in an underworld . . . The colliers bring it above ground with them, shovel it up.' The blackened land seems 'as if seen through a veil of crape'.

Lawrence is the greatest mystical novelist in English. His writing is built on the desirability of feeling, or knowing something, rather than *seeing* it. His story, 'The Blind Man', which he wrote in 1918, is explicitly about the desirability of sightless seeing. In it, a silent blind man teaches a knowing, sighted, over-confident rival how to feel. More importantly, Lawrence's fiction, in particular his short fiction, strives obsessively to make the invisible visible. In story after story, Lawrence writes about death or the moment of dying, of crossing over. In 'The Woman Who Rode Away' (1924), a woman ensnared and drugged by American Indians begins to sense a higher world beyond vision. She can hear 'the actual crystal sound of the heavens, as the vast belts of the world-atmosphere slid past one another'. The soldier who dies in 'The Prussian Officer' (1913) finds himself 'conscious of a sense of arrival'. The soldier who dies on the Front in 'England, My England', a story Lawrence wrote in a rented cottage in Sussex in 1915, is thrown into 'the great forgetting of death. To break the core and the unit of life, and to lapse out on the great darkness. Only that. To break the clue, and mingle and commingle with the one darkness, without afterwards, or forwards.' Lawrence's descriptions are sermons, mystic texts. And yet – and this is the wonder – they are not mystically vague but involve literal appearances, a kind of clumsy reality of the unseen. Partly this has to do with the kind of writer Lawrence was – he was not an ecstatic, and was suspicious of religious ecstasy. But it must also have to do with his increasing interest in theosophy and anthroposophy. Lawrence was exposed as a child to Methodism, and lost his faith, under the pressure of William James and Herbert Spencer, in 1908 and 1909. Kinkead-Weekes reports that in 1917 he read various hermetic and occult books. He wrote to Philip Heseltine that he had been reading Madame Blavatsky, but that he was not a theosophist. However, he wrote, he was drawn to the idea of 'a body of esoteric doctrine, defended from the herd'. In 1918 he was reading 'another book on occultism'.

But it seems likely that he had been exposed several years earlier to the ideas of the German anthroposophist Rudolf

Steiner (who is not mentioned by any biographer), who was giving lectures in Germany during this time. Steiner believed in the return of the dead and the recurrence of historical epochs. Lawrence consoled an aunt, in 1915, who had lost a son in France, with the Steinerian thought that the dead 'are not lost: they come back and live with one, in one's soul'. In his fine story, 'The Border Line' (1924), a woman breaks her journey in Strasbourg. Walking from her hotel in the evening, she sees the ghost of her husband, standing in a corner of the square. The simple insistence with which Lawrence endows this ghost, the unembarrassed surrealism, the daylight ordinariness of the ghost – all this carries the story, and allows the invisible an entirely natural domain.

Too little is made of Lawrence's occultism. For one sees in his writing not only many of the tropes of early Christian mysticism, but even at times a strain of Gnosticism (an early Church heresy which proposed a knowledge of God rather than a faith in Christ). There is the emphasis on the 'religious' elements – wind, flame, water and light. In one of his travel pieces, Lawrence described the arrival of light at sunrise as 'the light steps down' – an intensely religious formulation. (Swedenborg saw ladders of light ascending to and descending from heaven, for instance.) There is the stress on the heavens as a system of belts and wheels; and on the literal return of the dead. In various interpretations of the Apocalypse, we are told that time will stop when the Apocalypse comes: in Lawrence's repetitive mystical prose, the 'time' of the prose relaxes and is abolished. Above all, one finds again and again in Lawrence the idea of knowledge as a kind of secret, an occultism of the senses. Here, the Gnostic idea of 'knowing' the divine and being known via the spirit (pneuma) seems to combine with a hermetic or occult idea that knowledge is secret, hidden. Lawrence wrote to Lady Ottoline Morrell in 1915 that she should cheer up, because 'at the bottom one *knows* the eternal things, and is glad'. An exceptionally delicate passage in *Twilight in Italy* provides an example of the way in which so many of

Lawrence's descriptions are hidden sermons whose quarry is the secret of knowledge itself. Lawrence is sitting on a ledge. It is late afternoon, and suddenly, beneath him walk two monks, apparently in conversation. Lawrence cannot hear them, and he can barely see them. Instead, they must be divined:

> And then, just below me, I saw two monks walking in their garden between the naked, bony vines, walking in their wintry garden of bony vines and olive trees, their brown cassocks passing between the brown vine-stocks, their heads bare to the sunshine, sometimes a glint of light as their feet strode from under their skirts.
>
> It was so still, everything so perfectly suspended that I felt them talking. They marched with the peculiar march of monks, a long, loping stride, their heads together, their skirts swaying slowly, two brown monks with hidden hands sliding under the bony vines and beside the cabbages, their heads always together in hidden converse. It was as if I were attending with my dark soul to their inaudible undertone . . . I could hear no sound of their voices.

All of Lawrence's qualities as a writer seem to me to be gathered here. There is the brilliance of Lawrence's repetitions, so that the language becomes an abstract swoon, a religious nudging. There is the humble, funny, practical mention of the cabbages, beside which the monks walk. And then a verbal exchange occurs: Lawrence describes the vines as *naked* and *bony*, and then *both* the vines and the monks as 'brown'. He uncovers the monks, denudes them. He takes their cassocks off. For if the vines are like the monks, the monks become like the vines. The monks become 'naked, bony' and brown.

More importantly, the writer is feeling the presence of the monks, prayerfully. He cannot hear them, he can hardly see them, but he can feel them. They are 'hidden', yet Lawrence uncovers them. And he uncovers them religiously – by looking for the light they give off: 'sometimes a glint of light as their feet strode . . .' Underneath their cassocks, they glow. So Lawrence attends to the monks with his 'dark soul'. And what lights the path of this dark soul? The monks, who glow with light. Lawrence refers to the 'hidden converse' of the monks as they exchange words, but *this passage is really the 'hidden converse'*, for it enacts a secret exchange. On the one hand, Lawrence uncovers the monks by removing their trivial clothes, by stripping them to a state of nature (they are vines) and by illuminating them with light (they give off light, but Lawrence can only see them by the light they give off); on the other hand, and in an opposite direction, it is the monks who uncover Lawrence, who shine a light onto his 'dark soul'. Lawrence is dependent on the monks even as he conjures them into being on the page. This is a religious and literary humility with which Lawrence is hardly ever credited. Jesus said that he was the vine, and that we are the branches; in a sense, Lawrence, hovering out of sight, dependent on the monks and growing out of them, is a dark branch to their bright vine. All of this is to be found in Lawrence's *style*, which so many 'knowing' critics and readers so cheaply disdain as hysteria. I doubt that a more vitally religious passage of prose has been written by an English novelist in this century.

In November 1921, Lawrence received a letter from Mabel Dodge Sterne. She was an eccentric American philanthropist. The letter invited Lawrence to join a community in Taos, New Mexico. It is there that Lawrence would write the greatest book of his last years, *St. Mawr*, and one of his greatest mystical texts, 'The Woman Who Rode Away'. There, the ancient American vastness would be bent by the mystical vastness of Lawrence's prose, and he would give voice to a new landscape, to the 'vast, eagle-like wheeling of the daylight'. There he would become truly sick while breathing the fine high air. Physically he would wither; isolate, he would become as unapproachable as a cactus. Lawrence's ashes – they are thought to be his – are buried outside Taos. One goes up a long, five-mile track above the main road. It was winter when I went, a few years ago, and there was snow on the road. Mountains are ahead, and below are plains and canyons like throats, with massive rocky abandonments. In winter it is dulled, but in the summer it is religiously aflame and peppery red. It is this landscape that Lawrence would describe thus: 'It was always great, and splendid, and, for some reason, natural. It was never grandiose or theatrical. Always, for some reason, perfect. And quite simple, in spite of it all.' Of course, it is his writing he is really describing here. He had become the landscape.

T.S. Eliot's Christian Anti-Semitism

I

T.S. Eliot was an anti-Semite. Anthony Julius's programme, in his book *T.S. Eliot: Anti-Semitism and Literary Form*, is to assert the centrality of Eliot's anti-Semitism in his thought. Anti-Semitism, he says, was Eliot's inspiration, his muse; he was that rare anti-Semite, one who was 'able to place his anti-Semitism at the service of his art'; he 'trained himself to be an anti-Semite'. To conjure this centrality, Julius argues that anti-Semitism occurs at the heart of some of Eliot's greatest poetry. Julius is brave and occasionally right. His anger has the glow of righteousness. But it is the colour of simplicity. His book is tendentious, misleading, and unremittingly hostile. He has written an unstable book about an unstable subject; reading it is like watching a maniac trying to calm a hysteric.

First, there must be a conspiracy, and some long corridors. Julius contends that Eliot's anti-Semitism has been scandalously ignored or apologized for. 'Almost from the start, dissenting voices were rarely heard. . . .' But Julius passes over the amount of influential criticism there has been of Eliot's anti-Semitism. Since the publication of Eliot's three anti-Semitic poems in 1920, and certainly since the publication of Eliot's University of Virginia lectures in 1934, in a volume entitled *After Strange Gods*, readers have been aware of Eliot's tendencies. Stephen Spender attacked Eliot's anti-Semitism in 1935, and Lionel Trilling hinted at it in 1943, followed, over the next decade, by *The*

Saturday Review of Literature, Partisan Review, and the *TLS.* In the last twenty years, hardly a year has passed in which a book or essay has not appeared that has mentioned, and often censured, Eliot's anti-Semitism (these critics include Graham Martin, Roger Kojecky, Russell Kirk, William Empson, George Steiner, Christopher Ricks, Leslie Fiedler, Cynthia Ozick).

Julius announces that he is an admirer of Eliot's poetry, and that it is his admiration that draws him to this delicate subject. But his book is violently critical. Being praised by Julius is a brisk affair. The closest the book gets to the free pastures of praise is this: 'It is in the *Four Quartets,* and not in his prose criticism, that Eliot's conservatism finds its most considered, cogent expression.' Julius's business is to paint Eliot as racist, misogynist and anti-Semitic. The idea seems to be that the three demons are separate but pull together, like hard-working chefs, to prepare the feast of prejudice. But things are a little undercooked. For instance, Eliot's racism, for Julius, is as much a matter of silence as noise. His lectures to the University of Virginia, since they presuppose the racial uniformity of Virginia, 'overlook the entire Black population of the South'. Julius then reaches for two famous lines from 'The Dry Salvages', the third poem of *Four Quartets*:

> Time the destroyer is time the preserver,
> Like the river with its cargo of dead negroes, cows and
> chicken coops

Eliot grew up in St Louis, and as an old man recalled seeing the Mississippi in flood, when it flows at 'such speed that no man or beast can survive it'. In his essay 'American Literature and the American Language' (1953), he called the Mississippi 'the universal river of human life', and his noticing of the dead negroes catches the river's grim universal reach – both the river of life and the river of death. But Julius is scandalized that Eliot allows the dead negroes to be 'noted without emotion . . . Without censure the lines invoke the heritage of a commercial ("cargo") slave culture. This racism of prose and poetry [i.e. *After Strange Gods* and 'The Dry Salvages'] amounts to the adoption of the Confederate cause.' It is true that Eliot briefly praised the Conservative Agrarians of the early 1930s. But only an unhistorical critic could turn Eliot, the frail bloom of Boston Unitarianism, one of whose cherished books was his abolitionist grandfather's history of a black slave, into a surly Confederate! This is not merely a stubborn misreading of Eliot's lines (where 'cargo' binds together humans and animals, and precisely suggests how the river reduces those humans), but the kind of misreading that suggests the ticking of an ideological metronome. 'Without censure' – Julius expects Eliot's poetry to make ideological reparation for the slave trade. It is not allowed simply to describe.

Throughout his book, Anthony Julius is in such a rage that he whales his evidence into compliance. Consider this comment by Eliot on the poetry of Isaac Rosenberg, who died in the First World War, and whom Eliot called, in 1953, 'the most remarkable of the British poets killed in that war': 'The poetry of Isaac Rosenberg . . . does not only owe its distinction to its being Hebraic: but because it is Hebraic it is a contribution to English literature. For a Jewish poet to be able to write like a Jew, in western Europe and in a western European language, is almost a miracle.' Eliot's meaning is clear: Rosenberg was a distinguished English poet, but his particular addition to English literature was that he retained a Jewishness that was not assimilated; and this retention, within the pressure that the English poetic tradition exerts to surrender one's literary Jewishness, was almost miraculous.

But for Julius, this is an anti-Semitic 'libel' that allows 'Jews an aesthetic sense, and thus a measure of creativity, but deriving only from Jewish tradition'. He follows Eliot's quote with this extraordinary paragraph:

> Eliot's eccentric praise of the Jewish poet is consistent with his larger deprecations. 'That a Jew can do this!' registers the

surprise of the anti-Semite. What is it to write like a Jew? Richard Wagner explains: 'The Jew speaks the language of the country in which he has lived from generation to generation, but he always speaks it as a foreigner.' A Jew cannot compose German music; when he purports to do so, he deceives. The Jewish composer could only compose music as a Jew by drawing on the 'ceremonial music' of the synagogue service, a 'nonsensical gurgling, yodelling and cackling'. These 'rhythms . . . dominate his musical imagination'; they are irresistible. So while the talented Jewish composer is disqualified by his race from composing German music, he is disqualified by his talent from composing Jewish music. Rosenberg was luckier. He was able, by 'almost a miracle', to write in English 'like a Jew'. The difference between Eliot's anti-Semitism and Wagner's is defined, on this point, by the possibility of this 'miracle'.

This is characteristic of Julius's method. A passage of Eliot's is dropped into a stream of vicious anti-Semitic crudity, in the hope that the waters will mix. Almost every page of this book, which lavishly flows with examples of the anti-Semitism of people other than Eliot, attempts this guilt by immersion. But Julius makes Eliot mean the opposite of what he is saying. Wagner claims that the Jew tries to speak as a native but always reveals himself as a foreigner. For this reason he is incapable of great work. But Eliot praises Rosenberg for precisely the opposite quality. Rosenberg has retained a foreignness which Eliot considers a contribution and a miracle of self-preservation. If anything, Eliot implies that the Jew will always speak as a *native*, and that the struggle will be to speak as a *foreigner*. And Eliot is careful to suggest that Rosenberg's foreignness is not his only quality: 'does not only owe its distinction to its being Hebraic'. Julius reads the passage as if the phrase 'like a Jew' were simply not in the text, as if the passage read: 'For a Jewish poet to be able to write in western Europe and in a western European language, is almost a miracle.' This may be Wagner's belief, but it is palpably the opposite of Eliot's. Eliot is not praising Rosenberg for being able to write at all. The difference between Eliot's and Wagner's anti-Semitism is not defined by the word 'miracle'; it is defined by Eliot's not being, in this instance, anti-Semitic. At worst, Eliot's comment suggests a heightened awareness of Jewishness.

A critic who is inattentive to language in this way will not seem trustworthy, and Julius's book contains many bullied readings. Some of them are flicked off. For instance, in a brief discussion of Pound's anti-Semitism in the *Cantos*, Julius suggests that where Pound was incontinently anti-Semitic, Eliot was economical. 'Take Jewish Vienna: while *The Waste Land* renders it "unreal"' . . . the *Cantos* brood obsessively on it.' In a book one of whose themes is the silencing of Jews and the literary triumphing over them, we are supposed to attend here to Eliot's calm silencing of Jewish Vienna in *The Waste Land*. He renders Jewish Vienna 'unreal', and hence unreal also the Jewish lives it contains. Alas for Julius, nowhere in *The Waste Land* is Vienna marked as Jewish. The city's name appears only once, as one of a list of cities which may stand for the fragmentation, or perhaps the disordered superabundance, of civilization: 'Jerusalem Athens Alexandria/ Vienna London/ Unreal.' Nor, of course, does Vienna's unreality, even if it were anywhere identified as Jewish, have anything to do with silencing. Earlier in the poem, London is called 'unreal' in the famous, bleak, tolling passage in which the poet sees commuters walking across London Bridge:

> Unreal City,
> Under the brown fog of a winter dawn,
> A crowd flowed over London Bridge, so many,
> I had not thought death had undone so many.

The slow, lovely cortège of these lines makes hidden reference to Baudelaire and Dante: Baudelaire's vision is of a city of phantoms, and Dante's is of the living dead, those who know neither good nor evil. Eliot's London is unreal not because its people are silenced or dismissed, but because they are phantoms moving through a city of dreams. It is not that Eliot's modern city-dwellers have been silenced or thieved of reality by the poet; Eliot's point is that their lives do not have enough reality.

Eliot was not Wagner. He combined two strands of anti-Semitism: the fashionable contempts of his age and an unfashionable belief that whatever was outside the Christian Church was both heretical and, literally, deadly. 'If Christianity goes, the whole of our culture goes', he wrote in 1939, in *The Idea of a Christian Society*. 'If you will not have God . . . you should pay your respects to Hitler or Stalin.' Eliot's ecclesiastical petrification is necessarily wary of competing religions and hostile to all secularism. His critical prose, usually dementedly patient, is stirred to animus whenever those anti-religionists, H.G. Wells, George Bernard Shaw, Aldous Huxley, or Bertrand Russell, stray into his cloisters. ('These two depressing life-forcers' is his estimation of Russell and Huxley.) Jews, and especially 'free-thinking Jews', take their place in this procession of unfortunates. In one notorious passage in *After Strange Gods* (a book he did not allow to be republished), Eliot defined his Christian society: 'The population should be homogeneous; where two or more cultures exist in the same place they are likely to be either fiercely self-conscious or both to become adulterate. What is still more important is unity of religious background; and reasons of race and religion combine to make any large number of free-thinking Jews undesirable.'

This was uttered in 1933; it is indefensible. It sounds flippant, or worse, to suggest that Eliot did not want to be taken seriously at this moment. But Eliot's prose has a tendency towards a mocking chilliness of tone. He is at times puerile, delighting in pulling the wings off the sensitive secular insect. In *Notes Towards the Definition of Culture* (1948), he suggests that to discuss the preservation of Welsh as a language is 'really as much as to ask whether the Welsh, *qua* Welsh, are of any use?' Does one not here feel him relishing his nudity? Similarly, a footnote in his Norton lectures of 1932–3 calmly proposes this: 'The Roman and Communist idea of an index of prohibited books seems to me perfectly sound in principle. It is a question (a) of the goodness and universality of the cause, (b) of the intelligence that goes to the application.' In 'Thoughts After Lambeth' he likes to strike a Kierkegaardian note: 'You will never attract the young by making Christianity easy; but a good many can be attracted by finding it difficult; difficult both to the disorderly mind and to the unruly passions.' This language, with its pellets of precision, and its frozen demeanour, shocks contemporary readers because more than a century has elapsed since writers pronounced like this. In tone and thought there is little here that would have seemed unusual to Cardinal Newman. Eliot savours the shock of a word like 'intelligence', aware that most readers will find 'intelligence', in the matter of censorship and book-burning, trivial or irrelevant. Similarly, he squeezes the word 'undesirable' for its full sap of hidden prejudice, while holding the word to its exact volume of verifiable meaning: it is not that a concentration of free-thinking Jews is grotesque or impossible or disgusting, but not desirable, not ideal. This language buys its shocking effects through its glacial reticence. Of course, Eliot believed what he was saying in these instances; but he took pleasure, one suspects, at the idea that he might not be believed by others.

Julius, following several critics, argues that Eliot was tellingly attracted, when discussing non-Christian groups, to the excoriation of the Jews. But there is little evidence for this – all we have are the single passage in *After Strange Gods* that I have quoted, and a footnote in *Notes*, about the unfortunate nature of some of the 'culture-contact' between Jews and Christians, which was revised thus in 1962: 'It seems to be highly desirable that there should be close culture-contact between devout and practising Christians and devout and practising Jews.' All this mutuality of devoutness is sickly, of course, and merely adds free-thinking Christians to the free-thinking Jews already excluded from

Eliot's ideal society. But in truth, Jews are barely noticed in Eliot's writing about Christianity, and when they are, they are not awarded the fear and loathing that is reserved for Christian secularists like Russell and Wells. Eliot's obliviousness to the Jewish plight during the 1930s is a sin, but it is a different kind of sin from the anti-Semitism that Julius alleges. *The Idea of a Christian Society*, lectures published in 1939, makes no reference to Jews, and we may find this cruel or insensitive; but it does not, as Julius claims, 'disparage' Jews, or only by omission. I do not mean to soften the obnoxiousness of Eliot's anti-Semitism, not at all, only to argue against its *centrality* in Eliot's thought. Christian orthodoxy was his rock; all unorthodoxies issued from enemy territory.

Eliot's Christianity, he explained, was not emotional and religious, but intellectual and dogmatic. Reversing St Paul, he aphorized that in Christianity, the spirit killeth, but the letter giveth life. Eliot's family was of a distinguished Unitarian New England line. Unitarianism, from a dogmatic Christian position, is a religion of air. It is full of spirit and bereft of letter. It denies both the reality of the Trinity, and Jesus's claim to be the Son of God. It is optimistic, and with a spiny ethical emphasis on charity and good works. It is somewhat tiresomely untragic (we see this in Emerson). Eliot's grandfather, the Reverend William Greenleaf Eliot, was a leading abolitionist of his time. William Empson speculated that Eliot's anti-Semitism was the embodiment of Eliot's hatred for his father, a Unitarian businessman. Certainly, Eliot's Christianity – he was received into the Church of England in 1928 – was the dark to Unitarianism's light. (Responding to a correspondent critical of his words about free-thinking Jews, Eliot replied that Judaism without belief and observation descends into 'a mild and colourless form of Unitarianism'.) Eliot plunged into the magma of religious proposition even as Unitarianism fled from it. He worked upwards from the bottom through a chain of black excruciations. As a consequence of Original Sin, man is essentially bad. Man's religious existence will thus be the worship of correction

– 'thought, study, mortification, sacrifice', as he once described it. Tending toward disorder, he must covet discipline. Politically, this will mean order, and the order provided by institutions. For the Christian, that institution is the Church. Where there is no Christianity, there is heresy, disorder, anarchy – 'the anarchy of feeling' as he put it in his essay on Arnold and Pater. The Anglican thinkers whom Eliot admired, such as Richard Hooker (1554–1600) and Bishop Lancelot Andrewes (1555–1626), insisted on the oneness of the Church of England and the nation.

This may be cheerless, conservative, or reprehensible to modern ears. I should say that, as one brought up in an intensely Christian household, I find it repulsive, clenched, spiritless, and wrong. It is the very image of what Nietzsche called the Christian inversion of health. But our business is to scour it for anti-Semitism, not for charm. Judging it neutrally, one must observe that it is a vision of completeness, so that what is outside it must seem, to Eliot, incomplete. Eliot's anti-Semitism needs to be seen in this light. This was the mind that could write, about religious revivalism in the 1930s: 'Religion can hardly revive, because it cannot decay.' 'It cannot decay': Eliot's faith is a hard faith, and we may wonder at the theological usefulness of a critic of Eliot who can write, as Julius does, 'As late as *Notes* he was still insisting upon the determinative importance of Christianity', as if religion were like hypochondria, to be abandoned once secular medicines have brought release. *Of course* Eliot was 'still insisting' on this importance: he could insist on nothing else, because he could see no other. He believed. He spoke, once, of 'the incredibility of every alternative to Christianity that offers itself', and he used the word with customary formality: he could not believe in an alternative.

Some of Eliot's anti-Semitism, then, is dogmatic Christianity's anti-Semitism – not the anti-Semitism of the Church (the riots, the superstitions, the discriminatory laws, the complicity with the Holocaust), but the anti-Semitism of Christ himself. Clearly, Christianity must be structurally at odds with Judaism, and Judaism at odds with Christianity, for Christ claimed to be both a fulfilment and a supersession of the Old Testament: 'Before Abraham was, I am.' Jesus used Judaism to triumph over itself, which is the point of Jesus's disobedience of the laws of the Sabbath, a disobedience he justifies, when challenged by the Pharisees, by quoting David. For this illegality leads to a miracle: inside a synagogue, on the Sabbath, he cures a man with a withered arm, asking: 'Is it lawful on the sabbath days to do good, or to do evil? to save life, or to destroy it?' Julius, of course, rages against the anti-Semitism of St John, Marcion, Tertullian, and the early Church, and decides that 'the desire to sever Christianity from its Jewish origins is a project of many anti-Semites.' What this has to do with Eliot is never made clear, since Julius himself quotes Eliot stressing the connection of Judaism and Christianity. Eliot censured Simone Weil, whom he admired, for rejecting Israel. By 'denying the divine mission of Israel', wrote Eliot, she also rejected 'the foundation of the Christian Church'. Now, it is characteristic not so much of Eliot, as of his Christianity, that Israel is seen as the provider of Christianity. This will offend those who care about such things; it offends me. But this is not Eliot's anti-Semitism. It is Christianity's super-Semitism. Julius is blind to this theology of supersession, and, typically, storms in hysterical squalls: 'Here we are meant to infer that it was Israel's mission to found the Church; having done so, it should have dissolved itself' is his comment on Eliot's sentences. He offers no evidence for the second half of his allegation.

St Luke gives one of the Christian Church's most cherished stories of Israel's 'divine mission' in the second chapter of his gospel. It is known, in the Christian liturgy, as the *Nunc Dimittis*, and it is sung or spoken every day at the evening service called Evensong. Simeon, writes Luke, an old and devout man, 'waiting for the consolation of Israel', is visited by the Holy Spirit, who reveals to him that he shall not die before seeing the Christ child. Taken to the temple where Mary, Joseph and the infant Jesus are gathered, Simeon thanks God, saying: 'Lord now lettest now thy servant depart in peace, according to thy word: For mine eyes have seen thy salvation, which thou hast prepared before the face of all people . . .' The old man is ready to die, happy in the glory of Messianic completion.

Eliot put these words into verse in his poem 'A Song for Simeon' (1928). The poem is spoken by Simeon, as 'Journey of the Magi' (1927) is spoken by one of the three wise men. It is a dramatic monologue. It is a frail, somewhat blanched poem; minor, but touching. Simeon prays that 'the Infant, the still unspeaking and unspoken Word,/ Grant Israel's consolation/ To one who has eighty years and no to-morrow,' and ends in one of those Eliotian dying falls, the words repeated like the repetitions of ritual, so as to become a religious nudging:

I am tired with my own life and the lives of those after me,
I am dying in my own death and the death of those after me.
Let thy servant depart,
Having seen thy salvation.

Eliot's poem is faithful to Luke, save for the addition of some hyacinths, and Simeon's age. Eliot would not have greatly altered what is a canonical piece of Christian liturgy; indeed, he offers his poem as devout liturgy of its own kind. What mild Christian triumphalism there is in the poem – the Messiah who is Israel's consolation – is Luke's. And Luke's triumphalism has more to do with rejoicing, and with universal absolution, than with glee: 'thy salvation, which thou hast prepared before the face of *all* people . . .' But Julius, for whom the poem is obviously an obstacle (the anti-Semite poet who writes as a Jew), sees it as 'another one of Eliot's triumphs over Jews'. First, the title seems curdlingly significant: 'The song is *for*, not *of*, Simeon . . . The poem', he chides, 'merits Alasdair MacIntyre's wider criticism: "[t]he attempt to speak for [Jews], even on behalf of that unfortunate fiction, the so-called Judeo-Christian tradition, is always deplorable." '

Pass over the recollection that Eliot called one of his books, which contained an essay on the Elizabethan English divine, *For Lancelot Andrewes*. Pass over the thought that the critic who makes use of Alasdair MacIntyre's disparagement of the 'so-called Judeo-Christian tradition' later attacks as anti-Semitic 'the desire to sever Christianity from its Jewish origins' (had Eliot called that tradition 'so-called', Julius would stamp on him). Because Julius has more: 'Eliot gives the Jew lines that locate him, and by implication all Jews, wholly within the Christian drama. Incapable of denying its truth, but equally incapable of living that truth, Simeon welcomes death because his life is death.' He continues: 'Simeon does not know how to worship. Eliot allows him to condemn himself.' Yet Simeon does not welcome death because his life is death, but because his life has been gloriously completed, messianically irradiated. He is located 'wholly within the Christian drama' because, in a sense, he, like Israel, has been Christianized through his witnessing of the Messiah: he has been baptized into futurity. That the Jews were 'a chosen people' because they were chosen by God *to be Christians*, is a familiar New Testament idea, and St Luke means just this. This is, within the tradition, glorious because tenderly universal, embracing all. It is, of course, not anti-Semitic, unless the very idea of an actual and fulfilling Messiah is anti-Semitic. Only an unbalanced or unintelligent or tendentious critic would see it as a sinister 'triumph over Jews'.

2

After such knowledge, what forgiveness? Why should we trust a critic who seems to have such narrow access to justice? Julius is a lawyer by profession, and his prose style, when not sunk in troughs of research, has a judicial tread: 'This is an argument one can respect, though I reject it.' But more often, he insinuates. The New Criticism of the 1950s and its legacy, he writes, still 'protects Eliot'. Eliot 'wrote out of Symbolism for New Criticism' – as if Eliot, in Symbolism's dream-kitchen, were chopping poems to order. Or this on Eliot's criticism: 'At its best, it enlarged a particular tradition. In the context of his poetic achievement, however, Denis Donoghue's remark that its "flaws . . . or even its merits – are hardly worth talking about" is just.' At its best, Eliot's criticism did not merely enlarge a particular tradition, but founded a new one: his own. But we know what Julius thinks of Eliot's 'poetic achievement': 'The Love Song of J. Alfred Prufrock' is misogynistic; *The Waste Land* silences Jewish Vienna, and *Four Quartets*, when not racist, as in 'The Dry Salvages', offers merely the 'most cogent, considered expression' of Eliot's conservatism, a vision which Julius finds repulsive and tacitly anti-Semitic.

It is in this light that we need to examine Julius's claim that Eliot's anti-Semitism appears at the heart of his finest poetry. Why should we believe such a claim when Julius can find nothing warm to say about the poetry that is *not* tainted with anti-Semitism? This untainted poetry, incidentally, includes all the work for which Eliot will be remembered: 'The Love Song of J. Alfred Prufrock'; *The Waste Land*; *Four Quartets*; 'The Journey of the Magi'. It is not credible that Julius, the ferret of all forms of prejudice, would find Eliot's non-anti-Semitic poems to be somehow lacking, while finding Eliot's anti-Semitic poems (there are three, only) to be great or virtuosic! This would surely be perverse. But this is Julius's strategy, and it inevitably raises the suspicion in the reader that Julius is not telling the truth, that he likes none of the poetry, but that he needs to inflate the importance and the quality of Eliot's three anti-Semitic poems in order to be able to argue anti-Semitism's centrality in Eliot's work, and its thorough entanglement with Eliot's best poetry. In other words, the better the poetry in which anti-Semitism occurs, the better the anti-Semitism for Julius's case. For were Eliot's three anti-Semitic poems to be seen as minor, then so would Eliot's anti-Semitism.

The three poems are: 'Gerontion', 'Burbank with a Baedeker: Bleistein with a Cigar', and 'Sweeney Among the Nightingales'. They do not offer attractive reading, and Julius is at his best when supplying the dismal tradition of abuse from which Eliot's lines spring. In the best of the poems, 'Gerontion', an old man, confused, bitter, and frantic for the fertility of order, casts about himself and dribbles allusions – to Lancelot Andrewes, Henry Adams, Job, St Matthew's gospel, the Elizabethan poets:

> My house is a decayed house,
> And the Jew squats on the window sill, the owner,
> Spawned in some estaminet of Antwerp,
> Blistered in Brussels, patched and peeled in London.

These lines cannot be mitigated. True, 'Gerontion' is a dramatic monologue, and the old man is perhaps a bitterer anti-Semite than Eliot. (This is the usual argument in favour of Eliot's innocence.) But what we know of Eliot's anti-Semitism allows us to read, without unreasonable forcing, these lines as simultaneously lines of dramatic monologue and words congruent with Eliot's own internal monologue. More devastatingly, Eliot originally published the poem with 'Jew' in lower case ('jew'), enriching the typography only in 1963, when the Jew was suddenly allowed to walk tall in his own capital. This emendation is an admission of guilt. It was not Gerontion who changed the typeface, but Eliot.

Nevertheless, these are the only anti-Semitic lines in the poem, and though their foulness forces an arrest on us, we have to be able to free ourselves. 'Gerontion' is a poem with an anti-Semitic rash, but the rash is confined to a limb. It is a poem blemished. One cannot say this for 'Burbank with a Baedeker: Bleistein with a Cigar', which fawns at the Gentile reader, slobbering anti-Semitism. Bleistein ('Chicago Semite Viennese') is ridiculed, and the poem rises to this peak:

> The rats are underneath the piles
> The Jew is underneath the lot.

'Sweeney Among the Nightingales' does not crawl with distaste in quite the same way, though it features 'Rachel *née* Rabinovitch' who 'Tears at the grapes with murderous paws'.

Julius's discussion of the anti-Semitism in these three poems is valuable, though he does not relinquish his habit of mummifying all his details in strips of historical research. One notices, however, that while he states the quality of these poems as poems, his bag of superlatives is hardly full. While hating the anti-Semitism, he claims that the lines in 'Gerontion' 'economically render' various anti-Semitic themes. A little later, he refers to these 'charged, economical lines'. Later still, he compares Pound's anti-Semitism unfavourably with 'the charged economy of Eliot's anti-Semitism'. In 'Sweeney', he writes, Eliot, 'with great virtuosity . . . turns that material [i.e. anti-Semitic clichés] into art. He compresses it into a single, powerfully charged sentence.' But this 'art' appears to have only two qualities for Julius: it is economical, and it is charged (and this latter comes to us by definition anyway: anti-Semitic lines are bound to be 'charged').

Furthermore, Julius entraps himself. He must argue, on the one hand, that Eliot's poetic anti-Semitism is indebted to anti-Semitic clichés (Jews as rats, for instance), but he must also argue, on the other hand, if he believes these poems to be great and central, that the poetry is not itself clichéd, but original. For if *Eliot's* anti-Semitism were itself clichéd, it would not be great poetry. Inevitably, these two categories, cliché and originality, begin to slide towards each other, and at one point Julius admits that 'Gerontion''s squatting Jew, 'in his inability to find any permanent place of rest, is also Eliot's gesture toward that most fatigued of cultural clichés, the Wandering Jew. He gives the cliché a malignant twist in "Gerontion", and a comic twist in "Burbank" . . .'

There are readers of Eliot for whom these early poems, written before *The Waste Land*, are Eliot's most complex and daring. The poetry after 1920, for these people, is a trail gone cold. But Eliot's greatest poetry, in my opinion, is the poetry with no anti-Semitism in it. Is it impossible for an anti-Semitic poem to be a great poem? No, but it is harder for such a poem to be great, and Eliot's three poems provide the evidence. If we look at them as poems – one of Eliot's constant injunctions in the criticism that Julius deems negligible – we can only compare them unhappily with the poetry of *The Waste Land*. 'Gerontion', with its blemish, comes close to being one of Eliot's finer poems. The other two do not. We feel the pressure of a controlling malignity in these poems, where we feel the pressure of a helpless despair in *The Waste Land*. In *The Waste Land*, a desperate irony propels the lines; but in 'Burbank' and 'Sweeney' we feel the smaller category of sarcasm as the engine of the verse. In these poems ('Gerontion' excepted) the odour of light verse is merely smothered. And this is appropriate, for anti-Semitism is not mythic but colloquial: it belongs to, is owned first by, speech. Light verse is its home.

But the inhabitants of *The Waste Land* are mythical. Bleistein, Burbank, Rachel are made smaller than us, for we are supposed to condescend to them; they issue out of cliché. But in *The Waste Land*, Madame Sosostris, Phlebas the Phoenician, even the women in the pub, are enlarged. They include us, for their demise is ours:

> Gentile or Jew
> O you who turn the wheel and look to windward,
> Consider Phlebas, who was once handsome and tall as you.

The Waste Land is founded on the principle of enlargement. Blake, in his biblical epic poem *Jerusalem*, turned London into a city of impossible dreams, relishing the continuity between the world of biblical hugeness and the ordinariness, now radiant, of London's place-names: 'is that/ Mild Zion's hill's most ancient promontory, near mournful/Ever weeping Paddington?' Eliot learned much from Blake, and made London, as Blake did, larger than itself. London was not only London, but Dante's Florence, Baudelaire's Paris, and the Fisher King's sterile wastelands. Through allusion and counterpoint, London was lyricized – turned not only into Eliot's poetry, but into all of English poetry:

> And along the Strand, up Queen Victoria Street.
> O City city, I can sometimes hear
> Beside a public bar in Lower Thames Street,
> The pleasant whining of a mandoline

In *The Waste Land,* the banal – the young man carbuncular, the commuters crossing London Bridge – are at once condescended to, and somehow also pitied; for the stored pity of European poetry is brought to watch their ordinariness. And such people are pitied, unlike Bleistein or Rachel, because the poet pities, and include himself, too. The poet himself is 'unreal', he crosses the bridge with the other dead, he goes to Margate like the clerks and typists, and has his unhappy love affairs, and his unsatisfactory sexual encounter in Highgate. His familiarity with London is the mark not of his superior *flâneur*-like status, but of his Dickensian homelessness and ordinariness. (The poem has much more of Dickens in it than of Baudelaire.) The poet sits not in his fine Christian study, but in his 'empty room':

> The awful daring of a moment's surrender
> Which an age of prudence can never retract
> By this, and this only, we have existed
> Which is not to be found in our obituaries
> Or in memories draped by the beneficent spider
> Or under seals broken by the lean solicitor
> In our empty rooms

Just as Eliot went down into the theological magma for his rock, so we feel here that he has descended – made one of those 'rare descents' into the abyss which he wrote about in his essay on Matthew Arnold. What we bring back from those descents, said Eliot, is not 'criticism'. No, it is not criticism; and it is not disdain, and it is not condescension. It is the knowledge that far from the public rooms, far from the forms of life ('not to be found in our obituaries'), far from society itself with its cruelties, is a loneliness whose brutality is stronger than our powers, and which enforces on us gentleness, sympathy, and control. Here, at the end of *The Waste Land*, Eliot suggests a despair which cannot be renovated by the consoling verticalities of hierarchy and tradition. At the end of the poem, the thunder says three words in Sanskrit: 'Datta. Dayadhvam. Damyata.' – *Give. Sympathize. Control.* Eliot's anti-Semitic verse obeys only the last command of that austere triad.

George Steiner's Unreal Presence

George Steiner's prose is a remarkable substance; it is the sweat of a monument. Readers of his essays will be familiar with its imprecisions and melodramas; the platoon-like massing of its adjectives, its cathedral hush around the great works. Vladimir Nabokov once complained that one of Steiner's essays was 'built on solid abstractions and opaque generalisations'. But things are actually a little worse than that.

George Steiner has a fear of exhibiting even rhetorical ignorance, and this is accompanied by a superstitious worship of 'greatness', in which greatness is detached from its referent and has become a portable magic, like feng shui. 'An Uncommon Reader', in his book *No Passion Spent*, provides two amusing examples on successive pages. Steiner is discoursing on the decline of 'classic codes of literacy'. ('Do not even ask a relatively well-prepared student to respond to the title of "Lycidas".') Every true reader, he avers, 'carries within him a nagging weight of omission': the books he has not read. Apparently there are books that even George Steiner has not read. But he still knows that they are great: 'the eight volumes, unread, of Sorel's great diplomatic history of Europe and the French Revolution haunt me.' Or this, a page earlier: 'I have, a dozen times, slunk by Sarpi's leviathan history of the Council of Trent (one of the pivotal works in the development of western religious-political argument) . . . I shall never manage the sixteen thousand pages of Amiel's (profoundly interesting) journal currently being published. There is so little time in "the library that is the universe" (Borges's Mallarméen phrase).' David's lament for Jonathan, he tells us in his 'Preface to the Hebrew Bible', is 'unsurpassed in any poetry' – any poetry.

This greatness is memorialized in rippling and indiscriminate lists, whose habitual tic is a consumer's indefinite article. Just as one asks for a coffee, a Coke, a scotch, Steiner asks for 'a Socrates, a Mozart, a Gauss or a Galileo who, in some degree, compensate for man' ('The Archives of Eden'); or 'a Mantegna, a Turner or a Cézanne . . . a Racine, a Dostoevsky, a Kafka' ('Real Presences'). He charges that 'the pressure of presence throughout the world of the mind and of moral feeling exercised on civilization by a Marx, a Freud, even a Lévi-Strauss, is of a calibre which American culture does not produce.' This is not a trivial stylistic habit, though in fairness it may in part be the sound of a German locution turned into English. There is only 'a coffee', but there is no such thing as 'a Mozart'. There is Mozart, singular and non-transferable – a concretion, not a vapour. Steiner's use of lists, and his use of the indefinite article, suggests that the meal of greatness can be had in any order and in any combination; the important thing is to fill oneself up and to be bloatedly grateful. It may be that Steiner, detecting his own vulgarity in these matters, compensates by wrapping great works in veils. Since greatness is a magic, one must be wary of offending it, in particular by careless worldliness: 'if we choose, we can put on Opus 131 while eating breakfast,' he quivers in his book *In Bluebeard's Castle*. This is not supposed to be a good thing. Steiner is here denouncing the coarsening freedoms of modernity, specifically American modernity. One of his persistent sensations, doubtless accurate, is that reading as it was pursued a hundred years ago in bourgeois families has been superseded by listening to music. This technological proximity to great music is all very well, but one should not be too intimate with holiness. Steiner enunciates the dangers, in two languages: 'there can be an unprecedented intimacy, but also a devaluation (*désacralisation*).'

Steiner's melodrama of transcendence accounts for his air of excited gravity. He approaches each work as if leading a coup to restore a monarch to the throne. First he must synchronize his beating heart with the reader's. 'We are entering on large, difficult ground'; 'Here extreme precision is needed.' 'Let me be absolutely clear on this'; 'Again, this is a most complex topic.' Generally, the coup fails. The less precise his prose, the more it speaks of the importance of precision. An emblematic moment occurs in his essay 'Absolute Tragedy'. Steiner urges on us the blackness of our times ('This century has witnessed a carnival of bestiality'), and suggests that pure tragedy's lack of mercy may be our most appropriate literary form. 'If this perception can, must be dwelt on, if it must be "thought" (in Heidegger's active sense of that word), do there not attach to it the potential, the likelihood of a renascence of tragic drama?' 'Heidegger's active sense of that word' – here is the essence of Steiner. The operatic flounce, the sentimental wrestle ('if this perception can, must be dwelt on'), the allusion, quite irrelevantly, to Heidegger, followed by the ascription of the importance of thinking to the word itself rather than the demonstration of its activity. What is 'active' here except a pulse?

Great work, suggests Steiner, is to be worshipped and protected, and great work requires great questions. His commonest sentence is a question: 'Is it possible that . . .' 'Could it be that . . . ' Could it be that anti-Semitism is the Gentile's guilty revenge on the impossible demands of Mosaic monotheism, Christianity, and Messianic socialism, all Jewish 'inventions'? Could it be that great art not only thrives best in elitist structures, but in totalitarian regimes? Is it possible that great art does not merely co-exist with barbarism and evil, but in some way produces it? These are some of the questions of Steiner's work. He seems to relish the unanswerability of these questions, as if their unanswerability made them better questions, and as if the fact that nobody has answered them means that nobody has ever asked them. He is in love with the glamour of the unsayable. He has sensations rather than arguments. In his essay 'Real Presences', he notes that all value-judgments about works of art are unprovable and arbitrary. *'Anything can be said about anything'* he italicizes. Indeed. *And nothing can be said about nothing.* There are times, as Auden warned, when 'to ask the hard question is simple'.

His work since *Language and Silence,* published in 1967, has been ambitious, and engaged with several recurring questions. Steiner has felt, since the 1960s, that our age is 'in retreat from the word'. The word, for Steiner, signifies a certain authority of meaning and a body of assumed knowledge. This retreat is partly, and trivially, a matter of fashion. Education is no longer rooted in the Greek and Latin classics. We listen to music but do not read aloud to one another. Culture is now democratically accessible; most own paperbacks and few have libraries of hardback volumes. In place of what Steiner calls '*cortesia*' there is now 'informality'. Culture was once kept alive by stern schooling and by the cultivation of memory, especially through learning poetry by heart. This was the education Steiner received in the *lycée* system in Paris. 'Memory is, of course, the pivot', but in most students there has been an 'atrophy of memory'. Like so many, and quite forgivably, Steiner's thought bears the characteristic impress of a university teacher who has not recovered from the shock he received in the 1960s when the counter-culture (a phrase Steiner spits, when he can) ambled into his *cortesia*, and who has reinvigorated his earlier disapproval via an encounter with postmodernism, whose excesses seem to repeat philosophically what the 1960s attempted politically.

The retreat has deeper lineaments. Writers no longer write for the glory beyond death, so alleges Steiner: 'The very notion of *fama*, of literary glory achieved in defiance of and as rebuttal to death, embarrasses.' Above all, this is a crisis of meaning. Modernism snapped the idea of an essential link between a word and its meaning, and Freudianism has undermined our sense of intentional control over our meaning. Meanwhile, a belief in God, which guarantees final meaning and telos, has fallen away. The greatest danger, as Steiner sees it, is from the philosophical scepticism that travels under the name of deconstruction, postmodernism, or post-structuralism. The modernists strove against the decay of meaning, but deconstruction embraces it, embraces the free play of meanings. The text is a bubble of signifiers constantly revealing its own contradictions and wistful ambitions, and the contemporary critic's only job seems to be to prick it. Where modernism was unafraid to make hierarchies, deconstruction erodes them, and postmodernism simply ignores them. Truth is radically unstable; *Auctoritas* has gone.

There are too many professors of literature who see around them only collapsing vertebrae for Steiner's complaint to be other than conventional; and an argument on behalf of distinction – which is what Steiner's is – is surely cheapened by no longer itself having much distinction. It should be granted, in Steiner's defence, that he departs from these other complainers in three respects. He is philosophically more literate than most of them, dragging the heavy iron of the Germanic tradition into his corner whenever he can. (His book on Heidegger is creditable.) Second, he is much more open to new work, in various languages, than is usual among English-language critics. There are people who speak happily of their years at Cambridge University in the 60s, when Steiner filled lecture rooms and burrowed into his cellular erudition, prompting students to discover writers who were hardly known to them: Borges, Barthes, García Márquez, Beckett. An essay in *No Passion Spent,* written in 1982, on translation, shows Steiner passionate and unusually precise, arguing the merits of the Austrian novelist Thomas Bernhard and pleading for his translation into English. In 1982, only one of Bernhard's novels had travelled out of German. Now most of them are available in English, and Steiner surely had something to do with this. He speaks defensively of being only a 'courier', yet that is not an unworthy way for a critic to spend a life.

2

He differs from other Jeremiahs most spectacularly in his solution to the contemporary malaise, which he proffered in his

Cambridge lecture of 1985, 'Real Presences', and expanded in his book of the same title. The solution, for Steiner at least, is his doctrine of the Real Presence. Steiner thinks it is frankly theological; it is, alas, vaguely religious. His prose becomes diligently evasive in the course of this particular argument. Deconstruction, for Steiner, is a nihilism, and 'the summons of nihilism demands answer.' It is answered by faith. In the face of a deconstructionist who claims that *Madame Bovary* is just a set of signifiers, or Mahler's Fourth Symphony just some complex notations on staves, Steiner demands that we read and listen 'as if' – as if these great works have a transcendent meaning which is irreducible. This, suggests Steiner, is what Flaubert meant when, dying, he complained that 'that whore Emma Bovary' would outlive him. We will have to believe that these and other great works incarnate a meaning in the same way that in the Christian communion the bread and wine incarnate the flesh and blood of Christ (this is what the doctrine of the Real Presence refers to). Meaning is guaranteed, says Steiner, by a belief in the transcendent, in the divine. We cannot *know* this, but just as Pascal made his wager on God, we must make ours: 'Where we read truly, where the experience is to be that of meaning, we do so as if the text (the piece of music, the work of art) *incarnates* (the notion is grounded in the sacramental) *a real presence of significant being*. This real Presence, as in an icon, as in the enacted metaphor of the sacramental bread and wine, is finally irreducible to any other formal articulate . . .' A little earlier, Steiner refers to Descartes's *'sine qua non* that God will not systematically confuse or falsify our perception and understanding of the world' and adds that 'without some such fundamental presupposition' in regard to sense and value, we cannot understand great work. He calls this 'our Cartesian-Kantian wager, our leap into sense . . .'

So Steiner is saying, in effect: 'deconstruction has eroded our belief that texts mean anything; in opposition, I propose that, as Pascal wagered on God's existence, we must wager on meaning's existence. And I will wager on this in the same way that the Real Presence is a wager.' But this 'idea' is no more than the milk of optimism, and is soaked in errors. First of all, the Real Presence is not a wager like Pascal's (just as, it should be noted, Descartes's and Kant's proofs are not wagers either – Steiner is invariably at his loosest when invoking philosophers). Pascal wrote that we should force ourselves to believe in God even if we are doubtful about His existence, because if we are right, and God exists, we win heaven, and if we are wrong, and God does not exist, we have not harmed ourselves by believing in an illusion. How could the Eucharist possibly be a wager of this sort? The Christian, if he or she believes in the Real Presence, believes that the bread and wine of the Eucharist service refer to Jesus's body and blood because they incarnate them. This system of reference is in turn related to the larger incarnation, which is that Jesus refers to God, because Jesus incarnated Him. The Real Presence implies a wholly theological theory of meaning. It is not a wager, but a belief. Second, the Real Presence is not a metaphor, either. Yet this is what Steiner seems to think. Attend to his evasions: he writes that where we read truly, we do so not *because* the text incarnates meaning but '*as if*' it incarnates meaning. Again, he writes that we must follow Descartes's wager – but only vaguely: 'some such fundamental presupposition'. Any similar fundamental presupposition will do in Steiner's theory, as long as it is very fundamental. And while on the one hand the text is taken to 'incarnate' meaning, a word with a specific theological gravity of embodiment, in the next sentence this incarnation is made no more than an 'enacted metaphor'.

This is intellectually feeble. There are, broadly, three kinds of Real Presence belief. Catholicism believes that in the communion service, which repeats Jesus's last supper, the bread and wine become the flesh and blood of Christ ('transubstantiation'); Protestantism believes that Jesus's body is present in the bread and wine ('consubstantiation'); and there are Christians, like the Zwinglians of old, who believe that neither happens, but that the communion service memorializes Christ's last supper. It may be that Steiner is a Zwinglian, for only this last belief comes close to the idea of an 'enacted metaphor'. Most orthodox belief takes incarnation to mean what it says, because Christ's incarnation is taken to mean what it says. The Real Presence is founded on God-given truth; even the Zwinglian doctrine is founded on the possibility of memorializing God-given truth. None of these positions is a wager; none is, at base, an enacted metaphor, unless Christ be an enacted metaphor.

It is not pedantry to insist that Steiner employ his theological language with precision, for the Real Presence has a significant place in both theological and philosophical disputation of the last five hundred years. Indeed, most of that disputation has precisely concerned what for Steiner is so breezy a matter: the metaphoricity of this idea of theological meaning. The central struggle of the Reformation had to do with whether to treat the Real Presence as a literal embodiment of Christ, or only a symbolic one. These quarrels go back, in turn, to the old religious distinction between a sign and a symbol. A sign contains something incontestably certain, as in Heraclitus's saying that 'the Delphic god neither reveals nor conceals, but gives a sign.' A symbol has a softer, more merely commemorative meaning, as perhaps Steiner intends when he wrongly calls the Real Presence an enacted metaphor. Since the Reformation, the question of the Real Presence has taken on more than just denominational resonance. For Novalis, the Eucharist was an essential link in his theory of language and meaning. Emerson, on the contrary, resigned his Unitarian ministry after deciding that the Eucharist was no more than a 'symbolical action and expression'. In his sermon of 1832, 'The Lord's Supper', Emerson decided that the bread and wine could not possibly incarnate the blood and body of Christ. Jesus 'always taught by parables and symbols', writes Emerson, and the Last Supper was merely one of these parables, with no binding authority over believers. Hazlitt reports in his essay 'My First Acquaintance

With Poets' that Coleridge said that, as a Unitarian, he could not celebrate the Eucharist, because he did not believe in it.

Now all this matters because we can see that the Real Presence is invoked or refused exactly insofar as it denotes a theory of reference. Either the Real Presence is an incarnation, or it is only a symbol, and we will adjust our relation to it on the basis of this status. But what makes no sense is Steiner's middle position, in which the Real Presence is invoked as a bulwark against contemporary nihilism, but by a critic who does not apparently believe in it and does not use it theologically, but who merely uses it metaphorically. 'Incarnation' is not a word that should be used lightly, as Steiner does here. Not because to do so is blasphemous, but because to do so is meaningless. Incarnation promises the presence and guarantee of God. Nowhere does Steiner appear to believe in this final presence. His wager is not a wager on a final presence that might mean enough to guarantee meaning. Wagering on only 'a significant being' seems a mug's game. He is like a patient who reinfects himself by putting dirty bandages on his wounds. His own religiose language infects his theory of meaning, for it forces the very question which is necessary for a theological doctrine but which is entirely unnecessary outside it: does Steiner believe in God? Or does he not? Either Steiner is here wagering meaning on God, or he is merely wagering meaning by gambling with language. But if, as I suspect, Steiner is simply a metaphorical critic who imagines himself to be a theological one, what use is a theology that is never actually used? Novalis connected his belief in the Eucharist to his theory of meaning; but that is perhaps because he believed that Christ was 'the instrument of the Godhead' and the 'key to the world'. Steiner does not appear to believe as Novalis did. Nor should he have to – except that his own theory calls for such a belief. But there is no need for a theology if one only believes in a metaphor. Most secularists believe in a metaphor, and are not deconstructionists, sceptics, or nihilists. The binarism is not, despite Steiner's belief, between nihilists on the one hand and religionists on the other, between Jacques Derrida and the Real Presence. Ordinary non-believers, most of them, believe in Steiner's idea of metaphorical truth; they believe, as Steiner does, that words are more than marks on a page, that fictional characters have a mysterious life of their own, that music is a spiritual force. But they get by every day on precisely Steiner's metaphorical idea of truth-reference, which is a world of 'as if', a world in which words refer to things metaphorically, without expanding it into Steiner's theology, which would be a world in which meaning is religiously stabilized and guaranteed. There is simply no need for a theological language if it is only a language and not an actual theology. Secularists believe everything Steiner does, without having to invoke God. A 'leap into sense', which Steiner promises, is not the same as a leap into God, and does not have to be. A leap into sense is how the secular day begins for most of us. The sun rises, the birds begin their quarrels, the day takes its habitual creeping shape, we rise from bed – and we have leaped into sense, whether happily or unhappily. We do not need to 'wager' on this sense because all our life it has seemed a bet that has already been won for us: the sun rises every day.

It is not at all obvious that great criticism or great art needs Steiner's theological postulate to live in the stability of truth and the transcendence of beauty. Steiner ignores the many great post-Renaissance artists who have got along without either a theology or a language of theology, but who have radiantly made do with a theology of art. This is what Proust intimates in his essay on Ruskin, when he separates his own aestheticism from the Christian aestheticism of Ruskin, whose principal religion 'was religion', says Proust, and whose 'wholly religious life was spent wholly aesthetically'. Proust, who uses language exactly, calls Ruskin's aesthetic a 'supernatural aesthetic'. Steiner, who gambles with language, wants to have a supernatural aesthetic but without the obligation of supernatural belief. Ruskin worried about drinking tea while looking at Titians because Titian incarnated a Real Presence. Steiner fusses about eating breakfast while listening to Opus 131 because Opus 131 is an enacted metaphor . . . of something or other. Yet Proust's own example shines: it is entirely possible to revere and protect all the aesthetic and philosophical truths and values that Steiner adores, as Proust did, without becoming Ruskin or believing in Ruskin's God.

One feels that what Steiner is asking us to believe in is not the presence of the divine but the easier presence of undefined greatness. The test is easy to apply. Were Steiner proposing a doctrine of *meaning* it would have to be a universal doctrine. That is, if great work incarnates a Real Presence then minor or even bad work must do so also, for the divine cannot choose merely to be present in masterpieces. This is what a theory of meaning is: it is universal. Schubert's C major Quintet, which Steiner mentions ritualistically again and again, must incarnate meaning as, say, must a third-rate film. Ruskin worshipped, and wrote about, not only the stones of Venice but the stones and trees on simple hillsides, because both were incarnations of God's creativity. Nothing in the whole body of Steiner's work suggests that he could bring himself to apply his Real Presence democratically. And so one is tempted to suspect that Steiner is not advancing a theory of meaning at all, but a theory of value. Though he thinks he is opposing nihilism with faith, he is actually opposing it with nothing more than good taste. To Derrida and his like he is not in fact saying: 'Here is my religious theory of meaning.' He is saying: 'Here are the masterpieces I believe in, and this is why I believe in them.' A respectable cry, surely, but not a theory, and not a theology.

In fact, Steiner is dismissive of those who would hold him to theological accountability. At the end of his 'Preface to the Hebrew Bible', he wonders aloud if the Bible is literature only, or the bearer of divine witness and revelation. Those who believe the latter, he says, are 'fundamentalists'. Those who believe the former are secularists. Having vandalized each side of his binarism, he decides that we need a third position – his own metaphorical Real Presence doctrine. In fact, all that Steiner does here is bloat the Bible with mystery, but a mystery arrived at by the most vulgar route. What awes Steiner, and finally convinces him that the Bible is quasi-divine ('*as if* divine'), is that he cannot imagine someone writing the Psalms or the Book of Job or certain passages from I Corinthians – and *then going to lunch*. That really is his argument, accompanied by swirls and swoons. He can, he suggests, just about imagine 'Shakespeare remarking at home or to some intimate on whether or not work on *Hamlet* or *Othello* had, that day, gone well or poorly, as the case might be', and 'then enquiring as to the price of cabbages' – though this boggles his mind. But what he cannot do – or will not do? – is imagine the same about the writers of the Bible. 'The picture of some man or woman, lunching, dining, after he or she had "invented" and set down these and certain other biblical texts, leaves me, as it were, blinded and off balance.'

These texts make him feel somewhat religious; therefore they are somewhat religious. That is his thrust. He leaps into sublimity by deciding that the sublime cannot be vulgar, that you cannot write a Psalm and then eat. But he exaggerates vulgarity in order to exaggerate sublimity's lack of it; and in the end all he offers is a hedged secularism written up religiously. Elsewhere he has confessed to similar mystical goose-bumps in relation to Kafka. That the parable 'Before the Law' was written 'by a gentleman in a bowler hat going to and from his daily insurance business, defies my grasp'. And indeed it does. Truly, this is not thought, but a fear of thought.

3

The retreat from the word has one other component: the Holocaust. Here art blithely co-existed with utmost evil. 'We know of personnel in the bureaucracy of the torturers and the ovens who cultivated a knowledge of Goethe, a love of Rilke . . . Nothing in the next-door world of Dachau impinged on the great winter cycle of Beethoven chamber music played in Munich.' Heidegger wrote great philosophy almost within earshot of a camp. In his book *In Bluebeard's Castle*, and in several essays elsewhere, Steiner lays out the sensation that flows from this terrible knowledge. We can no longer believe in a necessary connection between high art and high behaviour. 'Voltaire and Arnold regarded as established the crucial lemma that the humanities humanize.' But we have lost this certainty. 'We have lost a characteristic élan, a metaphysic of "forward dreaming" (of which Ernst Bloch's *Das Prinzip Hoffnung* is the inspired statement).'

Perhaps, speculates Steiner, art encourages barbarism, for it wraps its audience in falsities which bloom larger for them than the dilemmas of reality. The obsessiveness of great art and thought promotes, perhaps, a mandarinism careless of the world. A recurrent image in Steiner's work is Archimedes, who would not relinquish his work on the algebra of conic sections even as the Romans came to kill him in his garden in Syracuse. Anthony Blunt, the British art historian and Soviet spy, inspired one of Steiner's best essays for *The New Yorker*, and in it he orates on the scandalous disjunction of civilized activity and treason: 'I would like to think for a moment about a man who in the morning teaches his students that a false attribution of a Watteau drawing ... is a sin against the spirit and in the afternoon or evening transmits to the agents of Soviet intelligence classified, perhaps vital information given to him in sworn trust by his countrymen and intimate colleagues. What are the sources of scission?'

As in much of Steiner's work, this is offered to us with first-night flamboyance, as if we were his virgins in knowledge. As in his discussion of religious faith, he erects rather melodramatic binarisms and does vulgar damage to precise thinking: philosophy or the death-camps; Watteau or treason; breakfast or Opus 131; a Real Presence or nihilism. More calmly, and with deeper understanding, writers and philosophers have long considered the irresponsibilities of art; it is a commonplace of theories of tragedy and the sublime. Hazlitt, in his celebrated essay on *Coriolanus*, pointed out that poetry 'delights in power, in strong excitement, as well as in truth', and that this 'gives a Bias to the imagination often inconsistent with the greatest good', that 'in Poetry it [the imagination] triumphs over Principle, and bribes the passions to make a sacrifice of common humanity.' Voltaire and Arnold certainly believed that the humanities 'humanize'; but did, say, Cardinal Newman and Herman Melville? Thomas Mann's novel *Doctor Faustus* is a great contemporary meditation on this theme.

Steiner has at times usefully reminded us of art's complicities with the inhumane. But Steiner is himself in love with the inhumane. This is not lightly said. The despotic negligence, the God-like separateness, the vicious mysteries, the sickness or madness of Weil or Kafka or Kierkegaard – these are the qualities Steiner cherishes. He wants to be the voice out of the whirlwind; and if this cannot be, he will spend his life chasing the whirlwind. The political system that seems best to protect the life of great art is elitist, anti-democratic, unjust, and possibly even totalitarian. This is where he would rather live, the better for whirlwind-chasing. In 'An Uncommon Reader', written in 1978, he notes that one country where the old codes of 'classic literacy' still hold – remembrance, learning by heart, *auctoritas*, fiercely held private libraries, a negligible competition from other media, and ideas to live and die for – is the (then) Soviet Union. Were Steiner to have to choose, he would choose, for art's sake, something closer to the Soviet dispensation than the American, democratic, meliorist version.

The very idea of speculating about choosing between these systems – as if such momentousness were up for grabs, as if this were all a kind of mutilated consumerism – is not only null but offensive. Since we are fortunate enough not to have to choose between tyranny and freedom, we should not choose rhetorically between them. But this is just what Steiner does in his notorious essay of 1978, 'The Archives of Eden'. He begins by charging America with having produced very little of great artistic or intellectual achievement. Its classical music is eccentric; its philosophy is limited, with no great work·done in the areas of metaphysics or ethics; its mathematics, where there has been real achievement, has been largely produced by imported Europeans; its fine art of any quality is simply an epilogue to European modernism and surrealism; in theology there has been no one of Karl Barth's stature. Only its literature has what he calls 'claims to classic occasion'. But in this century, 'the summits are *not* American: they are: Thomas Mann, Kafka, Joyce, Proust.' There is not, in America (to be Steiner-ish for a moment), a Stravinsky or a Schoenberg, a Kandinsky or a Picasso, a Heidegger, a Wittgenstein, a Sartre.

Steiner proceeds characteristically, eating his way through great works as a bat in flight blindly gobbles insects, at a hundred a minute. America, he decides, is a culture devoted to the custody of European work. It has the best museums and galleries, the greatest research centres, the finest holdings of manuscripts; but it is not a place where great new creation is going on. America has become, in the twentieth century, the richest and freest land on earth, while Europe has twice erupted into warfare and barbarism. This correlation between creativity and catastrophe suggests much about the relative qualities of these two societies, and the place that art is accorded in them. Steiner speculates that since art is always the preserve of the few, a society devoted to the liberation of the many, such as America, will not be the cradle for art's prospering. The American ideal is that of 'material progress and recompense. *Fortuna* is fortune.' (This, of course, is simply Tocqueville's speculation converted into Steiner-ish dogma.) Liberal democratic meliorism, says Steiner, is no home for the greatness that is always made by the few for the few. Such a society, aflame with 'libertarian cant', may actually conspire against the production of great work. Meanwhile, it seems to be the case that great art is produced either in conditions of elitism (Periclean Athens, Racine's France) or, in the modern age, in the nearest equivalent of this, which are the totalitarian regimes of Latin America or the Soviet Union. He quotes Borges, who once said: 'Censorship is the mother of metaphor', and Joyce who said: 'We artists are olives;

squeeze us.' He points out that the Russian novel in this century has an urgency and a desperation that American fiction cannot rival.

One of the many slynesses of Steiner's thought is that he affects the motions of argument while actually standing completely still. One is never in any doubt as to which side Steiner is on in this grotesque fight, but Steiner must pretend to see things from the American side. Of course, he simpers, there will be prices to pay on both sides. You can have torture, injustice, and restricted access in Europe; or you can have wealth, health, and the mindless pursuit of happiness in America. And to be sure, he pretends, only a monster would choose Europe. 'No play by Racine is worth a Bastille, no Mandelstam poem an hour of Stalinism.' America has done the *decent* thing: 'If a choice must be made, let humane mediocrity prevail.' Steiner would have us believe that he is merely being honest in laying out the costs. What he cannot stand are those – 'and they have been legion in American academe or the media' – who 'want it both ways'. For those who espouse the highest standards while preaching the liberal democracy that undermines those very standards, Steiner has only contempt.

There are a number of responses to this vicious incoherence. The swiftest and most majestic was provided by Joseph Brodsky, who knew at first hand the tyrannies that are only pornographic to Steiner. The two once appeared on a television programme. Steiner set out his anti-democratic stall. He spoke for fifteen minutes. He spoke in rolling discourses, hardly pausing for breath, almost high on his triumphalist evasions. He presented the argument of 'The Archives of Eden'. Then he stopped. Quietly, with thick dignity, Brodsky said: 'Yes, but liberty is the greatest masterpiece.' This is all that needs to be said. By insisting on his own lovely metaphor, Brodsky was reminding Steiner that although censorship may be 'the mother of metaphor', censorship is *not itself a metaphor*, is never only a metaphor. For when torture is discussed speculatively by an intellectual who has known only freedom, it is being discussed metaphorically. It is a rhetoric of choice indulged in by a man who is fortunate enough to have never had to choose; and his choice is for a system in which people have never been allowed to choose. He makes a choice for not being able to choose. His essay is thus an exhausted liberty. But it is also a nonsense. One cannot choose tyranny. No one would actually do so; so Steiner's argument is strictly meaningless. It is a question that cannot be intelligently asked. Steiner is like someone who, seeing a blind man in the street, says: 'I would rather be blind than deaf.' Yet notice his language. He despises those who 'want it both ways'. These are not people who, in the more usual phrase, 'have it both ways'; they *want* it both ways. The implication is clear. Steiner is the more honest for wanting it only one way, and this is the way of totalitarian regimes. He moves from the speculative to the prescriptive. It is as if Steiner, having speculated that he would rather be blind than deaf, asks to be forcibly blinded, the better to develop his hearing.

'If a choice must be made', he writes. But a choice must not be made; and has never been made. This rhetoric of choice pushes Steiner towards facile linkages: we want or choose a dispensation (America has apparently 'chosen' humane mediocrity); this dispensation uncomplicatedly 'produces' certain works of art and thought. Ironically, this great anti-American speaks a language of pure consumerism. Culture is a factory floor and he is the bullying foreman. But Steiner confuses elitism and totalitarianism. He begins by comparing Europe and America. By the end of the essay he is speaking of the Soviet Union. Most of his examples of European greatness are not Russian, yet the force of his melodrama is toward squaring off totalitarianism against American freedom. But much of European art, while laboured on in the midst of injustice, has been produced in conditions that are closer to democracy than to tyranny. And much ordinary art – Britain in the twentieth century: not one of Steiner's examples of greatness is British – has been produced in elitist, class-sodden cultures.

Steiner is not, in fact, making a political contrast at all, though he thinks he is. He is not setting banal freedom against special illiberality. He is comparing several very ancient societies with one relatively new one. This is not a comparison. Borges actually and politically repressed by a fascist regime is very different from Joyce merely wishing for repression. One lived in a police state, and one lived in democratic Europe. He thinks, for example, that it is a neat jibe to end his essay by pledging his faith in Archimedes's garden in Syracuse. 'My hunch is that it [the labour of greatness] lies in Syracuse still – Sicily, that is, rather than New York.' But the two Syracuses have much in common. Both are places of modern liberal democracy, even if the Italian version is corruptly unstable. What divides them is antiquity, not politics. Indeed, if one set out to become a great writer, perhaps Syracuse, New York would be quite hospitable. A very fine writer did grow up in Syracuse, New York, and briefly attended university there. This was Stephen Crane.

Had Steiner fought like with like – posed a newish totalitarian regime against a newish liberal one – what would have been America's proper rival? South Africa, perhaps. And this country gives the lie to the idea that totalitarianism produces, in some uncomplicated linkage, great work. On the contrary, in South Africa totalitarianism has produced an enfeebled literature. It is a literature whose constant subject has been, inevitably and limitingly, power and the corruption of society. About it, J. M. Coetzee said this in his Jerusalem Prize speech: 'It is a less than fully human literature, unnaturally preoccupied with power and the torsions of power . . . It is exactly the kind of literature you would expect people to write from a prison.'

Steiner complains that America is a museum culture. But Steiner is himself a museum of European monuments. In this museum all the monuments are in conspiracy with each other. One monument leads to another. Without Kafka, says Steiner, 'we would not have Beckett's clowns'. Without one monument a later one cannot exist. But those of us who cherish literary greatness as strongly as Steiner does, must also see that greatness is not always dynastic. The critic's truest wager is made not on an unarguably great God, but on the foundling, the unparented work. America is incomprehensible to George Steiner because it is a place which has produced masterpieces but not monuments on this order of frozenness. It is a country that has often set itself to the casting off of European monuments in order to create American masterpieces. George Steiner offers a parody of Europeanness while fighting a parody of Americanness. America eludes him. In America's museums are the great European works that populate Steiner's family of giants; but America's true vitalities fly.

Iris Murdoch's Philosophy of Fiction

English fiction since the war has been a house of good intentions. Inside it are thick theories and slender fulfilments. English novelists solemnize, in commentary about the novel, the qualities and virtues they most obviously lack in practice. They people their artistic gaps with desiderata. Thus Angus Wilson possessed a serious liberal politics, and an ethical respect for the individual, which illuminates his criticism of the novel; but he never really created a single character of free and serious depth. A. S. Byatt has written well about her desire to write what she calls 'self-conscious realism'; but her realism is seldom deep enough to warrant its self-consciousness. Margaret Drabble appears to want to combine Dickens and Woolf, to combine caricature and experimental forms, but can create neither vivid caricatures nor daring experiments. Martin Amis seems to want to borrow that very faculty – soul – about which he is most naturally, and most amusingly, ironic. And Iris Murdoch has written repeatedly that the very definition of the great novel is the free and realized life it gives to its characters, while making her own fictional characters as unfree as pampered convicts. Perhaps in our time only V.S. Pritchett has written the fiction his criticism desires.

A list of the weaknesses of English fiction since, say, Henry Green, would go like this: it has produced few characters of depth or life (only Mr Biswas, Jean Brodie, and John Self in almost forty years); it has been grossly, childishly explicit with symbol and allegory (Golding, Carter); the freedom of its characters has been too often muffled by bossy authorial intrusion (Spark, Drabble, Byatt); its comedy is too easy, too shallow, or too narrowly social (Spark, Wilson, both Amises); it lacks a tragic sense.

Though Iris Murdoch has rarely mentioned her contemporaries, this might be a list of Murdoch's own anathemata, of all the ways in which modern fiction falls short of the Tolstoyan ideal. 'Ultimately,' she has written in her essay 'The Sublime and the Beautiful Revisited', 'we judge the great novelists by the quality of their awareness of others . . . for the novelist this is at the highest level the most crucial test.' That her own fiction fails this test, indeed that it commits all of the sins she has proscribed, is not lost on her. The struggle between breviary and right conduct, the wrestle to turn a plan into a real city, is one of the admitted anxieties in Murdoch's writing about fiction. Indeed, it seems likely that her tendency to discuss fiction in somewhat armoured philosophical generalities at once exaggerates and acknowledges this gap. 'We no longer demand of people in books that they should be like real people, except in some minimal sense of verisimilitude,' she complains, and then confesses, rather movingly:

> And we may be tempted to forget how impossibly difficult it is to create a free and lifelike character, or to feel that this particular effort is worth making . . . How soon one discovers that, however much one is in the ordinary sense 'interested in other people', this interest has left one far short of possessing the knowledge required to create a character who is not oneself. It is impossible, it seems to me, not to see one's failure here as a sort of spiritual failure.

Murdoch's tendency to be philosophical before she is aesthetic, and her clipped relations with the aesthetic (so that she must see the failure to create real characters as a 'spiritual failure' rather than an aesthetic one), her humility, her anxious sternness, the gulf between her theory and practice – all this gives her writing about aesthetics an extraordinary interest. Her book of gathered non-fiction, *Existentialists and Mystics,* is surely one of the most substantial, rigorous, and suggestive collections ever produced by an English novelist. Murdoch's inspiring, unembarrassed hospitality to sublimity, her philosophical seriousness, and her free travel through literatures (she writes about Camus, Kant, Hegel, Sartre, Simone Weil) recalls sometimes the English nineteenth century, and sometimes, in the twentieth, that continental essayistic tradition which permits a writer like Thomas Mann or Jacques Rivière to produce a kind of fattened philosophy.

During the 1950s, Murdoch exchanged her existentialism for a loosely Christian Platonism, which has been the fabric of her worldview ever since. The shift was the product of reading Simone Weil. In a review of Weil's *Notebooks,* written in 1956, Murdoch praises Weil for avoiding both existentialism (whose offer of a freedom to choose Murdoch finds too 'consoling') and 'the English ethics of act and choice'. Instead, Murdoch praises Weil for her emphasis on 'waiting' and 'attention'. Weil meant by this a prayerful attention to a God-like Good, which is necessarily mysterious and beyond us, given to us and not made by us, revealed not to our intelligence but to our love. In Murdoch's version, this Good is less God-like than it was for Weil, because her impulse is less religious than Weil's. But the Good is certainly transcendent. In her essay 'On "God" and "Good"' (1969), she writes that 'the idea of the transcendent, in some form or another, belongs to morality', and adds that we need to retain 'a metaphysical position but no metaphysical form'.

Murdoch has an appealing, though vulnerable, metaphysics – appealing because vulnerable – which might be called daylight mysticism. It is a pudding of Plato, Kant and Weil. Looking around her, she feels summoned to a belief that 'there is more than this', that 'philosophers must try to invent a terminology which shows our natural psychology can be altered by conceptions which lie beyond its range . . . the Platonic metaphor of the Good provides a suitable picture here.' Actually, she does not really mean to demote the Good to only metaphorical status. On the contrary, she gives evidence of believing that the truth exists outside our metaphorical picturing of it, that our souls nudge a reality that lies beyond what we can see. This is not a philosophy of 'as if'. (George Steiner, by contrast, has a literary metaphysics – his Real Presence doctrine – that seems to be merely metaphorical, but which borrows a non-metaphorical religious language.) This transcendent reality, in Murdoch's vision, appears to resemble a retired God: 'God does not and cannot exist', she writes in her book of Gifford lectures, *Metaphysics as a Guide to Morals*. 'But what led us to conceive of him does exist and is *constantly* experienced and pictured. That is, it is real as an Idea, and also incarnate in knowledge and work and love.'

As with God, it is worth contemplating this transcendence: 'we can all receive moral help by focusing our attention on things which are valuable: virtuous people, great art . . . the idea of Good itself.' And as with God, this transcendent object is beautiful – indeed, it is beauty itself. 'Beauty is the visible and accessible aspect of the Good. The Good is not itself visible.' Truth is beauty, and where Murdoch differs from Weil (and, obviously, from Plato) is in her conviction that the Good finds clear, empirically discoverable incarnation in great works of art. Art, Murdoch might say, is the house of the Idea; it is where we can visit truth and spend the day with it. The best way to contemplate the Good, then, is to contemplate great art, for this contemplation is 'an entry into (and not just an analogy of) the good life, since it *is* the checking of selfishness in the interest of seeing the real.' When we read Shakespeare or Tolstoy (Murdoch returns fondly to these two, like someone returning to the city of her honeymoon), 'we learn something about the real quality of human nature . . . with a clarity which does not belong to the self-centred rush of ordinary life.'

Art, according to Murdoch, incarnates the Good, for two reasons: first, because through a picture of reality, it offers a grounded version of the truth and irreducibility of other people's lives; and secondly (and more abstractly), because art has an independence from us that cannot be altered or possessed by us. Art is truth because it reveals; and because it exists. In her essay 'Existentialists and Mystics' (1970), Murdoch goes even further. If the contemplation of art represents an entry into the good life, then the artist '*is* the good man: the lover who, nothing himself, lets other things be through him.'

On the face of it, Murdoch's metaphysics would seem to be too aesthetic and her aesthetics too metaphysical. Her philosophy, for instance, would be swiftly singed by proximity to the empirical. Murdoch does not really argue, against the claims of relativism, for the existence of a transcendent truth or reason. She simply asserts this transcendence. Her long essays begin sternly but soon undergo a rich degradation, into polemic and command. She is a literary thinker, trained in philosophy but exercised by art. Imperatives are her syntax, and metaphor her logic: 'philosophers must try to invent a terminology'; 'prose must recover its former glory'; 'moral philosophy should attempt to retain a central concept' (the concept of the transcendent). Though she says that she is not a critic, her favourite way of doing philosophy is to take Kant or Plato and submit them to amorous critical re-interpretation, as if their philosophical worlds were clumsily suggestive, like those of the great novels. Thus she decides that Kant's theory of the sublime *ought* to be his theory of the beautiful, and his theory of the beautiful *ought* to be a theory of tragedy. (Murdoch believes that tragedy is the highest art-form.) Once she has decided that, she can proceed to invent her ideal Kantian aesthetics. A philosopher who refers slidingly, indeed evasively, to the importance of 'the idea of the transcendent, *in some form or another*' (my italics), who is hungry enough to talk loosely of the 'moral help' we can get from attending to the Good, is not one who wants to win, but rather is content to gamble, her arguments. And, one feels, she would admit this: clearly, she loves to conjoin aesthetics and ethics, because art is the felt reality for 'the hygienic and

178

dehydrated analysis of mental concepts which we use in this city' (she means Oxford). Art, as it were, is a London to philosophy's Oxford.

Murdoch's hungry metaphysics can perhaps survive on the alms of assertion, but her aesthetics cannot. She is at her most calmly assertive, most serenely philosophical, when in the midst of aesthetic argument. One misses the grain of actual criticism. Aesthetics, I believe, does not really exist – it is always a form of criticism – and so all aesthetic arguments need to stop at local stations. The discussion of specific works is the only valid aesthetics. As Coleridge has it in chapter XIV of the *Biographia Literaria*, the answer to the question 'What is poetry?' is so nearly the answer to the question 'What is a poet?' that 'the answer to the one is involved in the solution to the other.' Of course, since all criticism is itself ultimately subjective, Murdoch would not actually avoid assertion if she exchanged aesthetics for criticism proper. But if she were writing criticism her assertion would at least be rationally softened.

Instead, Murdoch's aesthetics have a strange, quasi-philosophical circularity. At the beginning of 'The Sublime and the Good', she takes issue with Tolstoy's idea that we should first fix our aesthetics and then, in the light of that theory, choose the artworks which fit it. As Murdoch rightly demurs, this is the wrong way round: 'our aesthetic must stand to be judged by great works of art which we know to be such independently.' She goes on: 'So let us start by saying that Shakespeare is the greatest of all artists, and let our aesthetic grow to be the philosophical justification of this judgment.' But this is illogical. If one simply *knows* 'independently' that Shakespeare is great (though Murdoch never tells us whence comes this independence: nor can she, of course), then one cannot test one's aesthetic by recourse to Shakespeare. Murdoch promises to make her aesthetics provisional – but provisional on an aesthetic certainty secured without the help of aesthetics. 'Independently': Murdoch does not know Shakespeare to be great via any aesthetics (for she clearly proposes this independent knowledge as something apart from aesthetics), but via philosophical certitude. She *knows* that Shakespeare is great, philosophically. Shakespeare represents the Good. In other words, her aesthetics is not aesthetics at all, but is philosophy. Once one has discovered this, both her arguments about fiction and her fiction itself glow more clearly for us. In particular, the puzzling gap between her theory about fiction and her own practice as a novelist comes to seem less puzzling. For her aesthetics are precisely the expression of a philosophical ideal, serenely meditated in an Atlantis of the mind.

In one rather austere sense, her own novels must then seem irrelevant as practice, for they are just shards of this ideal. For if one just knows Shakespeare to be great, then one also knows that, out of sight, there is an even greater artist, the Idea of the artist. In this view of things, one could not only never be as great as Shakespeare or Tolstoy, one could never be as great as fiction itself; one could never be as great as the Good. *Thus one could never be great at all.* Perhaps some such excessive Platonic scrupulosity on Murdoch's part infects her practice as a novelist; it may explain the apparent wildness, even the carelessness, of many of her novels, not to mention the almost disrespectful fecundity of her imagination. Of course, a novelist could never think of her novels as irrelevant. So a simpler explanation for the gap between theory and practice might be to suggest that it is we, not Murdoch, who see a gap. We see a gap because we read Murdoch's commentary on fiction as a species of aesthetics, and then watch her novels enact a different aesthetics, or fail to enact the desired aesthetics. But if we read Murdoch's commentary as a species of philosophy, and her novels as hapless enactments of philosophy, as necessary metaphysical failures or lapses (recall that Murdoch feels that the inability to create real characters is a 'spiritual' failure not an aesthetic one), then the novels are the logical philosophical product of Murdoch's commentary.

Murdoch believes that Shakespeare and Tolstoy are the greatest artists for metaphysical and ethical reasons. For Murdoch, 'morality, goodness, is a form of realism', and this realism means attending as truthfully as possible to 'other people and their claims'. Ethics means the annihilation of self before the irreducibility of other people. This belief can be found throughout her fiction. In *The Nice and the Good,* John Ducane realizes that 'the great evil, the dreadful evil, that which made war and slavery and all man's inhumanity to man, lay in the cool self-justifying ruthless selfishness of quite ordinary people.' It is the novelist, according to Murdoch, who can best deliver us from the tyranny of ourselves: 'The novelist is *par excellence* the unprejudiced describer of *le monde vécu.*' In a marvellous denunciation of T.S. Eliot Murdoch wonders if Eliot has ever admired and enjoyed a novel. Eliot, Murdoch complains, doesn't want us 'to attend to other people'; he wants us to attend to God. 'So it is not surprising that he makes no place for imaginative prose literature which is *par excellence* the form of art most concerned with the existence of other persons.' Murdoch has returned to this repeatedly. In 1970, she writes: 'Art (good art) used to silence and annihilate the self. We contemplated in quietness something whose authority made us unaware of ourselves.' Shakespeare and Tolstoy created the freest, most densely real characters, she says; they also have, as artists, that undisarrayed impersonality – the artist 'who, nothing himself, lets others be through him' – that Murdoch prizes so dearly. So they are the greatest artists, and the nineteenth century the optimal playground for the greatest novelists (Balzac, Dickens, Eliot, Tolstoy). 'The most obvious difference between nineteenth-century novels and twentieth-century ones is that the nineteenth-century ones are better,' Murdoch catechizes somewhat sharply. In the nineteenth century, the individual is seen in all his social and ethical fullness, against an entire society. At its highest levels, the novelist's ability to penetrate the otherness of his characters is indistinguishable from love. This is Murdoch's most passionate emphasis:

> Art and morals are . . . one. Their essence is the same. The
> essence of both of them is love. Love is the perception of

individuals. Love is the extremely difficult realisation that something other than oneself is real. Love, and so art and morals, is the discovery of reality . . . The enemies of art and of morals, the enemies that is of love, are the same: social convention and neurosis . . . Fantasy, the enemy of art, is the enemy of true imagination: Love, an exercise of the imagination . . . The exercise of overcoming one's self, of the expulsion of fantasy and convention, which attends for instance the reading of *King Lear* is indeed exhilarating. It is also, if we perform it properly . . . painful.

It is stirring to read a novelist who believes so acutely in the destiny of fiction, and in its renovation in our time. But it is stirring only as personal faith. An aesthetics that announces, with Oxonian briskness, and merely in passing, that 'the highest art is not music, as Schopenhauer, who was not very concerned with particular human beings, imagined, but . . . tragedy, because its subject–matter is the most important and most individual that we know' can only be taken as personal faith. To demote music aesthetically because it is not 'concerned with human beings' is to demote it via non–aesthetic criteria for failing to be something it has no power to be. It is like faulting a lemon morally for not tasting sweet.

Again, Murdoch's conception of virtue is only asserted. Moreover, it seems limited. Why should it be the case that the highest ethics is the suppression of self, or that the greatest artists gloriously smother their personalities? (Think of Melville, of Dostoevsky, and of the wholly personal T.S. Eliot.) Murdoch's Christian emphasis on unselfish virtue recalls Nietzsche's gibe about George Eliot in *The Twilight of the Idols*, that she had got rid of the Christian God, but only clung more fiercely to Christian morality. The difficulty is that if one does not share Murdoch's idea of virtue, one may not share her wholly ethical idea of what makes fiction great. For example, if she believes that the artist is 'the lover who, nothing himself, lets other things be through him', then this may explain her own lack of interest, as a novelist, in surfaces, in the pigments of reality, in all the textured distractions that should obstruct the free flow of otherness. It may illuminate why she appears to attend so little, as a novelist, to her prose, which seems good only by accident, and is often careless. Only this can explain that baffling moment near the end of her celebrated manifesto, 'Against Dryness' (1961), when Murdoch, lamenting that English fiction no longer seems '*written*', and arguing, movingly, that fiction must 'recover its former glory', alights upon Camus as the ideal. 'All his novels were *written*.' Camus! Now Camus was a great writer, but he was a great truthful blunderbuss, whose novels have an almost cherishable aesthetic clumsiness. Who is so eager for philosophical conversation between his (largely unfree) characters to begin that his descriptive linkages from set-piece discussion to set-piece discussion are rudely formulaic, and who abandoned description altogether in *The Fall*. It is hard to see how Camus represents a prose of 'eloquence' or richness, unless one's ideal in this regard is coolly renunciatory. And perhaps, metaphysically speaking, a rich prose would be precisely that assertion of self which Murdoch finds neurotic and unvirtuous. Perhaps her novels are the aesthetic sacrifices to her stern metaphysics?

Likewise, it seems significant that while it is philosophically important for novelists to attend to other people, Murdoch has little interest in the aesthetic quality of that otherness. She uses Tolstoy and Shakespeare, in a sense, to close aesthetic discussion. Once they have appeared in the argument, there is no need to examine *what* it is the great novelists do with their free characters. It is enough for these characters to exist, independently of their creators. Again, perhaps just such an idea is enacted in Murdoch's novels, which are full of characters who are clearly not their author, but who often seem savagely meaningless in any way other than in their histrionic freedom. They mean their freedom, they perform in the theatre of it. But it is often hard to find any other meaning in them. This is most clear in Murdoch's treatment of her demonic characters –

people like Mischa Fox in *The Flight From the Enchanter*, Father Carel in *The Time of the Angels*, and Julius King in *A Fairly Honourable Defeat*. The demonism which such characters threaten represents, for Murdoch, an important philosophical sin. Such people are enchanters, fantasists, controllers. They do not attend to the reality of other people, but distort other people into false statuary. Every critic who writes about Murdoch canters loyally in Murdoch's path, remarking on the centrality of such demonic people in her fiction. Very few remark on how undemonic such people actually seem in the novels. One reads Murdoch's fiction happily reminding oneself that such people are supposed to be horribly menacing. In fact, Murdoch's conception of demonism – that which opposes the Good, presumably – seems precisely too philosophically refined to be truly threatening. Murdoch clearly believes that great fiction stages wars between good and evil, but her evildoers never have the felt demonism of, say, Henry James's malefactors. Gilbert Osmond is truly evil; Mischa Fox is theoretically evil. James seems to know what to do, aesthetically, with such people, and binds them deep into the aesthetic structure; Murdoch seems only to lease them to the novel before reclaiming them for philosophy.

But as Murdoch would note, it is easier to write philosophy than to write even philosophical novels. Nevertheless, it is frustrating, if one cares about English fiction, to see a novelist so well-equipped artistically, skidding around on this hard philosophical ice. Of all the post-war English novelists, she has the greatest intellectual range, the deepest rigour. She takes her place, however awkwardly, in a tradition of flexible, homemade English Christian Platonism which includes Ruskin and George Eliot and Virginia Woolf. Woolf, in some ways, was the rebel who had to overthrow her father's moral Platonism and make the Good an aesthetic category only, and one discoverable only by a highly aestheticized fiction. Murdoch may be seen as the rebel to Woolf's rebellion, closing down Bloomsbury's aesthetic mysticism (art is never for art's sake, always for life's sake, she has written) in favour of a moral, 'hard idea of truth'. In doing so, Murdoch joins herself to the George Eliot who, writing of Ruskin in 1856, sounds exactly like Murdoch: 'The fundamental principles of all just thought and beautiful action or creation are the same,' writes Eliot, 'and in making clear to ourselves what is best and noblest in art, we are making clear to ourselves what is best and noblest in morals . . . all truth and beauty are to be attained by a humble and faithful study of nature, and not by substituting vague forms, bred by imagination on the mists of feeling, in place of definite, substantial reality.' Had Murdoch's aesthetics been more aesthetic, her fiction might have been less philosophical.

Martin Amis: The English imprisonment

For much of this century, English literature has been at furtive war with its American pretender. It has been a fight for the throne, a race to see who would lead the age. Virginia Woolf, in an essay about American fiction published in 1925, conceded that the Americans were now like the Elizabethans, 'coining new words'. In England, she thought, the word-coining power had lapsed. Yet she judged American literature 'an expressive ugly vigorous slang', and hoped that 'the English influence may well predominate'. But the English influence did not really predominate. Lawrence, Woolf, and Henry Green were the last great English novelists, the last true magi of language, the last serious European modernists. It is as if, in 1945, a treaty were signed that simply ended verbal and formal ambition in English writing for thirty years. During the 1950s, 60s, and 70s, English fiction lacked a novelist of the power and centrality of Bellow, of Camus, of Pavese. (V.S. Naipaul was the only really important novelist working in England at this time.) During this period, and until the early 1980s, when Salman Rushdie, Martin Amis and Kazuo Ishiguro began to constitute a new generation of novelists, English fiction had fallen into facetiousness, miniaturism, and metaphysical complacency. In particular, there had been a failure of language, of 'word-coining power'.

Martin Amis's importance in English writing is that he is one of the few writers of his generation to have recognized these enfeeblements. He has produced a true literary slang, fattened on contemporary swill. For better or worse, one of the methods of transformation, as befits a writer who has argued that this has been the century of the American novel, has been to Americanize his prose and placements. In *Money* (1984), he let the grotesque pornographer John Self frolic in Manhattan. *London Fields* (1989) was partly narrated by an American writer. For the prose, Saul Bellow, Amis's greatest influence, has provided the radiant emergencies necessary for the task. Or rather, Amis has taken from Bellow what is most easily imitable. Bellow may well have given Amis his Swiftian theme, as well as his fondness for lurching italics, when he has a character say, for example, in *The Adventures of Augie March*: 'The big investigation today is into how *bad* a guy can be, not how good he can be.' From Bellow, Amis gets his streaming syntax and parenthetical interruptions, his boisterous plurals and compounds. More problematically, Bellow has lent Amis the example of his peculiar seriousness. From him, Amis has learned to drop his characters deep into the tank of the contemporary and watch them flail. John Self, in *Money*, is 'addicted to the twentieth century'; the vibrant thug Keith Talent, in *London Fields*, is 'modern, modern'. When, in his novel, *The Information*, we encounter a phrase such as 'the press of sense data'; or, 'he also made mental preparations. The state Richard sought was one of disparity readiness'; or, 'Mrs. Verulam was a modern person, and routinely traded in information', we hear not only Bellow's high melody but his high themes – his own 'disparity readiness'.

Amis also brings a very English comic talent to his writing, with all the strengths and weaknesses of that tradition. It is the line of comic burlesque that connects Fielding to Thomas Love Peacock to Dickens. Amis has the old English interest in the grotesque and the evil. This tradition allows for authorial asides and jokes. It also allows, alas, for a certain vulgarity, or simplicity. Amis has Dickens's tendency toward caricature, towards applying a comic collar so tightly to his subjects that they lack aeration; like Dickens, he loves lists; and like Dickens, he ripples and writes in fluent surges, in comic riffs. Unlike Dickens, however, he is often at his best in these riffs. The stylistic principle is repetition and inversion, as in this chorus from *Money*:

You just cannot park around here any more. Even on a Sunday afternoon you just cannot park round here any more. You can doublepark on people: people can doublepark on you. Cars are doubling while houses are halving. Houses divide, into two, into four, into sixteen. If a landlord or developer comes across a decent-sized room he turns it into a labyrinth, a Chinese puzzle. The bell-button grills in the flakey porches look like the dashboards of ancient spaceships. Rooms divide, rooms multiply. Houses split – houses are tripleparked. People are doubling also, dividing, splitting.

Just as, say, Dickens founds Mrs Gargery's funeral in *Great Expectations* on the principle of inversion – the funeral is funny when it should be solemn, and ritualized when it should be spontaneous – so Amis's joke here twirls away from a simple comic inversion: from the nonsensical idea that there is no space to park while there is space to doublepark.

The Information is about literary rivalry, though not about American and English rivalry, except insofar as the novel registers that literary success for English novelists now means a successful twelve-city author tour in the States. Gwyn Barry is the author of a novel called *Amelior*, some ill-written liberal froth about a group of people who get together on an unnamed island to talk about solving the world's problems. Morally spotless and awfully written, it is very bad and very successful. In the opinion of Richard Tull, his rival and old Oxford friend, '*Amelior* would only be remarkable if Gwyn had written it with his foot.' Tull, from whose viewpoint most of the novel is written, has dedicated himself to Gwyn's destruction. As a writer, he has been spectacularly unsuccessful. His dauntingly modernist novel, called *Untitled*, 'with its octuple time scheme and its rotating crew of sixteen unreliable narrators', lies unread on his agent's desk. (Of course, he and Gwyn share an agent.)

Richard spends most of his time reviewing books: 'He was very good at book reviewing. When he reviewed a book, it stayed reviewed.' He dribbles away a day a week at a vanity publishing firm called The Tantalus Press. They publish not just 'bad literature. It was anti-literature. Propaganda, aimed at the self.' And his novels are the kind of books that need subsidies of not only money but generosity: 'If you homogenized all the reviews . . . then the verdict on *Aforethought* [his first novel] was as follows: nobody understood it, or even finished it, but, equally, nobody was sure it was shit.'

The comedy in this novel is simple, a little puerile, often very funny. But it is a self-mutilating comedy. *The Information* is trapped in its destructive patterns of repetition and inversion. Such is the nature of the burlesque pair as Amis establishes it, that the novel's jokes come in identical and unbreakable sets, like plastic tableware. It is an implacable rule of the book, for instance, that Richard Tull will fail at every attempt he makes to destroy Gwyn Barry. He tries to have him beaten up, but the attackers mistake Richard for Gwyn and beat him up instead. It is another implacable rule that no one can read Richard's novel, *Untitled*, without becoming physically sick. This is repeated throughout the book, so that no one ever finishes *Untitled*. And it is a rule of the novel that we only ever see Richard reviewing enormous and friendless biographies of minor poets with titles such as: *The Soul's Dark Cottage: A Life of Edmund Waller*, or *The Character of Sir Thomas Overbury (1581–1613)*.

These are Amis's comic routines. Whenever Gwyn's fortunes increase, Richard's decline: while Gwyn is short-listed for a huge American prize called the Profundity Requital, Richard's agent develops a migraine on page seven of *Untitled*. When Gwyn is sent on a royal publicity tour in the States, Richard is sent with him to write a long profile of 'Gwyn On Tour'. So the book is a revenger's comedy: as in a cartoon – as in *Tom and Jerry* – its rivals exist for each other. The point of such cartoons is an uncancellable frustration. The building block is repetition. As long as the novel remains cartoonish, the structures do their work; but when *The Information* seeks any kind of real seriousness, they are a prison. Since Richard and Gwyn exist for each other, they are – exactly like Tom and Jerry – dull when separated. And, since they exist so severely for each other, they hardly exist at all for the reader. One expects to be able to peel them off the page.

The literary world, with its pieties and *putti*, its fake gods and grounded angels, is a fine hall for Amis to sack, and he lays about himself very happily. Still, it is perhaps too quiescent a target. The satiric defenestration is rather easily performed. Richard's agent tells him that 'writers need definition. The public can only keep in mind one thing per writer. Like a signature. Drunk, young, male, fat, sick: you know.' Richard hardly needs to be told this. He has his own theories about diminishing returns in literature. He has been working on a book called *The History of Increasing Humiliation*, a book 'accounting for the decline in the status and virtue of literary protagonists. First gods, then demigods, then kings, then great warriors, great lovers, then burghers and merchants and vicars and doctors and lawyers. Then social realism: you. Then irony: me.' He has his novel published in the States by Bold Agenda Inc., a shadowy publishing giant who have decided that their image needs correction – political correction. Their new fiction list begins with *Untitled*, and two other books: *Hush Now* by Shanana Ormolu Davis and *Cowboy Boots* by John Two Moons. Richard is included because the failed white male modernist is rare, too, now. He later discovers that the firm has published only a few 'courtesy copies'.

So here we are, once again, in Amis's own dwindling and scarred world. London, where both Richard and Gwyn live, is seen under an apocalyptic cloud, much as it was in *London Fields*, raging and Americanized by crime. As in most of Amis's fiction, the chosen area is Notting Hill Gate and the West London hinterland. Amis is by now the Napoleon of Notting Hill and must return to the scene of old victories; but one feels this revisited ground is becoming too heavily grooved. And

Amis does not write especially well about London in his new book. *London Fields* yielded the sublime fantasy of grey-hooded city pigeons in 'their criminal balaclavas', and had marvellous slashes of description, particularly of West London's balding and dismal parks: 'the untouchable youths in their spikes, the meteorology of the sky, the casteless old wedged into benches'. Now, apparently, the elderly have been mugged off the page. Richard takes his twin sons, Marco and Marius, to what he calls 'Dogshit Park'. The untouchable youths are still there, though: 'While snorting and giggling, one pale youth was also managing to taunt his dog *and* cat crisps.' (This is Amis at his most serrated; in a stroke he conjures a recognizable inner-city aimlessness.) Here there is jogging and crime: 'the multiple single mothers in crayon-colour beachwear, the splat and splot of English skin . . . the joggers pounding the outer track in scissoring shellsuits of magenta, turquoise . . . past the flat-roofed park toilets where a boy younger than Marco had recently been raped while his mother tapped her foot on this same piece of asphalt . . .'

Since *Money*, Amis has painted a world of vaporized motivation and collapsed subjectivity. The more intellectually respectable parts of this are to be found in Bellow; Amis's interest in ecological crisis, millennial fatigue and – in the new novel – the stars and quantum mechanics, is his own. *The Information*'s cast of characters – which in addition to Richard and Gwyn includes thugs, hustlers, aristocrats, the human furniture at the local pub, the illiterate and the morally myopic – are either hollow or bloated with false self-consciousness. All of them have been mentally colonized by the contemporary media, especially trash television; all of them are happy sponges for 'the press of sense data'. In Richard's local pub, the regulars know that Richard is different, a literary man, an intellectual. They need a nickname for him. They call him Cedric, after the host of an 'intellectual' gameshow on television – 'often, in such quandaries, a TV tie-in can grant clarity.' Naturalness has disappeared, and with it naturalness of literary representation:

'The black kid cannot just be black anymore. Nobody can just be somebody anymore. Pity about that.'

As in Bellow's work, the writer sends out his surrogates, his porous scouts, bloodily sensitive to the culture's moral swerves. Where Bellow is suggestive, though, Amis tends to tell us: 'Congratulations: here was the culture, and he was living in it, to the full.' England has declined, it seems, like Richard's literary genres; it is a story of increasing national humiliation, from moral pastoral to urban *policier*. Hearing birds singing outside his study, Richard reflects: 'Say birds were just parrots and learned their songs from what they heard: those trills and twitters were imitations of mountain rivulets, of dew simpering downwards through the trees. Now the parrot had left its jungle and stood on a hook in a pub shouting "Bullshit!" '

Of course, this is the novelist that is being described here, not the bird. Since the black kid cannot just be black anymore, and the birds cannot just be birds anymore, the novelist cannot just be a novelist anymore. The novelist has lost his dewy innocence, too; the novelist no longer trills and twitters; the novelist shouts 'Bullshit!' a lot. Politely put, the novelist ironizes. The late twentieth-century collapse, Amis seems to be saying, means that this is all he can still do. The calamity of the situation, however, demands that he stay ahead of the game, as the novelist used to. But what are his resources? Only irony is left, suggests Amis. This is the usual defence of the postmodern condition: the melting of those stabilities that enabled the writer to act as if he were omniscient now throws him in the soup with the rest of us. Being a postmodernist – there is a character called Martin Amis in this new book too – Amis has already hammered out his protective armour. He has Richard reflect on his weaknesses as a writer, in particular the fault that 'he wasn't innocent enough. Writers are innocent. Tolstoy was certainly innocent. Even Proust was innocent. Even *Joyce* was innocent.' Well, this is Amis's excuse, rather than his project. For Amis's greatest weakness as a writer is not that he is not innocent enough, but that he is too knowing. His work seems to say: 'the novelist no longer knows anything with certainty in the old George Eliot sense; but he can still be knowing.' Yet the opposite of innocence is not knowingness, it is guilt. In literary terms, this could be a despairing irony, a sense of shared existential entrapment (as Camus shares his characters' entrapment) or shared grief (as Bellow laughs and cries with his characters). One can accept that the old bird-twittering innocence is gone. But Amis is too clever. He is always an adjective ahead of his subjects; always an adjective ahead of wonderment.

This separates him from his greatest literary influence. Amis rides a brief crest of satiric advantage over his subjects, but Bellow shares the deeper current of comic pathos. Bellow's heroes have fallen, certainly: Herzog asks Heidegger, despairingly, 'When was our fall into the quotidian?' But they and their creator measure their fallenness without glibness. They grasp at greatness; they go about their business under the beady eye of eternity. 'We human creatures should be at play before the Lord – the higher the play, the more pleasing to God,' is how the narrator of *More Die of Heartbreak* puts it. Bellow's heroes resist their diminished inheritance for they are 'a kind of being filled with death-knowledge, and also filled with infinite longings'. In their longing is their absurdity (their intellectual vanities, their confusions, peccadilloes), but also their nobility. Amis's heroes have no nobility. Theirs is the comedy of devils, already on the other side. Bellow's is the comedy of displaced angels.

Still, Amis is occasionally capable of wonderment. At his best, his satiric knowingness is not just cleverness, but a deep literary gift. He has a hospitable ear for cadence and rhythm, and for paradox. It is the old English balance between composure and collapse. The prose, insisting on degradation but never enacting it, writes better than the world lives. There is a perfect list, in this novel, of bookshops encountered by Richard in the States: 'The Muzaked and mallish, the underlit and wood-panelled and pseudo-Bodleiac, the disco-Montparnassian.' Only a very good writer would hear how rhythmically, how tightly that final 'disco-Montparnassian' buttons up the sentence. Or this, probably the best paragraph in the novel, in which Richard and Gwyn set out on their flight to the States:

> Richard sat in Coach. His seat was non-aisle, non-window, and above all non-smoking. It was also non-wide and non-comfortable. Hundreds of yards and hundreds of passengers away, Gwyn Barry, practically horizontal on his crimson barge, shod in prestige stockings and celebrity slippers, assenting with a smile to the coaxing refills of Alpine creekwater and sanguinary burgundy with which his various young hostesses strove to enhance his caviar tartlet, his smoked-salmon pinwheel and asparagus barquette, his prime fillet tournedos served on a timbale of tomato and a tapenade of Castilian olives – Gwyn was in First.

This passage is as good as Pope, and just as calculatedly literary. Amis controls the mock-heroic tone perfectly, as well as the daintiness of paradox that this style requires ('prestige stockings' and 'celebrity slippers'). Different registers jostle: the savvy and journalistic ('non-wide and non-comfortable') with the formal and literary ('strove to enhance'). Gwyn is princely on his 'barge', and the word is chosen to jolt us backward to another great set-piece of rich travel, Enobarbus's description of Cleopatra on *her* barge, in *Antony and Cleopatra*.

Yet bewilderingly, for much of this novel, Amis squanders his talent in vulgarities and easy hits. He seems happy to fall under the table and roll around in farcical sawdust. Again and again, he falls into comic jags and riffs. Some are crude and some are funny. That Amis's novels fall so naturally into comic recitatives tells us something about these books' nature. There is a failure to connect these recitatives to a larger music. They are sealed – against each other, and hence against living with each other inside the novel. This is because they are units of the already known. For Amis at such moments, the world does not exist to be torn into novelty, it exists to be smartly slapped around a little. He puts down his riffs and they invite no answers back. He has killed off his subjects with words. Thus, Richard compares the uniformity of the English literary scene with American diversity: 'Not like America, where spavined Alabaman must mingle with Virginian nabob, where tormented Lithuanian must extend his hand to the seven-foot Cape Codder with those true-blue eyes.' But this is far too uncomplicated. The language wants to be sophisticated and it is certainly knowing; but Amis is not transforming anything here. These people exist in the catalogue, already indexed and adjectivally tagged ('spavined', 'tormented').

Stylistically, *The Information* is confusingly variegated. There are moments when Amis reminds us that he can indeed see the world and make it fresh for us: a bike messenger seen in 'his city scuba gear'; or 'a loose flock of city birds [that] reared up like a join-the-dots puzzle of a human face or fist.' But whole sentences – indeed, whole scenes – are soused in vulgarity and silliness. The reader can actually catch a paragraph turning, like a penitent, away from crudeness into richer and more refined habits: 'The doors were open to the evening traffic of Notting Hill Gate. Along with the seams of cigarette smoke, the pub vapours and pub humours, the pie waft and the yeasty burp of beer, there was also the breath of cars like a grey mesh at table height.' The 'yeasty burp' is itself only a burp; but the 'grey mesh' of traffic fumes is a phrase of poetry.

Were the novel content to be only a comic romp, none of this would matter. But Amis would like *The Information* to tell us important things: about the nature of literary rivalry and the male midlife crisis. Amis has always had an uneasy relation with his themes, with deep matter, with seriousness. His novels tend to swallow their themes whole like snakes, so that their shapes and outlines can still be seen. In his collection of stories, *Einstein's Monsters*, Amis swallowed nuclear warfare. *London Fields* was nibbled with sermons about eco-crisis, global warming and apocalypse. Its characters appeared to act as if under crisis, but this was only because Amis would keep on telling us they did. In *The Information*, we have left the weather for the stars. Amis looks heavenward as eagerly as Isaiah. He is forever comparing his characters to stars and to their glittering entropy. And with what portentousness! 'He [Richard] looked up . . . the usual metropolitan sky with its six or seven stars weakly guttering. Raw land can do nothing about them but cities hate stars and don't want their denizens to be reminded of how it really goes with ourselves and the universe.' Since we are not reminded enough, Amis reminds us again and again that everything 'was made in the stars: in stars that explode when they die . . . This is to put Richard's difficulties in context. The context of the universe.' Ah, Richard's difficulties. We hear much about them. Richard's difficulties are not just literary. He is dragging himself through a midlife crisis. Richard is forty, and his hair is falling out, and his bones are sighing, and his ego is tousled. His sexuality is sleepy but stubborn. Being forty, he is privy to 'the information, which is nothing, and comes at night'. The information, apparently, tells him that he will die. Meanwhile, the streets yield *their* information: 'Before, girls looked at him and showed interest or no interest. Then for a while, they looked past him. Now they looked through him . . . Because he no longer snagged on the DNA. Because he was over on the other side, and partly invisible, like all the ghosts who walked there.'

The sentimentality of that last passage is characteristic. Without fail, at every moment that Amis addresses this subject, his cooling system breaks down. His supplies of hipness and cleverness run dry. He becomes lachrymose, self-pitying, bleating. He wants to squeeze a pathos that is not there, which we do not feel. Men of Richard's age, according to Amis, slobber and snivel in their sleep. When their partners ask them what the matter is, they reply: 'Nothing. No it isn't anything really. Just sad dreams.' Richard cries in his sleep. He used to be suspicious of female tears, 'but now he was forty, and he knew'. And now even the climate is sprightlier than Richard: 'Now that he was forty, he feared the cold. Now he was forty, something animal in him feared the winter.'

The problem here is partly that such moments of soul-expansion sit uneasily with a narrative of comic burlesque. Richard hardly exists: why should we grieve for a ghost? The deeper problem is that this is not a literary subject adequate to the weight with which it is loaded. It is strange that Amis would think that a receding hairline and an inability to pull the girls supports any analysis, let alone that it is worth putting in 'the context of the universe'. Perhaps this is the genre-withering and hero-decline that Amis had in mind put into action, a story of increasing humiliation: Shakespeare's Richard II worried about his crown; Amis's Richard worries about his double crown. Had Amis put any metaphysical lather on this, and turned Richard's midlife crisis into a larger apprehension of death – had he made 'the information' something other than mere informa-tion – it might have worked. But it is difficult not to laugh at Richard and his ontological pomposity, while aware that Amis wants us to cry at it. It is difficult not to laugh, that is, until a significant rent in the novel toward its end. Richard is thinking about women crying. Women, he thinks, understand about time and mortality:

> They knew they would be half dead at forty-five. This information did not fall in the path of men. Men, at forty-five, were in 'the prime of life' . . . They get the Change. We get the Prime. And this is the reason why our bodies weep and seep in the night, because we're half dead too, and don't know how or why.

Recall that Richard is only forty; it is Amis himself who is forty-five at the time of writing this novel. And it is Amis who speaks here, for himself and his generation and his battered gender. ('We' vs. 'they'.) The reader smarts at this intrusion and is then sad for its author. Perhaps this is why Amis is unable to write about Richard's midlife crisis without – in stylistic terms –

bursting into tears? Is this private grief the reason for the sentimentality in a writer who is never sentimental? Certainly, it explains the impression the novel gives of something incompletely digested, something painful and a little embarrassing.

As a writer, Amis speaks distinctly. The creation of a partly Americanized yet English comic voice has been his great achievement, and this is not negligible, for it has led Amis part of the way out of the English verbal prison of the 1950s, 60s and 70s. But Amis has re-imprisoned himself in the English burlesque. He does not speak to his reader; we are not swayed by his creations. And it is this same comic voice, which appears so emancipatory, that is actually gagging its creator. *The Information* is full of brilliance and flame, but it is an essentially unserious novel – or perhaps we should say, since it speaks with a distressingly personal note, that it is serious only to Martin Amis. His burlesque smothers gravity, his knowingness seals feeling. In particular, his novels are deprived of true struggle, because his characters struggle only with situations, and not really with themselves. His comedy tends towards burlesque because it is situational rather than characterological.

Comedy in literature arose out of satire, and in particular out of the exposure of hypocrisy; this is the case from Lucian to Chekhov. Amis is interested, in a general way, in the hypocrisies of our age, but personal hypocrisy interests him little, because he is not especially interested in motive. Of course, great comedy exceeds its origins (which are dramatic, or stage-origins), and at its highest is nothing less than a form of metaphysical irony. Comedy is tragedy, incognito. Great comedy has its roots in individuals, and lives on the principle not that people are funny, or that situations are funny (which is the assumption of *The Information*), but on the contrary, that people and situations are serious. Ruskin noted, in his *Lectures on Art*, that burlesque is an absolutely English art: 'There is one strange, but quite essential, character in us – ever since the Conquest, if not earlier – a delight in the forms of burlesque which are connected in some degree with the foulness of evil.'

He went on to say that into the most beautiful passages, English writers will often slip 'momentarily jesting passages'. These jests degenerate 'into forms of humour which render some of quite the greatest, wisest, and most moral of English writers now almost useless for our youth. And yet you will find that whenever Englishmen are wholly without this instinct, their genius is comparatively weak and restricted.' This is the finest description available both of Martin Amis's qualities, and of his English imprisonment in the burlesque. A writer as good as this must find an escape; Martin Amis needs to get beyond the information.

Thomas Pynchon and the Problem of Allegory

It is a problem for allegory that, while going about its allegorical business, it draws attention to itself. It is like someone who undresses in front of his window so that he can be seen by his neighbours. Allegory wants us to know that it is being allegorical. It is always saying: watch me, I *mean* something. *I* mean something; I am being allegorical. In this, it is very different from most fiction. (It resembles bad fiction.) Why does anyone tolerate it? In literature, we rarely do. It is forgiven its hieroglyphics when it overcomes itself and behaves like great fiction (Kafka, Mann, some Dickens); when it elaborates complex truths (Dante, Kafka again); or when it explodes itself in the hunt for allegorical truth (Melville). It is tolerated when it is not only a map, but a landscape, too.

Thomas Pynchon is the most allegorical American writer since Melville, and, for better or worse, the clear inheritor of Melville's broken estate. But his novels behave like allegories that refuse to allegorize. They pile up meanings and disown them at the same time; it is no accident that Pynchon so loves the shaggy dog story, which does the same. Thus he has created readers who think he is a great occultist, and readers who think he is a visited hoaxer. His novels are manic factories which seem alive, but which are actually rather static, because they do not move. Yes, they move meaning around, they displace meanings; but they do not inhabit meaning. The factory has no products. Readers of Pynchon often mistake bright lights for evidence of habitation. One saw this in the reception of *Mason & Dixon*, which drew gasps for its bright wonders: here is a novel, wrote reviewers, set in the eighteenth century in which we see the first English pizza being made; a dog that talks; two clocks having a conversation; a vast octagonal Gloucestershire cheese; George Washington smoking a joint; a mechanical duck; a crazed Chinese man who lectures everybody in sight on the magic of feng shui; a giant Golem; and a severed ear that moves. They listed these things as if they were scenes not objects, as if they constitute the *movement*, the workings of the novel. That the book merely contains these things, holds them in a lively grid, was taken as wonderful; they were listed as simple natural marvels, whose presence was in itself meaningful. There was no need to ask what these marvels were for. They were read as signs; they were taken allegorically. Signs were taken for wonders.

There are delights in *Mason & Dixon*, and some wonders. Chief among them is Pynchon's language, which is notionally a pastiche of mid-eighteenth-century prose, but is in fact a beautifully flexible alloy, capable of bending calendrically, to take in early eighteenth-century styles, as well as late twentieth-century incursions. The novel's story is told by one Reverend Cherrycoke, who accompanied the surveyors, Mason and Dixon, on their trip to divide Pennsylvania and Maryland in the mid-1760s. Verbally, he is metaphorical, sententious, rounded, periodical, and lawless. All this is to the prose's good. It is the novel's achievement to create a prose, when it is working well, that seems not so much antiquarian as pristine – an original American language before it knew itself as 'an American language'. One is reminded of John Berryman's Elizabethan-American in *The Dream Songs*. Indeed, the capitalized nouns which are flaked all over the book begin to seem like the capitals of line-breaks: the prose is like a poetry that was written out in prose by mistake:

Below them the lamps were coming on in the Taverns . . .
the wind was shaking the Plantations of bare trees, the River

ceasing to reflect, as it began to absorb, the last light of the Day. They were out in Greenwich Park, walking near Lord Chesterfield's House, – the Autumn was well advanc'd, the trees gone to Pen–Strokes and Shadows in crippl'd Plexity, bath'd in the declining light. A keen wind flow'd about them.

But this language, despite its beauty, is only a refined game. On its own, it is not enough to make a novel great. The limitations of *Mason & Dixon* are the limitations of allegory. *Mason & Dixon,* which so often delights and moves, is not a novel, and deprives itself of all the flexibility of a novel. For it functions as an allegorical picaresque, rolling the brougham of itself from implication to implication, taking on extra implications at one town, and throwing off a few at the next. It tamps its characters down into little plots of meaning, then uproots them. Its characters exist to dispense lessons, ideological or philosophical. Although they have a certain alluring liveliness, they do not exist as people (one is unlikely to be really surprised by them). As usual in Pynchon, there are scenes that mean too much and scenes that mean too little. Thus the Mason-Dixon line, which the eponymous heroes are drawing, is made to stand for several things: the good rule of law and the tyrannical rule of law; freedom but also imperialism. George Washington smoking cannabis is no doubt supposed to instruct us in the importance of presidential liberality. But the octagonal Gloucestershire cheese and the mobile ear are just diversions, scattered throughout the book – these act like the money that politicians used to throw to voters from the cart: they distract us from the truth.

Pynchon is famous for his fantastic comedy. But too much, even in this benign book, seems willed, unfree, a hysteria that he forces onto his scenes because without it they would not really exist. It is the difference between the comedy of character and the comedy of culture. Pynchon does not, or cannot, do the former; what he can do, often powerfully, is to make the culture vibrate at high speed, and whip comedy from the rotations. To be fair, his two protagonists, Charles Mason and Jeremiah Dixon, have some presence as human beings. Both are English. Mason is from Gloucestershire, a melancholic deist in long mourning for his dead wife Rebekah, and essentially conservative in temperament. Dixon is from the north of England, near Durham. He is a Quaker, an instinctive radical and populist, who finds himself appalled by the cruelties of American life (Indian-killing and slavery) even while enamoured of its rebellious volume. Mason and Dixon are a double act; most of their reality is complementary. They are most full as characters when they are acting as halves to each other. Mason is gloomy, Dixon is cheery; Mason is sophisticated, Dixon a bumpkin; Mason is an astronomer (he looks up), Dixon a surveyor (he looks down), and so on. The comedy Pynchon extracts from this is familiar, and occasionally touching. The novel opens with the pair voyaging to South Africa, to the Cape of Good Hope, to chart the Transit of Venus. (Since everything is always connected in Pynchon, the two also conduct some transits of Venus on land too, in the shape of the highly-sexed Vroom sisters, who tease them, Fielding-style.) At this time, Mason and Dixon are hardly on speaking terms, and cannot look each other in the eye. But they are not long in Capetown. By the end of the novel, by which time they have spent more than four years in America and are badged with all kinds of adventure, they have developed a deep fondness for each other.

This pattern has the guiltless simplicity of celluloid. It seems likely that Pynchon is burlesquing the buddy movie – the novel ends with the two men, now retired from their surveying labours, fishing together on an English river, grumpy old men, but learning to talk about their wives and children. This is a reduced comedy, comedy in prison. It relies on fixed forms and the fixed escape from those forms. For example, the picaresque. The two heroes are invited to come to America to survey the state boundaries, and there they move from adventure to adventure – and this has the ridged, repetitive quality of the picaresque: however dissimilar each new adventure is from its predecessor, it resembles it in its mere adventurousness. But the variety becomes homogenous; one would like these fattened incidents to shrink into life; the road to become a current. There is a bloating familiar in other Pynchon books – a weakness about knowing when to stop accumulating.

The comedy is fixed in other ways, too. Pynchon's most usual trick is to confront the apparently antiquarian eighteenth-century form with unexpected modernities, such as pizza, or the Malayan *ketjap* (ketchup) with which Dixon lathers his food, or a woman asking: 'Hallo, d'you think he'll get much of a hard-on, then?' There are puns ('Suture Self, as the Medical Students like to say'), and some sublime sillinesses (twins 'nam'd Pitt and Pliny, so that each might be term'd "the Elder" or "the Younger," as might day-to-day please one, or annoy his Brother'). The comedy is most funny when least knowing. Too much of it works simply at the level of reader-registration, a ticket-punch whereby we acknowledge the prompt presence of a Pynchon joke: for instance, a writer of sea yarns called Pat O'Brian; or the moment when Dixon goes into a Philadelphia coffee-house and asks for 'Half and Half please', the punch coming a second later, when he clarifies: 'Mount Kenya Double-A, with Java Highland . . .' Or when a character called Mrs Eggslap quotes Tammy Wynette's 'Stand By Your Man': 'Sometimes, 'tis hard, to be a Woman.' (Again, this is rarely comedy about people; it is comedy between cultures, the old and the new, and between the writer and his text.)

One of the least funny and least likeable scenes involves Mason and Dixon's meeting with Colonel George Washington at Mount Vernon. It is emblematic of Pynchon's comic vision elsewhere – its desperation, its desire to squeeze meanings, its inability to resist a kind of comedic harlotry. Washington is first seen 'talking real estate', as Pynchon has it. He offers the English visitors some dope, while dispensing realpolitik about why Americans will always kill Indians. Washington likes to say 'Proclamation-Shmocklamation' and 'It's makin' me just meeshugginah', a habit traceable to his African servant, Gershom, who is Jewish. At first we see Gershom serving coffee, and Pynchon notes only that he has 'an ambiguous expression'. But a moment later, Gershom breaks in fondly: 'Don't bother about that Israelite talk, anyhow . . . it's his way of joaking, he does it all the time.' The scene ends with Gershom singing 'Havah Nagilah, a merry Jewish Air, whilst clicking together a pair of Spoons in Syncopation'. This moment feels characteristic of many others in Pynchon's work: the expected is disrupted by the zany, and a purchaseless benignity falls over the whole scene. At such a moment, one realizes why so many of Pynchon's characters, here and elsewhere, have an irritating habit of breaking into song: the principle of Pynchon's comedy is the principle of the stage-musical. Everyone gets to sing their song, however meaningless. Pynchon's comedy floats in the watery democracy of the musical, the idea that everyone sings as well as the next person, that many tunes are better than one tune. Gershom turns and reveals – how nice! – that he is not really a slave, but a mild Jew. Of course, the novel *is* a warmly democratic form, in the sense that all characters are noticed. But there is a difference between descriptive charity and comic subsidy, which is the difference between real comic sympathy and the lease-lend of allegory. For Pynchon wants something back from Gershom for Gershom's twirl on stage; he wants Gershom to signify, politically.

Pynchon's comedy is either dystopian or utopian. This is a moment of utopian wish-fulfilment: oh, if the whole world were like this! Gershom must pay us back by fulfilling our wish. And thus it is, in part, that this scene is not funny, and has no stringency. Because it is not human comedy, it is not freely given – characters allowed to exist in 'the irresponsible plastic way' in James's lovely phrase. The comedy is not given at all. It is extracted from the characters, at their expense. Who cares, in Pynchon's world, for a George Washington or a Gershom who might move us? This is the agenda of Pynchon's writing: scenes like this one can be strictly meaningless on the surface, because they are supposed to represent something underneath their surface. The comedy is not about the people involved. It is about a cultural moment, about an idea, or ideal. It is the comedy of culture; a moment not of free fiction but of unfree allegory. Pynchon's characters do not move us, because they are not human; they are serfs to allegory. Dickens might have powerfully shaded in Gershom the servant, given him a moment of quick particularity, and thus released him. But Pynchon's Gershom is a servant all right; he is Pynchon's servant. Pynchon's characters exist to generate meanings or to dissipate meanings. One sees here, as throughout his work, that he is forced to award his characters an extraneous flamboyance because they cannot generate interiority. They must be theatrical, because all they are for is to enforce meanings.

Allegory, and the confusion of allegory, is the principle of Pynchon's fiction; and it drives this book, in particular its explicit politics. The America in which Mason and Dixon travel resembles the America of *The Crying of Lot 49*; there is not such a great distance between 1766 and 1966. Both are ruled by what Pynchon once called 'an emerging techno-political order that might or might not know what it was doing'. America is both pure possibility and deep degradation, in Pynchon's vision; his diagnosis moves between the wildly dystopian and the wildly utopian. The degraded America is the country Pynchon wrote about in a short essay on 'Sloth', in 1993, for *The New York Times Book Review*. In the mid-eighteenth century, he wrote, America was 'consolidating itself as a Christian capitalist state'. In *Mason & Dixon*, the Christian capitalist state has been seeding itself, it seems, by laying waste to the land. Both Mason and Dixon are shocked by the subjection of the Indians, and by slavery. In South Africa they saw a similar tyranny. 'Whites in both places', thinks Mason, 'are become the very Savages of their own worst Dreams . . .' Dixon recalls 'the iron Criminality of the Cape' and 'the beefy contented faces of those whites', but decides that 'far worse happen'd here', in America. The Reverend Wicks, narrating the novel, plunges this truth home:

'the word *Liberty* . . . was taken in those Times to encompass even the darkest of Men's rights, – to injure whomever we might wish, – unto extermination, were it possible . . .' As Mason and Dixon make their way along what they call 'the Visto', the eight-foot-wide trench they cut between Maryland and Pennsylvania, they meet various Indians and slaves. They are tutored in corruption. Near the end of the book, Dixon decides that he is no better than these white Americans, 'having drawn them a Line between their Slave-Keepers, and their Wage-Payers . . .' For in cutting a line between a slave state and a free state, he has simply shared in the general illusion that slavery is 'ever somewhere else' – in South Africa, or in Maryland – 'but oh, never in Holland, nor in England, that Garden of Fools'. 'Where does it end?' he asks. 'No matter where in it we go, shall we find all the World Tyrants and Slaves? America was the one place we should *not* have found them.' This is the busted dream Pynchon writes about in *The Crying of Lot 49*, a land 'with the chances once so good for diversity'.

What troubles is not the relative ordinariness of these ideas, but their lumpy deployment in fiction. Mason and Dixon's blotter-like receptivity to every bloodstain of American capital-ism seems a little convenient, artistically. They might be freer as characters if Pynchon allowed them to put up some resistance to Pynchon's view of things. But that would be fiction, not allegory. Of course, they do respond to the freedoms and unscored music of early American life. Pynchon enjoys the democratic anarchy of American religious life. There are insane German sects and dour Puritans and strict Quakers and busy Catholics, all of them at stormy war with one another. Politically, there are British patriots and American rebels and mild indifferents. The Indians are fighting the Americans who are fighting the British; and beneath it all, the dried powder of slavery, ready to fire. In the usual Pynchon way, this world is furrowed with paranoia. Each American suspects the next of being an agent or spy. The Jesuit network is especially feared, and Mason and Dixon's cutting party is joined by a mad Chinese, Captain Zhang, who is on the run from the Jesuits. Indeed, it emerges that most of the surveying group are agents of one power or another, including Mason and Dixon, as Dixon observes. To a sceptical Mason, he declares that both of them are paid employees, and therefore agents, of the British crown. They are servants of the oppressor of both black and white Americans.

So this is America in the 1760s. But really, it is the thickly sown lot of Pynchon's mind. For the wartime London of *Gravity's Rainbow* is a similar place, less a city of one noble British defence than the site of internecine paranoias, a city of shadowy groupings and official acronyms: 'Everyone watching over his shoulder, Free French plotting revenge on Vichy traitors, Lublin Communists drawing beads on Varsovian shadow-ministers, ELAS Greeks stalking royalists, unrepatriable dreamers of all languages hoping through will, fists, prayer to bring back kings, republics, pretenders, summer anarchisms that perished before the first crops were in . . .' (Pynchon's inability to stop accumulating meanings finds its verbal embodiment in his fondness for lists and descriptive catalogues.) And this is the California of *The Crying of Lot 49*, where Oedipa Maas voyages among secret groups and inflamed syndicates, trying to read the signs and clues that Pynchon throws to her.

Paradoxically, it is in this sea of paranoia that the drowning may be saved. Pynchon seems to cherish the contradictory energy of diverse paranoias because of their lust for confusion. Their busyness confounds the single ruling order, the 'techno-political order'. In *Mason & Dixon*, a young radical praises the jumbled street music of America, especially 'the Negroe Musick . . . 'tis there sings your Revolution.' In *Lot 49*, Oedipa realizes that 'The only alternative was some unthinkable order of music, many rhythms, all keys at once . . .' What is the vehicle of this plotlessness, this new music? It is the novel – more, the sliding

chromaticism of Pynchon's novels. Against the plot of government stands the musical novel, with its many plots or tunes. In
case we miss this, Pynchon uses his characters to remind us.
Pynchon's fiction elaborates an allegorical politics. In it,
partial truths are forced into a bent absolutism. It is a system
whose vents, whose partialities and flaws, seem only to make it
stronger, like medieval astronomy. Pynchon's world is a
planetarium devised by a myope. The forces of evil, in
Pynchon's vision, are the straight, the linear, the rule of
governance. Mason and Dixon, though likeable men, are agents
of fixity. Dixon remembers that back in England, he laid out the
boundaries that enforced the hated and unfair system of land-
enclosures: 'He had drawn Lines of Ink that became Fences of
Stone.' However, underneath the soil is where the anarchy of
non-linear freedom lives. 'Down Below, where no property
Lines existed, lay a World as yet untravers'd.' Captain Zhang,
with his love of feng shui, reminds the surveyors that their line
'acts as a Conduit for what we call *Sha*, or, as they say in Spanish
California, Bad Energy . . .' The Mason-Dixon line is like a
dragon's tooth across the free flesh of the land, he warns. The
Reverend Cherrycoke explains that Pennsylvania and Maryland
are white man's abstractions. They do not exist, but are merely
'a chronicle of Frauds committed serially against the Indians
dwelling there'. By contrast, the forces of good – who may be as
crazy as the forces of evil – are all those who drift out of the
reach of governance and rule. Dream is the utopian space of
resistance. *The Crying of Lot 49* ends by praising 'drifters' who
live as if in exile from America. In *Gravity's Rainbow*, Tyrone
Slothrop is thrown back onto 'dreams, psychic flashes, omens,
cryptographies, drug-epistemologies, all dancing on a ground of
terror, contradiction, absurdity . . .' In the paranoia of dreams,
there you feel free. In *Mason & Dixon*, all the uncharted
America west of the Mason-Dixon line is the land of dream,
'serving as a very Rubbish-Tip for subjunctive Hopes, for all
that *may yet be true* . . .' These dreams are 'safe till the next

Territory to the West be seen and recorded, measur'd and tied in . . .'

It is a sign of how greatly Pynchon's indexical intelligence intimidates his readers, and in particular of his powers of evasion and self-subsidence, that few question the banality, or worse, of these ideas. But one of the advantages of the utopian is that it is impossible to fulfil. Pynchon's utopian good is good exactly because it has no body, because it resists body and form. It is the uncharted. It is futurity or dream. It dwarfs one's known littleness. Similarly, Pynchon's evil works in his fiction as an inverted utopia, a dystopia that has no streets or fixtures, that cannot be named. In *Gravity's Rainbow*, Slothrop, an American intelligence officer based in wartime London, is obsessed with the idea that 'they' are out to get him. He wonders if 'they' will explode a rocket over London with his name on it. But 'they' are not the Nazis, who are actually sending rockets to London. No, 'they' embrace 'possibilities far beyond Nazi Germany'. But we never find out who 'they' are.

Only very occasionally does Pynchon become specific; only rarely, in effect, does he come out of hiding. Perhaps it is well. For Pynchon's *Times* essay on Sloth, in which he attempts to give body both to the forces of evil and to the forces of resistance, is dismayingly incoherent. In it, he suggests that in mid-eighteenth-century capitalist America, time – clock-time – became a tyrannical linearity that ruled all citizens. Only the 'ungovernable warp of dreams', or a secularized form of the old sin of sloth, can counter time. The modern equivalent of enforced linearity, he suggests, is television. How might we fight this televisual governance? By using the VCR! 'We may for now at least have found the illusion, the effect, of controlling, reversing, slowing, speeding and repeating time – even imagining that we can escape it.' And then, in a characteristic move, almost as if Pynchon has seen that he has revealed too much, that he has been *spotted*, that without novelistic clothes he looks like the editorial board of *Social Text* or *Screen*, he retreats. He seems to mock the very idea he has proposed, to disown his own allegory. When he writes, for instance, that 'Sins against video time will have to be radically redefined', it is difficult not to hear Pynchon's snicker. He is having us on. Or perhaps not. But he has certainly disappeared. In this way, Pynchon covers his allegorical hide. At first sight, he seems to avoid a too-schematic war of good and evil by confiscating the identity papers of both sides. Perhaps, Pynchon asks, good and evil are one side, not two. How would we ever know? The real forces of government are as invisible as the unreal forces of dream, and it is the fate of Pynchon's characters to search a landscape of toppled signs. This, Pynchon suggests, is the real terror of modern society, this cloud of unknowing. Thus, in *Mason & Dixon,* the English surveyors are good men serving a bad King. The line they draw is a gesture of imperial rule, yet it also rules between good and bad, between free men and slaveholders. Captain Zhang, who complains so bitterly that the Mason-Dixon line is a bad force, is himself a bad force, a monomaniac in a world that should be plural and drifting. Above all, Pynchon's fiction promotes the importance of the many-voiced (the dreamers) over the single-voiced. Pynchon believes in the importance of plurality. He resents lines, and therefore struggles to diversify his own sometimes schematic fictions. He fends off any single allegorical line or reading. He wants his people to have many choices, including his readers, and he thinks that this is pluralism. Oedipa Maas is waiting for the end of normative America, 'waiting for a symmetry of choices to break down, to go skew . . .'

But Pynchon's allegories are somewhat tyrannical. He may long for the many-voiced music of the fabulist, but his novels enforce a strict binarism even as they imagine themselves to be deconstructing this binarism. Oedipa may want 'a symmetry of choices to break down', but Pynchon's very fiction is built on a symmetry of choices. Either utopia or dystopia; either governance or dream; either too much meaning or not enough meaning. At the end of *Lot 49,* Pynchon offers Oedipa a choice: if the shadowy organization (called 'The Tristero') that she has been tracking exists, she will join it and escape, because she cannot wait any longer for America to mend its ways. But if the organization does not exist, then she must live in America. And if she must live in America, she will have to be paranoid. At first, Pynchon seems to be suggesting that this ordeal of choice is what is wrong with America: it is America that forces us to choose between exile or madness. But since we cannot verify that such a choice need exist (the novel leaves open the possibility that the Tristero is merely Oedipa's hallucination), since Pynchon's vision is itself so ungrounded, all we can say is that this ordeal is Pynchon's problem, not America's. It is his fiction, not America, that offers secrecy or dissolution as the only choice.

Pynchon's novels have a certain power – the agitated density of a prison. But can one construct and deconstruct allegory without producing incoherence, and an incoherence that seems evasive rather than suggestive? In *Moby-Dick*, Melville came close to destroying his book, by loading its circuitries of significance with so much energy that the novel was in danger of meaning too much and therefore too little. In *Moby-Dick*, the whale is both good and evil, it is truth and it is blankness. It is a thousand things. But what is at stake in the novel is supremely human; it is the fate of one's soul. Melville used allegory to hunt down truth, and in so doing he exploded allegory into a thousand pieces. Pynchon uses allegory to hide truth, and in so doing expands allegory into a fetish of itself. Melville raced with the danger of nothingness while running after truth. Nothingness was a wound in truth's side. But what is left when allegory does not believe in the possibility of truth is not allegory but merely *the allegorical*; or a dogmatic faith in the allegorical. What is left are novels that draw attention to their own significations, which hang without reference, pointing like a severed arm to nowhere in particular.

Against Paranoia: The case of Don DeLillo

I

To call *Underworld,* Don DeLillo's large novel, a failure might seem an act of slightly flirtatious irrelevance. The book is so large, so serious, so ambitious, so often well-written, so punctually intelligent, that it produces its own antibodies and makes criticism a small germ. Moreover, Don DeLillo's huge endeavour represents a promise to restock the novel's wasting pedigree in our age, and few want to see the promise broken. It is easy, and rightly so, for big books to flush away criticism.

But DeLillo's novel, despite chapters of great brilliance, does not gather its local victories as a book this large should. Instead, it enforces relations between its parts which it cannot coax. Curiously, it is at once distractingly centrifugal and dogmatically centripetal: its many characters dissolve an intensity which the novel insists on repeating. Its big, broken structure moves back and forward through all the decades since 1951, travelling from Arizona to the Bronx to Kazakhstan and back again, and the book intends to be a collection of lavish fragments, set down in a maze: for fifty pages we are with Nick Shay, the central character, in Phoenix in the 1980s; for another fifty in the Bronx with a group of charitable nuns, again in the 1980s; then we move back to 1974, where we spend time with Klara Sax, a conceptual artist, in New York; then back to Harlem, in 1951; for 120 pages we visit Nick's childhood in the Bronx of the 1950s – and so on. But the effect is of subtraction not addition.

With the exception of Nick Shay, we do not spend enough time with the many characters for their lives to seem more than a rattle of months on the page. Nick exists, greyly; but fictionally speaking, he is a stranger promoted above his station. Despite the amount of superb description DeLillo spends on Nick's childhood Bronx (an origin he shares with his author), it would be hard to describe him once the novel has ended. The novel mistakes him for an interesting enigma. Thus it is that one can read, unmoved at the deepest levels, more than eight hundred pages.

But even as it fritters outwards, *Underworld* sucks inwards. In every scene, DeLillo uses his characters to force home his themes, or to do so by exaggerating his themes into comedy. DeLillo has often seemed to me a didactic writer who wants to be honoured for not being one. *Mao II*, his last novel, was a geometric sermon. In *Underworld,* everything always comes back to a few ports: nuclear war, the secret power of the American government, the paranoid state in which the bomb put us all, and the ambushing power of the postmodern image-culture. The book is neurotically webbed – not surprising, perhaps, for a novel which seems to believe that 'everything is connected'.

Indeed, *Underworld* proves, once and for all, or so I must hope, the incompatibility of the political paranoid vision with great fiction. (That private paranoias can generate great fiction is obvious from Stendhal, Dostoevsky, Svevo.) Why is political paranoia so bad for the novel? In part because it is a mysticism facing a form that naturally repels it. Paranoia has an unlicensed freedom which outraces fiction, whose formal task is to establish a licensed freedom. At a simple level, this can be seen in DeLillo's language, which is so often richly exact. Yet when DeLillo writes about secrets, about hidden plots and political viruses, his language becomes a thick scrabble. It sickens into vagueness. The culture of secrets encourages a pomposity in DeLillo and his characters. In *White Noise,* he smartly burlesqued a portentousness he seems now to respect. The difficulty is that the paranoid character is necessarily pompous; he is always at the centre of all his plots; he worships himself really, is the brass god of his own mysticism. This can make characters seem a little ridiculous, something DeLillo knows – his novel is full of madly paranoid people some of who are made fun of. Too often, however, DeLillo appears to offer a solemn endorsement; his spiralling lyricism represents that endorsement. In one scene, Brian Glassic, a colleague of Nick Shay's who works with him at a firm called Waste Containment, stands before a huge garbage landfill on Staten Island:

> To understand all this. To penetrate this secret. The mountain was here, unconcealed, but no one saw it or thought about it, no one knew it existed except the engineers . . . a unique cultural deposit . . . and he saw himself for the first time as a member of an esoteric order, they were adepts and seers, crafting the future, the city planners, the waste managers, the compost technicians, the landscapers who would build hanging gardens here, make a park one day out of every kind of used and eroded object of desire.

Brian is standing before garbage the way Ruskin stood before Rouen Cathedral. He is having an epiphany, and DeLillo does not seem to think it silly or hubristic of him. Yet it is only by seeing garbage, preposterously, as a 'secret' in the first place that he is led into these moist decodings, and into glamorous untruth. One notices that Brian/DeLillo assumes that garbage only comprises 'object[s] of desire'; whereas garbage contains objects of indifference, convenience, and hatred. In this way paranoia leads the novel astray.

In like manner, Sister Edgar, a nun who runs a charity in the Bronx, is a bit eccentric, but hardly insane. She puts on latex gloves before doing her rounds among the AIDS patients. The world seems to her a brew of hidden viruses and acronyms – 'Acquired Immune Deficiency Syndrome. Komitet Gosudarts-vennoi Bezopasnosti. Yes, the KGB was part of the multiplying swarm, the cell-blast of reality that has to be distilled and initialed in order to be seen.' Her gloves are protection, writes DeLillo, against 'the viral entities hidden within, submicroscopic parasites in their soviet socialist protein coats'. Now, it would seem that DeLillo is presenting us with a crank. But it is precisely DeLillo's little surge of lyricism – 'in their soviet socialist protein coats' – that gives one pause. This is not how a nun would express herself, even a cranky nun. It is how DeLillo expresses himself. Which is not to say that DeLillo believes that the Bronx is, or ever was, full of KGB agents; only that DeLillo's verbal investment in this idea exceeds its worth and thus appears to credit it. Paranoia, it seems, makes language go for broke, alas in both senses of the phrase.

The problem can be reformulated. If, when DeLillo writes about 'parasites in their soviet socialist protein coats', he neither believes that his character would think like this; nor believes it himself; nor is expressing an actual truth, then DeLillo is squandering language on a game. This is expensive frivolity. And as it happens, Sister Edgar *is* a kind of game. Though she appears often in *Underworld*, she is not supposed to be real. She is supposed to be a female counterpart to J. Edgar Hoover; as it were, Hoover in drag. It is Hoover, whom DeLillo introduces early in the novel as a man obsessed with viruses and bacteria and the KGB, who is speaking through Sister Edgar. It is Hoover's paranoid vision which DeLillo's lyricism flatters.

Political paranoia, then, makes characters unreal, because the unreality of their interests colours them and claims them, like the chameleon in the joke that explodes when it is placed on Scottish tartan. A character's private paranoia, such as Svevo's Zeno, has a named source in the actions of other individuals, and therefore a reality, even if it is unfounded. Political paranoia's unreality is its necessary sourcelessness. Not all DeLillo's paranoid characters are as unreal as Sister Edgar, and some are mocked. What is striking is how many paranoid people there are in *Underworld*, and how this multitude drives so many perforations of unreality into the book's form that its truths come to seem ragged and uncertain, while its untruths have an airy consistency.

It is worth trying to list the examples of paranoia, so as to give a sense of how repetitive, thematically, is the novel. We meet J. Edgar Hoover at the start of *Underworld*. He is part of a huge crowd attending the 1951 Giants–Dodgers game. The *New York Times*'s front page celebrated Bobby Thomson's home run as 'The Shot Heard 'Round The World'. On the same page, it was reported that the Russians had detonated their first nuclear bomb, in Kazakhstan. DeLillo has said that these two shots provided him with the fuse of his novel. Hoover is informed, mid-match, of the Russian success. DeLillo comments: 'There is the secret of the bomb and there are the secrets that the bomb inspires, things even the Director cannot guess . . . because these plots are only now evolving. This is what he knows, that the genius of the bomb is printed not only in its physics of particles and rays but in the occasion it creates for new secrets. For every atmospheric blast . . . for every one of these he reckons a hundred plots go underground, to spawn and skein.' This is the novel's task: to tell the secret history, the plots of a generation forced underground by the bomb. The bomb was administered by paranoiacs; and it turned Americans into paranoiacs. DeLillo follows the lives of a group of people affected by nuclear power and connected directly and indirectly with the 1951 baseball game: there is Nick Shay, a teenager in 1951, who now works for a firm that gets rid of nuclear and other waste; his brother, Matt Shay, a mathematician who does the physics for nuclear weapons in New Mexico: 'There were people here who didn't know where their work ended up . . . Everything connected at some undisclosed point down the system line.' Matt has a bad trip in which he remembers his service in Vietnam, and recalls that the cans of agent orange resembled cans of frozen Minute Maid. Matt 'felt he'd glimpsed some horrific system of connections in which you can't tell the difference between one thing and another, between a soup can and a car bomb, because they are made by the same people in the same way and ultimately refer to the same thing . . . And how can you tell the difference between orange juice and agent orange if the same massive system connects them at levels outside your comprehension . . . Because everything connects in the end.'

There is Nick's black colleague, Big Sims, who believes that the census is a fraud because it hides the real numbers of black people in the country. He tells Nick about a boat that has been at sea for two years, trying to find a country poor enough to accept its load of possibly contaminated waste. There is Detwiler, who used to be a 'garbage guerrilla' and who thinks that the boat contains a shipment of CIA heroin. Detwiler, too, believes that 'everything is connected'. There is the artist Klara Sax, who is building an enormous installation in the Southwest desert, by painting hundreds of B-52 bombers which are now retired but which used to carry nuclear bombs. She fears the bomb as something that 'outimagines the mind'. There is a preacher glimpsed on a street corner in Harlem in 1951 ranting, Farrakhan-style, about the masonic insignia on the dollar bills. There is Marvin Lundy, a baseball fanatic who has paranoid fantasies, and who thinks that there were 20,000 empty seats at the baseball game in 1951 because 'certain events have a quality of unconscious fear. I believe in my heart that people sensed some catastrophe in the air.' He points out that 'when they make an atomic bomb . . . they make the radioactive core the exact same size as a baseball.' There is a showing, in 1974, of the Zapruder film of Kennedy's assassination. There is Sister Edgar.

After a while, DeLillo's attitude towards these people, some of whom are supposed to be crazed, comes to seem irrelevant; their bulk amounts to a pedagogical statement. Though they are all different, their differences are burned away by the scandal of their sameness. DeLillo's anxiety about having anyone of substance in the novel unconnected to his central theme is not only irritatingly airless but itself begins to seem a little paranoid, as if he can only employ characters who are loyal to him and his agenda. I am not saying that if one writes about many paranoid people one becomes oneself paranoid; only that a novel speaks its themes not only in what it says explicitly, but in what it accumulates gently. A theme is not only spoken but is consolidated, and this consolidation betokens a paranoid vision. The novel comes to seem complicit with the paranoia it describes. That is to say, the *form* of *Underworld* is paranoid.

Nick Shay is intended to be the character who counters these shabby emergencies of fantasy. He is not a paranoiac, and will not surrender. DeLillo tells us that he does not believe Klara Sax's view of history as 'a matter of missing minutes on the tape. I did not stand helpless before it . . . A single narrative sweep, not ten thousand wisps of disinformation . . . I believed we could know what was happening to us. We were not excluded from our own lives.' But Nick is not a full or interesting enough character to carry much weight. And besides, the form of the novel is against him. The novel does indeed read like 'ten thousand wisps of disinformation'.

2

Such an agglomeration of paranoid people makes the reader weary about discrimination, and thus deprives this novel of one of fiction's great goads. Paranoia must necessarily do this to fiction, for it silences judgment. One might call this the logic of pampered ignorance. If what you start out from is what you do not know, this is an infinitely extendable mystical spectrum. One can always not know more. Paranoia approaches knowledge from behind, so that anything can be connected with anything. It is a dogmatic occultism. Yet fiction's task is to show where connections seem to end, the better for their vivid spread. Henry James saw this in his preface to *Roderick Hudson*. 'Really, universally, human relations stop nowhere, and the exquisite problem of the artist is eternally but to draw, by a geometry of his own, the circle within which they may happily *appear* to do so.' It may be that this novel's immense size has to do with the paranoid vision's inability to stop collecting connections.

Fiction is the avenger of paranoias. The very form of fiction is in tension with political paranoia, and paranoia will always tend toward an explicitness of form. Paranoia, by its nature, has to be expressed. It is an odd paradox of paranoia that all its attention is towards what is hidden, but it exists only when it is given coarse voice. In fiction there is no such thing as a quiet paranoid; the neurosis is essentially voluble. Fiction exists the other way round. Fiction's attention is toward what is tangible; yet it exists most effectively when its themes are unspoken. An ideal fiction has a kind of thematic ghostliness, whereby the novel marks its meanings most strongly as it passes, as it disappears; rather as on a street snow gets dirtier, more marked, as it disappears. Fiction's meaning is all that cannot be said; paranoia's is all that can be said, because it exists only in the saying. It therefore has to be spoken explicitly, either by characters or author or both. The delicacy of fiction is much stronger than the fattened feebleness of paranoia. Paranoia will always try to get fiction to speak about paranoia. As in *Underworld*.

Don DeLillo is a serious artist whose pointed stewardship of the novel in our culture, and pleasure in the chafe of fictional language, is cherishable. But his very defensiveness of the novel leads him, as far as one can see, into a philosophy of history which may weaken the novel, and into a battle with the culture which the novel can only lose. Again, the problem is that DeLillo veers towards a complicity with the very culture he wants to defend the novel against. Yet DeLillo's struggle with the anaconda of postmodern America, if not his personal theory of that struggle, is representative of much American writing since 1960, when Philip Roth famously argued that American reality was more vivid, and hence more fictional, than American fiction. DeLillo is not isolate; where *Underworld* fails, it fails collegiately.

For some time DeLillo has been brilliantly obsessed with the image in our culture: its sucking power and the tantric theft of aura by television and culture. *White Noise* was a funny and acute razing of a generation of academics who had been robbed of their epistemological innocence. They say things like: 'We were kids. It was too early in the cultural matrix for actual screwing', and test each other on where they were when James Dean or Elvis died. DeLillo's own prose is nervously alert to this image-corruption, and squeezes it for ironic effect – as when, for instance, he describes one of these academics as having 'the innocent prewar look of a rural murderer'; or when, more superbly, in *Mao II*, he writes of drivers sitting in cars caught in a Manhattan jam, 'slumped in the gloom like inmates watching daytime TV.' At such moments, DeLillo properly steals new fictional life back from a culture that is depleting fiction.

DeLillo seems to argue in his recent work that the peculiarity of our time is that the culture has become a kind of debased novelist, has overtaken the novelist. *Mao II* suggested, unconvincingly I think, that the novelist used to 'alter the inner life of the culture', but that this soul-stealing power no longer belongs to novelists. Instead, it belongs to terrorists ('they make raids on human consciousness'), to the new power of crowds ('The future belongs to crowds'), to the nightly TV news ('News of disaster is the only narrative people need. The darker the news, the grander the narrative'), to paranoiacs of all stripes, and to cult-leaders such as Mao and the Reverend Moon. All these forces act on the mind's unconscious in the way fiction used to because they share with fiction a certain fictiveness. They invent realities, shape them, as the novel used to, and rub them into the collective unconscious. In *Underworld*, DeLillo is more specific. The image-culture is still powerful in this book, but now the charge is against the state. The state is a novelist. For when the Americans discovered the bomb, they infiltrated our dreams. Klara Sax, the performance-artist (and not a character whom DeLillo seems to mock), explains: 'I think that if you maintain a force in the world that comes into people's sleep, you are exercising a meaningful power . . . The poets wrote long poems with dirty words and that's about as close as we came, actually, to a thoughtful response. Because they [i.e. the inventors and managers of the bomb] had brought something into the world that outimagined the mind.' Later in the book, a group of druggies watch the Zapruder footage of Kennedy's assassination with 'an acquired sort of awe . . . it was amazing that there were forces in the culture that could outimagine them.'

DeLillo appears to suggest that the paranoia of the state is greater than the paranoia of the individual; and both act like novelists (the crucial word is 'outimagine'; paranoia is imaginative work). DeLillo made this explicit in 1997, in an essay in *The New York Times*, 'The Power of History'. There he argued that great historical figures have a kind of fictionality because they leave the historical record to bristle in myth and memory. Nevertheless, DeLillo argued, Hoover was a real man, and surely a historical novelist who wants a Hoover in his book (or Sinatra, Jackie Gleason, and Lenny Bruce, who all appear) runs the risk of 'distort[ing] the lives of real people?' Well, DeLillo answers, 'not as much as the memoirist does, intentionally, or the biographer, unintentionally. That's the easy answer. The deeper reply begins with a man who distorted the lives of real people as a matter of bureaucratic routine.' DeLillo is a little opaque here, but he appears to suggest that since Hoover 'distorted the lives of real people' (that is, kept almost-fictional files on people), the novel can fight back with its own distortions, and keep a kind of file on the age. In other words, since Hoover acted like a bad novelist, it is time to act like a good novelist, and defeat the likes of Hoover on his own turf. DeLillo may not intend an equivalence between the fiction-making powers of history and the fiction-making powers of fiction, but he has produced one. The danger is obvious. For Hoover may have acted *like* a novelist, but he was not a novelist. DeLillo both acts like and is a novelist. The distinction, rather than the equivalence, between Hoover and DeLillo, or between the state and the novel, seems worth keeping. To say that Hoover acted *like* a novelist is a respectable metaphorical exaggeration. But to say that the novelist should act like Hoover is to suggest, in effect, that Hoover was a novelist. To suggest that Hoover was a novelist is to believe in your own metaphor to the point of turning history into metaphor. It is to say that history does not just make fiction, but *is* fiction. And to suggest that the novelist acts like Hoover is to surrender the novel to Hoover's terms even as the novelist prepares to fight Hoover. It is to be more paranoid than Hoover himself.

DeLillo feels he needs this equivalence so as to do better battle with the fictionality of the culture; he is taking on protective camouflage. But his vision does come close to turning history into fiction. Bill Gray, in *Mao II*, says this: 'There's a curious knot that binds novelists and terrorists . . . Years ago I used to think it was possible for a novelist to alter the inner life of the culture. Now bomb-makers and gunmen have taken that territory. They make raids on human consciousness. What writers used to do before we were all incorporated.' Gray is something of a paranoiac, of course. But DeLillo seems to agree with him. Yet it is only possible to think that novelists and terrorists do the same thing if you so expand your idea of 'the inner life of the culture' that all the outer life of the culture has disappeared. It is in the outer life – real, unimagined life – that people lose their limbs to bombs; it is in the inner life that people grant their souls to Dostoevsky. When DeLillo threatens to make history fictional, and the culture a novelist, he awards the culture a power it does not have. He flatters the state. (Which is why George Will's gibe that DeLillo is a leftishly 'bad citizen' is not only wrong because a writer does not need to be a good citizen; but because paranoia anxiously preserves the status quo, is in fact conservative because it assumes the battle is always lost.) DeLillo may not mean to do this. It is born, one suspects, of an anxiety about the destiny of the novel in our time. DeLillo wants the novel to win. If history acts like fiction, then perhaps the historical novel can defeat history; the truer fiction can win. This is a paranoid vision in which history is a plot to bring down the writer. Again, this is made explicit in 'The Power of History'. The novel, he writes there, 'has lately grown desperate for attention'. The culture would seem to be stronger than fiction. But the novel can fight the culture: 'At its root level, fiction is a kind of religious fanaticism with elements of obsession, superstition and awe. Such qualities will sooner or later state their adversarial relationship to history.' A little later he goes further: fictional language, he says, 'is stronger than the weight-bearing reality of actual people and events. It has a necessary existence, while the source material is exposed as merely contingent.' Fiction is 'stronger' than reality.

This is Bronx-fed Valéry. It is fin-de-siècle decadence, brawny aestheticism. Fiction a kind of 'religious fanaticism'! What obscurantism from a writer not notably religious! This is a dangerous aestheticism if it leads to the idea that fiction is stronger than reality only because reality is a weaker fiction. For if the novelist believes that reality is weak fiction he may stop caring about the quality of the reality in his novels. If the novelist, however unwittingly, has conceded a battle he cannot win to the greater fictional power of history, his fiction may become too fictional. And there are signs in DeLillo's recent work that this is the case. *Mao II* was a desperately unreal book, a collection of conceptual episodes. It had a portentousness that made it vulnerable to comedy. That novel was dominated by the very images it sought to overpower; one retains no character from that book, but what remains vivid are the photographs that DeLillo spread into his text – and which the text made almost fictional – of mass Moonie weddings, of the crowd-destruction at the Hillsborough stadium, of the millions at Ayatollah Khomeini's funeral. The fictionality of the image defeated the reality of the fiction.

The vast crowd of paranoiacs in *Underworld* certainly robs the fiction, and the reader, of crucial meters of discrimination. The book acts like realism, but feels like hallucination. A great deal of human life passes through its corridors, but this life seems overshadowed by what is going on in the classrooms of paranoia – lessons in civic surliness. One notices how often DeLillo is drawn to create inhuman, or exaggeratedly human, set-pieces: the 1951 baseball game; the 200 B-52 bombers in the desert; the landfill on Staten Island; graffiti in Manhattan; a cancer clinic in

Kazakhstan where the ruined victims of radioactivity roam and loll. He seems to enjoy describing these large occurrences because in doing so he is, in some way, describing his own art. Sometimes, *Underworld* seems a scrapbook of billboards, full of stiff importances. Only in one great, long passage, the 120 pages which beautifully draw DeLillo's childhood Bronx, does DeLillo relax his clench, and write about nothing so important as human consciousness. Here he writes fiction as it should be: a free scatter through time, unpressed, incontinent, unhostaged; surprised by the shock of its unhindered passage through frontiers it, and not history, has invented.

In the nineteenth century, Stendhal, in *The Charterhouse of Parma*, and much more acutely Tolstoy, saw the novel as the form that would examine the religion of history and show it to be a superstition. *War and Peace* sought to overturn Hegel's idea that Napoleon was the world-spirit on horseback. Fiction would shake history's certainties, it would show that we cannot control history, that to be in the army at Waterloo or Austerlitz was to be part of an entanglement you could not understand. The religion of history would be fought with the secularism of fiction. Real lives in Moscow and St Petersburg would lay bare, would humanize, the myth of the faceless armies of millions. The family would illuminate the army. (Tolstoy, despite his religious dogmatism, always treated the novel as a thoroughly secular form.)

In his way, DeLillo is the inheritor of this struggle. But he cannot win it within the mystical confines of the paranoid vision. Paranoia believes that there are forces that act beyond our control. This was Tolstoy's view of history, except that Tolstoy believed that we ourselves create these uncontrollable forces. When Tolstoy decided that this was his view of history, as he did at the end of *War and Peace*, there was no difficulty about showing, as a novelist, characters living within this world – for this is how we all live ordinarily, and always have done. Naturally enough, DeLillo has his own American anxiety; you cannot have the calm growl of a Tolstoy in late twentieth-century America, nor should you. But the paranoid vision incorporates a certain restless despair that makes the creation of rounded individual characters impossible. Paranoia acts as a falsely religious stimulant, both to novelists and their characters. Thus it is that DeLillo fights history with the religion of the novel, and speaks of the novel as a 'fanaticism, with elements of obsession, superstition and awe' – an extraordinary inversion of the sober nineteenth-century legacy, and a superstitious cul-de-sac for the novel. Living in America, inheriting a dread that American reality is too powerful for American fiction, he responds by crawling very close to an outright denial of reality's groundedness, while exaggerating the strength of fiction's potential resistance to that reality. If Tolstoy fought superstition with the daylight of realism, DeLillo merely fights superstition with a new superstition. He fights the religion of history with the religion of fiction.

John Updike's Complacent God

The enormous gap – in interest, substance, and turbulence – between Herman Melville and John Updike, both God-involved novelists, is one measure of our broken estate. Surely John Updike is one of the least tragic major writers; and of all theological writers, one of the most complacent. It is hard to picture a moment of real anguish, or agony, in his work. His fiction certainly seeks to dramatize questions of faith and belief, but it cancels genuine drama, because it is unable to give the devil the best lines – or indeed, any lines. His fiction stages theological arguments which are foreclosed. Doubt, or its opposite, fervency, is not taken seriously in Updike's work. All of his books suggest a belief that life will go on, that it will be thickly unvaried, that things will not come to a stop. The very form of the Rabbit books incarnates a belief that stories can *be continued*. For Rabbit, and indeed for his creator, there is too much alluring and sweetly tormenting data to allow him to jump mental bail and run wild. That quality of fattened paganism in Updike, which finds the same degree of sensuality in everything, whether it is a woman's breast or an avocado, paradoxically stabilizes and stills him as a writer. In this sense, Updike, like Rabbit, is always at rest, despite his visual greediness. Melville was a truly metaphysical writer. Updike is only a theological writer. (Just as Hawthorne was a theological writer, and in some way could not understand Melville's intensity and suffering.)

Updike's lyric capacities have been praised, and need not

detain us here. It should go without saying that he is, at his best, a fine pupil of Nabokov; and at his worst, his prose is a harmless, puffy lyricism, a seigneurial gratuity, as if language were just a meaningless bill to a very rich man, and Updike adding a lazy ten percent tip to each sentence. Instead, let us examine his strange theological serenity, the stainless quality that ensures that his books never quite agitate us (or, on the other hand, never quite console us) as great works do. Updike is not, I think, a great writer; and the lacuna is not in the quality of the prose, but in the risk of the thought. Updike's serenity and his deep indebtedness to the textures of the actual may flow from his own religious belief. Updike is a Christian with a particular loyalty to the Protestant theologian Karl Barth. Barth's teaching emphasizes God's free grace, and man's inability to affect that grace. According to Barth, God chose to reveal himself in Jesus Christ, and in no other way can we reach God. Creation is a gift, and we are the blessed recipients of this gift. But we should not infer from creation that God is our creator; it is no good, says Barth, looking in the world for proofs of God's presence (to do so is traditionally called the argument from design). We know that God exists because of Jesus Christ. Yet creation surrounds us, and we can see that, as Barth puts it in *Church Dogmatics,* 'creation is the formal presupposition of the covenant in which God fulfils the will of his true love.' Though Barth never quite says this, what he suggests is not so much an argument from design (for Christ is our proof), but a *reassurance from design.* We look around us, and in everything we see a reminder, not a proof, of God's relationship with us.

Is not this Updike's essential view? For him the world does indeed seem to exist as a divine visual gift, and as a consolation or reassurance, rather than as a proof. While the idea of reality as a proof would suggest intensity, Melvillean torments and doubts, reality as a reassurance suggests mildness. And perhaps, also, the difference between proof and reassurance is one between activity (the zeal to define) and receipt (the gift of God). Updike is not a writer whose characters ever doubt their

existence or who doubt the existence of the world. All of
Updike's work sings this hymn of receipt, and one novel in
particular dramatizes an argument around it. *Roger's Version*
(1986) arranges an opposition between an Updike-like follower
of Barth and an earnest young evangelist. Dale Kohler, the
evangelist, argues that biology and the new physics can prove
the existence of God. A world this complex must have been
created by God, says Dale. He proposes to use his computer to
establish a mathematical proof of God. He applies to Roger
Lambert, a professor of divinity, for a research grant. Roger
flinches from Dale's ardour and literalism. For Roger, God
could never be proved. Nor could reality ever be a sufficient
argument for God's existence. Roger feels, in the world around
him, God's marvellous echo rather than his calculable presence.

It is bold of Updike to address such large questions; but he
rigs the entire novel – and thus they are not really questions.
Dale is, throughout, a repulsive character; Roger Lambert, a
genial, mild professor. Roger is troubled by Dale Kohler, but
hardly in crisis. His faith is faint, but strongly faint –
complacently faint. The novel takes his side, presents *his* version.
Over the course of the novel, Dale's excitable need-to-prove is
rather too tidily killed off. Dale loses his faith at the end of his
labours, but Roger Lambert's faith is hardly affected, partly
because he has so much faith in the natural world that Updike
provides for his delight. As it happens, I am in agreement with
Updike and with Roger Lambert: the urge to prove God's
existence is hopeless. But it is not Updike's theological position
that dismays, nor is it that one religious version beats another; it
is the way the novel appears to dramatize two positions while
never actually exerting itself to do so with any felt strenuous-
ness. Indeed, Updike seems to mock excitability itself, to close it
off, to drown it in perfect language. *Roger's Version* poses an
argument that is never brought to any pitch of true importance.
Cannot one say because of this that the novel is theologically
complacent? For insofar as the need-to-prove is not really
credited (Dale's position), then the fervour that would produce

the need-to-disprove (the fervour that might propel atheism) is not really credited either.

This book may be compared with a novel written by Updike ten years later, *In the Beauty of the Lilies* (1996), whose largest failure is its inability to imagine atheism and the loss of religious faith. Like *Roger's Version*, *In the Beauty of the Lilies* is a novel that refuses to be interrupted, theologically. The first section describes a Presbyterian minister's loss of faith. The minister is the Reverend Clarence Wilmot, and he suffers his abandonment in Paterson, New Jersey, in 1910. The Reverend Wilmot announces his crisis, and asks to be relieved of his duties. He is unable to find decent work, and spends the rest of his life as a door-to-door salesman of encyclopedias. With time on his hands, he becomes an early devotee of the movies, and 'the incandescent power of these manufactured visions'.

The novel thus quickly establishes its own movement, from God to gods, from the sacramental to the sacramentalized, the aesthetic. This, suggests Updike, is modernity's journey. Truth surrenders to the depiction of truth. The movies, and references to them, form one of the girders of the book, which covers most of the twentieth century in its four sections. Reverend Wilmot's granddaughter, Essie, will become, in mid-century, a celebrated film actress; Essie's son, Clark, will die in a kind of movie of his own, a heavily televised conflagration at a religious compound in Colorado, clearly based on the disaster at Waco, when David Koresh's religious cult was destroyed in flames.

The Reverend Wilmot loses his faith; but the reader finds belief hard, too. Clarence's crisis does not live for us because Updike is at his most calm and efficient when he needs to be most turbulent. Clarence loses his faith, supposedly, in an absolutist swoop: 'the Reverend Clarence Arthur Wilmot, down in the rectory of the Fourth Presbyterian Church at the corner of Straight Street and Broadway, felt the last particles of faith leave him. . . He was standing, at the moment of the ruinous pang, on the first floor of the rectory.' Already, this has an air of preciousness rather than difficulty. Clarence loses his faith in the same rapid way he might have gained it – by conversion. But would a priest ever lose his entire faith, every 'last particle', as swiftly as this? The heavy upholstery of the passage, gesturing towards nineteenth-century solidity ('the Reverend Clarence Arthur Wilmot'), seems arch, uneasy, inappropriate. And then Updike swaddles everything too gorgeously: 'With a wink of thought, the universe had been bathed in the pitch-smooth black of hopelessness.' But these warm splashes of insight do not sound very hopeless. Do a wink and a bath sound so arduous?

A little later, Clarence stands in his study surveying his shelves of theological and other classics, now redundant. These sturdy volumes, thinks Clarence, 'were ignorant but not pathetic in the way of the attempts of the century just now departed to cope with God's inexorable recession: the gallant poems of Tennyson and Longfellow, phrasing doubt in the lingering hymnal music . . .' Does this sound like the Reverend Wilmot's language or Updike's? It is supposed to be a kind of inner monologue on Clarence's part. But it sounds as if Updike is reviewing Clarence's loss of faith for *The New Yorker*, and writing the review at his desk on a fine calm morning in Massachusetts: 'God's inexorable recession' is a phrase of placid summation, certainly not the words of a man in the process of losing his faith; and 'gallant' is a word of placid condescension.

It is as if words themselves might protect against crisis. Clarence's loss of faith never quite shakes him enough. Perhaps Updike, this acolyte of plenitude, *finds it hard to picture absence*, especially the absolute absence Clarence is supposed to be feeling. For as soon as Updike begins to picture it, he fills the emptiness with words and images. Absence is simply absent in this book. Part of the difficulty here is Updike's customary tranquil aestheticism, which so swells the textures of his books that it is hard for the reader to imagine any of Updike's characters feeling metaphysically abandoned. For they always have the world to comfort them, which is a kind of religion in Updike's work. The world's textures are what redeems us for all our deficiencies. Treating the real like food, Updike's characters consume more of it when miserable. Reality fattens the soul.

Updike, unlike Beckett or Bernhard, never appears to doubt that words can be made to signify, can be made to refer, to mean. He is a prose writer of great beauty, but that prose confronts one with the question of whether beauty is enough, and whether beauty always conveys all that a novelist must convey. At times, his fondness for an expensive phrase obscures, because it marks the moment at which he inserts himself oppressively. For instance, in *Roger's Version*, a passing girl is described as 'poignantly breastless'. It is an absolutely Updikean phrase, and elicits, initially, a grateful submission to Updike's high verbal powers. On second thoughts, however, it is meaningless. There is nothing necessarily poignant about a breastless woman, and anything so poignant is unlikely to be caught so swiftly in that one easy adverb. The phrase is too small genuinely to capture poignancy; while the word, 'poignantly', is too large, too poetic, to describe the relatively trivial sensation of seeing a flat-chested woman. This is, in fact, lyric kitsch, something Updike's prose descends into too often. This kitsch is sentimental, and false. While sentimentally sympathizing with a passing character, it actually condescends to her; anyone who did find this woman poignant would not use the word 'poignant'. (It is much like saying 'Oh how quaintly undernourished' about a beggar.) In *In the Beauty of the Lilies*, 'God's inexorable recession' is another, similar example of Updike's self-insertion. Elsewhere, Clarence hears, on the streets of Paterson, 'operatic ribbons of Italian, rapid stabs of Yiddish, mushy thrusts of Polish'. Again, these are an author's phrases, not Clarence's. They distance, rather than focus, the sound of these languages, and the result, for all its apparent fanciness, merely validates cliché: Italians are musical, Jews fast-talking, Poles incomprehensible. Such writing bestows rather than discovers. It runs away from disturbance of any kind, and so makes disturbance harder to depict.

To such tendencies, *In the Beauty of the Lilies* brings all the cognitive idleness of historical fiction. The historical novel, as practised nowadays, is merely science fiction facing backwards, with all the attendant crudities. Updike's book moves through this century's decades, and it forces smooth pacts between its characters and historical events. The danger in such novels is that characters will be no more than pacts themselves, composite agreements between colour and expectation. And in particular, the writer will have to ensure that his characters do not act simply because historical events demand that they should (dancing the Charleston in the 1920s, going off to Spain in the 1930s, becoming anti-Communist in the late 1940s, and so on). Alas, Updike's characters in this book are historically exemplary. History is used not to challenge but to confirm a character's essence. And one has the feeling that history is nothing so much as Updike's slathered detail. Essie, Clarence Wilmot's grand-daughter, enters a local beauty contest as a teenager. It is the late 1940s, and anti-Communism is in the air. On stage, she makes a pro-Communist statement and loses. Afterwards, she is rueful, and Updike decides on her behalf: 'She didn't really mean to defend Communists. She couldn't even picture one, or imagine why anybody would want to overthrow the American way of life, with its hemlocks and hollyhocks and soda fountains and new Studebakers without front fenders, just creamy smooth sides.' This sigh of notation, autographed with its characteristic clearing of the throat (the 'with its' prelude), is wholly Updike's. Again, we see Updike establishing what would seem to be a third-person interior monologue, the author entering Essie's mind, and turning the sentences over to her. But Updike cannot relinquish, he must insert himself. Who but Updike would imagine 'the American way of life' in this coolly rhapsodic way? A sixteen-year-old girl? And why should Updike be so certain that a teenager in a flush of radicalism could not possibly imagine a political alternative to the American way? Why is Updike so condescendingly sure that Essie 'couldn't even picture' another way of life? Is it not, in fact, Updike who cannot actually picture a Communist, Updike who cannot picture an alternative to the creamy plenitude he has himself created? Essie is unable to imagine an alternative because Updike is unable to picture a reality more powerful than his own. He is unable to picture the opposite of his own reality, which might be absence.

Again, one wonders if Updike has any capacity to register absence, and in particular, God's absence. One recalls *Roger's Version*, in which Updike hardly bothers to give the idea of God's absence anything more than a thought. For one of the oddities of *Roger's Version* is that what appears to be a clash between a sense of the fullness of God (Dale) and a sense of the absence of God (Roger) is actually a clash between two comparative fullnesses of faith, one fervent and one serene. And serenity wins. Both Dale and Roger are full of God; Updike strives to paint two presences. But he fails to draw a convincing picture of Dale. Only the complacent, unfervent, pornographic Roger is convincing in this book. And, as I suggested above, insofar as Updike cannot really picture Dale's fervency of belief with any kind of sympathy, he cannot picture the negative equivalent, the inverse fervency that might produce atheism. We can rephrase this: insofar as Updike cannot picture fervent theological fullness, he cannot picture fervent absence.

Is it possible that in some way Updike cannot really imagine God working in a life? If Updike cannot really imagine this, he cannot really imagine God's terrible absence from a life. After all, the fervent believers in both *Roger's Version* and *In the Beauty of the Lilies* are the obnoxious Dale, and the obnoxious cultists, clearly based on the fanatical followers of David Koresh who perished in flames in 1992. Fervency forces Updike into caricature. Updike's version is Roger's, a mild, manageable relation with God.

Updike is an oddly calm Barthian, a writer for whom God is unlikely ever to be a flaming presence or a flaming absence. This converts Barth's rather chilly, tragic view into a more serene theology. But how is it that Updike is mild about God's presence while clearly irradiated by reality's presence? This is precisely where Barth may be a useful way of reading Updike, since Barth suggests that we should not restlessly infer the existence of God from reality but simply be grateful to reality for its constant confirmation that God exists. The result, in Updike's work, is a mild gratitude for reality rather than an irritable searching after metaphysics. I hope it is clear that I am not requesting that Updike be an atheistic novelist, nor even a Melvillean doubter, merely that he *be a novelist*, abandon himself to negative capability, and depict something he does not like: fervent belief and fervent unbelief. Certainly, it is a lost opportunity in American fiction that one of the few theologically literate novelists remains so unexercised by the tremor of faith.

The Color Purple: Toni Morrison's false magic

Since fiction is itself a kind of magic, the novel should not be magical. The creation of characters out of nothing, their placement in an invented world, is chimerical; and for this reason one rarely wants the novelist further to ripen these chimeras in a false heat. The argument against magical realism in fiction should not be an argument about what is real and unreal, but an argument about belief. Fiction demands belief from us, and this request is demanding in part because we can choose not to believe. But magic – impossible happenings, ghoulish returns – dismantles belief, forcing on us apparitions which, because they are beyond belief, we cannot choose not to believe. Belief is a mere appendix to magic, its unused organ. This is a moral problem. One can hardy claim that magical realism corrupts our sense of reality, for at any moment we can close the novel. No, magic is most likely to corrupt our ability to judge *un*reality, it is likely to seduce our scepticism until it expires from unrequital; and hence magic corrupts our ability to judge fiction, which is a measured unreality. Fiction is threatened by magic (and vice versa). This is why most fiction is not magical, and why the great writers of magical tales – E.T.A Hoffmann, Gogol, Kafka – are so densely realistic.

The argument against magical realism is also an argument against Toni Morrison's fiction, because she is America's leading representative in these particular vaults. Morrison's talent – and she certainly has great novelistic talent – has been to combine magic, myth, and history, and to make of this a dignified superstition. Her fiction, at best, is an examination of this superstition, and at worst, its ready choir. In the best parts of *Song of Solomon* and *Beloved*, Morrison uses her fiction to narrate an African-American history which, because it has so often not been written or officially recorded, has become a necessary superstition – a myth, made of oral tellings and retellings. Her prose, with its flushed, oral cadences and vernacular stammer, attempts to become another of these retellings, a myth that is written down but which reads as if it were spoken. In her most acute moments, Morrison works against this collusion, by telling stories about people who are suspicious of mythical history. In *Song of Solomon*, Milkman travels to the South to explore the origins of his imposed last name; the strongest character in the new novel is a woman who defies her town's self-legend, and destroys the town's family tree she has been copying.

Paradise, her new novel, is a choir for superstition, and rarely an examination of it. It is a novel babyishly cradled in magic. It is deeply sentimental, evasive, and cloudy. It slights truth. It forces magic and pure rhapsodies on its characters like a demented anaesthetist bullying patients with laughing-gas. For all its soak of anguish, it is a novel that actually wishes everyone to have good feelings. It tells the story of the clash between a stern, religious all-black town in Oklahoma, founded in 1950 and called Ruby, and a convent of women about seventeen miles away from this town. One day, in 1976, a group of men from Ruby invade the convent and attempt to kill the women; these women, who are apparently cultish and strange, have become scapegoats for the town's own failures. The novel explains how this false blame gestated. This tale has been criticized for its political schematism – controlling men, incapable of tolerating female difference, murder the good feminists – and certainly, Morrison is hardly afraid of the explicit. We read of 'men finding it so hard to fight their instincts to control what they could and crunch what they could not'; a woman in the town helpfully summarizes the nature of the convent's female threat: 'Not women locked safely away from men; but worse, women who chose themselves for company, which is to say not a convent but a coven.' The women are witches to these men. The women, for their part, enjoy the way that their convent 'felt permeated by a blessed malelessness, like a protected domain . . .' One of the murderers sweetly confesses, at the end of the book, that he was raging against 'the needy, the defenseless, the different'.

Yet the novel fails not because Morrison schematically loves the women in the convent and hates the men of Ruby. It fails because she loves both sides, men and women, all of her characters, too indulgently. She stifles them with warmth. Morrison has an odd addiction to sweeteners. Though she occasionally depicts a squabble or two in the convent (just to show that all is not always well in paradise), the general atmosphere is ridiculously comforting. Consolata, or Connie, is a grandmotherly figure who sits in a room in the basement of the convent and looks after her damaged flock. 'Who hurt you, little one?' she asks Pallas, a sixteen-year-old newcomer, who has fled from a faithless man in California. For Pallas, Connie conjures 'images of a grandmother rocking peacefully, of arms, a lap, a singing voice . . .' The women hold dreaming sessions, and dance in the rain; there is nothing as wonderful as the 'rapture of holy women dancing in hot sweet rain', Morrison reminds us.

But Morrison does not ration her ardour to the convent. In Ruby also, 'the light falling from the April sky was a gift'. One of Ruby's inhabitants, Soane Morgan, recalls how children were baptized in the early days of the town, 'when baptisms were held in sweet water. Beautiful baptisms. Baptisms to break the heart, full of major chords and weeping and the thrill of being safe at last.' Outside Ruby, the light also falls like a gift, and there are more warm feelings and rhapsodies. Mavis, one of the women who ends up at the convent, is driving to California. She picks up a female hitcher called Bennie, who sings all the way: 'Songs of true love, false love, redemption; songs of unreasonable joy . . . Mile after mile rolled by urged and eased by the gorgeous ache in Bennie's voice.' Later in the book, Mavis is reunited with her daughter Sally. The two look at each other across the table in a diner: 'their eyes met. Sally felt the nicest thing then. Something long and deep and slow and bright.'

To select these sentimentalities is not to deny characters their sunspots of rhapsody, or even their confusions of rhapsody. But in all these cases Morrison's prose is lushly complicit with the rapture she is describing; and in most of these instances the lyricism starts and finishes too abruptly to be anything more than a careless shower. It is Morrison's own prose that is 'full of major chords and weeping'. These are not 'songs of unreasonable joy' so much as songs of unreasonable prose.

The difficulty with Morrison's 'poetry' is that it ignores the preparations, the flat stealth, the argument, that narrative demands. For instance, Mavis's encounter with Bennie lasts only a few lines. We have never see Bennie before, and we never see her again. The lyricism squandered on Bennie's singing ('the gorgeous ache in Bennie's voice' – this is an absolutely vulgar phrase) is not only sentimentally abrupt, but evasive. In place of a real Bennie, who might exist, even for only a paragraph, in descriptive links, Morrison rushes a generalized 'effect', a mood, on the scene instead. One imagines Morrison thinking: 'How can I make this little scene memorable, mournful, beautiful?' And Bennie disappears from the reader. Morrison's lyricism, in its evasive abruptness, is like a rich man stuffing money into our pockets while refusing to look at us and shouting all the while: 'Here, take this, and feel good.'

The world of *Paradise*, despite the pretence of its sombreness, is a cosy world because it lives on infusions of good feelings; and because uncertainty does not really inhabit it. On the contrary, *Paradise,* like a good deal of contemporary so-called 'poetic' fiction, lives in the magic kingdom of fairy-tale, in which happenings have an unexplained extremism which seals them from rational inspection. We are in the world of vibrating resonances. Small children love this kind of storytelling because although terrible things may occur in fairy-tales, the terrible is always wrapped in the continuing consolation that the terrible cannot be explained, and that it thus has no connection with our lived world. The childishness of magical realism has to do with its pre-psychological certainty: for the child, there is little difference between 'They all lived happily ever after' and 'They all lived unhappily ever after.' The consolation is that neither state will fail because neither can explain itself. These are the consolations of Morrison's novel. When something happens it is always a dumbfounding extremity. Time, and the argument of time, is always obliterated by the slicing reply of myth. 'Soaking in happiness, she folded the letter back in the envelope, put it in her shoe and carried it for the rest of her life.' 'Then, after a few seconds of total silence, he began to hum the sweetest, saddest sounds Rector ever heard.' 'At the door, her knuckles lifted for the knock, she heard sobbing. A flat-out helpless mothercry – a sound like no other in the world.' 'Wine-soothed, they slept deep as death that night.' 'The girl thought Sweetie was crying, and a black woman weeping on a country road broke her heart all over again.'

The result is, again, an evasive opacity. Two instances will suffice. Halfway through the novel, Morrison tells the story of an incident in the life of Billie Delia, one of the young women of Ruby. When Billie Delia was tiny, one of the town's elders used to bring her a racehorse to sit on. Too small for underwear, the little girl loved the feel of the horse under her skin. Then, when she was three, on a Sunday, the elder once again brought the horse. This time, the little girl was wearing panties. When she saw the horse coming, she ran out into the town's main street, and 'pulled down her Sunday panties before raising her arms to be lifted' onto the horse's back.

In a magical world, this incident becomes ominous: 'Things seemed to crumple after that. She got an unintelligible whipping from her mother and a dose of shame it took her years to understand. That's when the teasing began . . . Suddenly there was a dark light in the eyes of boys . . . Suddenly a curious bracing in the women, a looking-away look in the men. And a permanent watchfulness in her mother.' But this notion of fairy-tale upheaval – 'suddenly' – is unconvincing. Even in a conservative town, it would not be a strange sin for a three-year-old girl to remove her underwear. Would men refuse to look at her because of this? Fifty pages later, Morrison suggests that Billie Delia was treated oddly because she was lighter-skinned than anyone else in Ruby. But the explanation is overwrought. It merely defers explanation. For, like the incident of the panties, it is just another datum of unreason, and yet offers itself as the sole cause of Billie Delia's downfall. Besides, it comes too late to be novelistic. And it is precisely the novelistic that Morrison neglects. Had she described this incident, had she suggested that it was the beginning of a slow change, had she linked it to other incidents – had she, in short, conducted a *narrative* – we might believe in this moment, and we might have a clearer sense of Billie Delia's quiddity. But Morrison insists on a mythic swirl, in which something is suddenly and mysteriously changed for ever, as if life were a child's chemistry set.

Another instance of myth-making offers a larger problem, because some of the novel's structure of motivation rests on it. Connie, the irenic 'mother' of the convent, has a passionate affair with Deacon Morgan, one of the town's most upright citizens (he is also married). Deacon abruptly ends the relationship after Connie bites his lip and draws blood. 'Don't ever do that again', he warns. But there is no 'again'. In this charged moment, the passion dies: 'his eyes, first startled, then revolted, had said the rest of what she should have known right away . . .' Morrison comments that Deacon could not possibly endure 'a woman bent on eating him like a meal'. So the woman is a man-eater, and the man is not strong enough for the woman; we get the point. Fifty pages later, at the end of the book, Deacon is one of the avenging men who storm the convent. After the crime, he confesses to the pastor that he needed to expunge his 'shame', and that he had to 'erase both the shame and the kind of woman he believed was its source. An uncontrollable, gnawing woman who had bitten his lip just to lap the blood it shed . . . a Salome from whom he had escaped just in time . . .'

In a sense, the entire novel turns on this coin of parable; the entire novel flows from The Bite. Deacon and his like think of the women as bloodsuckers, and must erase the shame of their dependence on such women. But this entirely unnovelistic explanation is at once over-explicit (parable-like) and unconvincingly enigmatic (mythically extreme). It manages to be both at once because it refuses the daylight of motive. We are not encouraged to wonder why Deacon might recoil so finally from such a minor abrasion. Morrison does not require our belief; she wants to ravage our scepticism. She wants to boil motive in the broth of myth, and make it disappear, to cancel 'because' from the language. There is no need of 'because' in Morrison's world: Connie bit Deacon; and then Deacon took his revenge: that is all we need to know. Again, despite the apparent severity of the story, magic powders it with consolations. How much easier it is to swallow this tale than to examine realities. How entirely do a real, accountable Deacon and Connie disappear into the tale of The Bite. And how eagerly, once again, Morrison's language colludes with this opacity, frothing itself into meringues of magic. For if one might just about accept that Deacon is madly hasty, one certainly does not accept the support he gets from Morrison's own relishing language: 'an uncontrollable, gnawing woman who had bitten his lip just to lap the blood it shed'.

Too often, Morrison is so besotted with making poetry, with the lyrical dyeing of every moment, that she cannot grant characters their own words. She is in love with *her* words, and it is too bad if these words coincide somewhat awkwardly with the words of her characters. It might seem at first that the reason that Morrison's characters do not really exist is that she loves them too much, and in so doing hotly hugs the life from them. But in fact Morrison loves her own language more than she loves her characters, and appears to view them as mere spokes of style, who exist to keep her lyricism in motion. This explains why Morrison so often squanders her considerable talent for interior monologue, or stream-of-consciousness. At her best, in certain portions of *Beloved*, Morrison demonstrates a real capacity to enter a character's mind, and to let her own style be bent, in the course of interior monologue, by the needs and palpabilities of actual characters. Of course, interior monologue is essentially inner speech, and Morrison has been, from the beginning, a fine recorder of speech. Her dialogue is often acute and alive as her commentary is not.

But in this novel, she uses interior monologue not as a window but as a funnel; she blows her own exhortations into her characters' privacies. In this respect, for all the former similarities, Morrison could not be less like Faulkner. *As I Lay Dying* is a great book because Faulkner, like Joyce and Woolf (and presaged by Chekhov), uses the innovation of stream-of-consciousness to allow his characters to forget themselves, to break free of the author's incessant memoranda, to be in their own verbal confusions. That this confusion, this freedom, is granted by the novelist, is a trivial paradox: how else could it exist? It is because this paradox is unavoidable that the novelist approaches stream-of-consciousness so gingerly but also so fatalistically. Thus Faulkner's five-year-old Vardaman speaks to the reader as a five-year-old could not. He is enriched by Faulkner, yet he must continue to seem, skeletally as it were, a little boy. The literary delicacy lies in an enrichment which can at any moment become a reduction.

Morrison is mostly reduction in this book. Again, she fails when she makes her language collude too eagerly with her character's thoughts. Deacon, for instance, has a reverie about his childhood in the town of Haven, which was a dry-run, before the war, for Ruby. Deacon is given to self-exhortation and self-legendizing. Hearing schoolchildren reciting a poem he learned as a child, he drifts into memory. Morrison, hovering

somewhere between third-person narrative and interior monologue, indulges him:

> But none of it was as good as what they had learned at home,
> sitting on the floor in a firelit room, listening to war stories;
> to stories of great migrations – those who made it and those
> who did not; to the failures and triumphs of intelligent men –
> their fear, their bravery, their confusion; to tales of love deep
> and permanent. All there in the one book they owned then.
> Black leather covers with gold lettering; the pages thinner
> than young leaves, than petals. The spine frayed into
> webbing at the top, the corners fingered down to skin. The
> strong words, strange at first, becoming familiar, gaining
> weight and hypnotic beauty the more they heard them, made
> them their own.

Remember that Deacon is not supposed to be a reliable
assessor of his own traditions. It is Deacon who leads the men to
the convent. But why, if Deacon is exhorting himself, should
Morrison so lavishly collude with him? For this passage is just
esteem-building, preaching. Morrison is so keen to exercise her
own lyricism – 'the pages thinner than young leaves, than petals'
– that she bullies her way past Deacon. Like so much in this
book, in doing so she compresses the individuality, the freedom,
of her characters. Does – can – a real man exist inside this halo
of pride? Does this utterly clichéd iconostasis – the fireside hush,
the big book with its 'strong words' and thin pages, the devoted
auditors – enable us to see anything at all, with any specificity? It
will not do to reply that this is intended to be the fantasy of a
deluded man, in love with his own rigidities. First of all, if this is
a delusion, then Morrison has failed to give the delusion any
uniqueness or body. And secondly, Morrison is deluded herself:
she is in love with the scene, her language is a helpless flummox.
    This kind of writing is everywhere in the novel, and it
multiplies as the book reaches its bloody conclusion. Near the
end, the convent women, who are all damaged in some way,

use a form of story-therapy to purge themselves of their hauntings. They sit in the building's cellar and conduct 'loud dreaming'. They also draw shapes of themselves on the floor, and use these shapes as a form of art-therapy. They have seances, and are visited. As usual, Morrison's prose beomes solemnly reverent: 'They spoke to each other about what had been dreamed and what had been drawn. Are you sure she was your sister? Maybe she was your mother. Why? Because a mother might, but no sister would do such a thing.' Here the novel finds its perfect medium. Nowhere does Morrison explain what is meant by 'such a thing'. She does not have to. Why should the novel crumble its magical potencies into dusty explanation? In the half-light of the seance, where everything is beyond belief, the novel's false magic finally comes to rest. Here, at last, is a world in which the puncture of reality need never be felt. *Because a mother might, but no sister would do such a thing.* Here the novel achieves its greatest desire: an objectless sentence, pure throbbing verb. Finally, Morrison has stopped speaking to her readers, and is only speaking to her characters.

Toni Morrison puts one in mind of Auden's poem 'The Novelist'. The poet, writes Auden, can rush forward 'like a hussar', but the novelist must eschew such acceleration, and learn to be 'plain and awkward'. In this novel, Morrison is forever rushing in sentimental garments, with no thought of the plain and awkward clothes that carry a narrative, that make its solemnities moving and not simply ridiculous. Above all, she oppresses her characters with her own essence, so that she seems, preposterously, to be secretly proud of them all. It is true that her parable is schematic. But in fact, in the end, there are not good people and bad people in her book; there are only good people. Her lyricism cannot help telling the story of the collision of two loved and honoured worlds, the town and the convent. *Paradise* is no battle at all; it is a warm battle-hymn.

The Monk of Fornication: Philip Roth's nihilism

Until recently, Philip Roth had begun to cage his dangers, routinize his obsessions. His characters still shouted at each other, but too argumentatively to offer any argument to the reader; or too symmetrically not to cancel themselves out. Jewishness, women, Israel, the burden of fiction-making, the antagonistic self: his characters had become parlour soldiers, and the novel simply the piano around which they gathered to sing their little rages. His men had their campaigns of sex, but the sex was no longer subversive or important, as it had been in *Portnoy's Complaint*, and had come to seem merely inevitable. It was a little tedious to follow Roth's fictional games, ghosts, and handprints.

But *Sabbath's Theater*, Roth's extraordinary novel, shares little with this recent history. Its male protagonist is not Philip Roth in disguise, nor is he (apart from his Jewishness and his New Jersey origins) proximate enough to his author to excite suspicion. There is more sex, more male outrage, more filth in this book than in any of Roth's earlier work, but the sex here is important, even desperate, and not merely victorious, as it had tended to be; and the outrages are not only opportunistic.

In *Sabbath's Theater*, Roth's menace is uncuffed and at large. It gathers in the character of Morris 'Mickey' Sabbath, who is a moving army of disgusts. Sabbath is a great hater, a walking insult. He is now in his mid-sixties, bearded, heavy-bellied and deep into a second, sexless marriage to an alcoholic. For pleasure, he has his glorious relationship with his lover Drenka, a Croatian-American with a tendency towards malapropism. He has been unemployed for years, but survives on a flowing stipend of hate. 'Despite all my troubles, I continue to know what matters in life: profound hatred', he tells his wife. Sabbath defaces life; he tears his days from their peaceable volumes and scrawls his filthy footnotes over every page. Sabbath is a former actor, director, and puppet artist who behaves like a genius: 'He'd paid the full price for art, only he hadn't made any.' He is a dispensary of free enmities and he sprinkles his pollutants across the novel. He rages against the Jews, the Catholics ('Jesus and Mary and Joseph and all the gang there in the manger . . . the whole fucking Catholic schmeer that we all need like a fucking hole in the head') and the Japanese, who shot down his beloved elder brother, Morty, in World War Two. He delights in his holiday from rationality. When his wife asks him why he hates the Japanese so much, he replies: 'Because of what they did to Alec Guinness in *The Bridge on the River Kwai*. Putting him in that fucking little box. I hate the bastards . . . When I hear the word Japan, I reach for my thermonuclear device.' He has stopped following the news: 'The news told him nothing. The news was for people to talk about, and Sabbath, indifferent to the untransgressive run of normalized pursuits, did not wish to talk to people. He did not even want to know who the president was of the United States. He'd rather fuck Drenka, he'd rather fuck *anyone*, than watch Tom Brokaw.'

This novel alludes often to *King Lear*. As a young man, Sabbath played Lear in his own production. When Drenka dies of cancer, Sabbath flees his wife and drives to New York, where he has a Lear-like breakdown, and wanders the streets recalling lines from the play. As Lear, so Sabbath crumbles from a misanthrope into a nihilist, and his hatred becomes comprehensive where before it had been indiscriminate. Now he hates everyone, especially himself. 'All I know how to do is to antagonize', he moans. He wants to die, and reads books about death and funerary practices in the world religions. Like Lear, he must first be exposed on his metaphysical heath. And indeed, Sabbath's life has been sourly fugitive; he has run from various sexual scandals to the moral quarantine of rural Massachusetts. In New York in the 1950s, the young Sabbath – 'a squat man, a sturdy physical plant, obviously very sexed-up and lawless, who didn't give a damn what anybody thought' – ran a street theatre opposite the gates of Columbia University, in which he used his fingers as puppets. But he could not keep those fingers off the pretty girls in his audience, and an indecency charge was filed against him. When his unhappy first wife, Nikki, disappeared in peculiar circumstances, Sabbath quit New York with his new lover, and later wife, Roseanna. In Massachusetts, however, he lurches into disgrace again, at the local college where he teaches theatre. A student whom he has seduced tapes one of their bouts of phone sex. Sabbath is sacked, and the tape becomes a standard work for various women's pressure groups. (Roth obligingly provides a transcript of the tape.)

Sex – sex with the enterprising and inexhaustible Drenka, but anyone will do, really – both heals and salts his life-wounds. Sex gives Sabbath a reason to live, confronts the great refusing force in him. But sex is also the very emblem of this refusal, for it so violently mocks everything. Sabbath, after all, wants to fuck the world, literally and figuratively. Sex is the badge of his militancy as a man, and each new offence merely reveals another unoffended area. 'Yes, yes, yes, he felt uncontrollable tenderness for his own shit-filled life. And a laughable hunger for more. More defeat! More disappointment! . . . More disastrous entanglement with everything.' Sex seen in this way is as interminable as life, and as entrapping. Feeling suicidal in New York, Sabbath rues that 'Something always came along to make you keep living, goddamnit!' This something is sex. Sabbath cannot escape sex. He lives within it as certain great painters are said to live within one colour; everything he does is sex-tinged. Even when he is not thinking about sex, he is thinking about sex. 'Never, never would he voluntarily depart this stupendous madness over fucking.' Roth relishes this madness, and it *is* a madness, something that, like the medieval carnival, inverts the world. In the ancient nihilistic way, Sabbath trades in opposites:

he wants to die rather than to live, for living is a sickness, not a health. Similarly, sex is a sacred slayer, a liturgy of errancy: 'The core of seduction is persistence. Persistence, the Jesuit ideal . . . You must devote yourself to fucking the way a monk devotes himself to God. Most men have to fit fucking in around the edges of what they define as more pressing concerns . . . But Sabbath had simplified his life and fit the other concerns in around fucking . . . The Monk of fucking.' This passage tells us, in effect, that Mickey Sabbath is not supposed to be real or representative, any more than Zarathustra is supposed to be real, or Dostoevsky's Prince Myshkin (and certainly it is hard to believe that, in real life, a man would masturbate over his mistress's grave, as Sabbath does in this novel); no, he is an exceptional figure, emblematically and offensively named, a philosophical icon of the inverted spiritual life, a priest of spiritual unhealth, a strike *against* the 'Sabbath'.

Sex here exists as the most tangible index of the rage for disorder. And what disorder, what mischief! When Drenka comes to Sabbath, asking him to look over a speech her Croatian husband has written for the local Rotarians, Sabbath sabotages it. Realizing its deep boredom – it is about rural innkeeping – Sabbath advises that it should be three times as long; and he tells Drenka that her husband is misusing English idiom. The phrase in English, he explains, is not 'nuts and bolts', it is 'nuts and bulbs'. He advises appropriate correction, which is duly followed. The speech is a disaster. (Sabbath enjoys Drenka's own verbal slips: 'when the shithouse hit the fan'; 'the boy who cried "Woof!" '; 'alive and cooking'; 'let him eat his own medicine'; 'crime doesn't pay off'; 'the whole kitten and kaboozle'.) After Drenka's death, Sabbath leaves his wife and drives to New York, and is taken in by his friendly and upright colleague, Norman Cowan. He thanks Norman by trying to sleep with his wife, Michelle. Norman catches him masturbating over a graduation photograph of their daughter Deborah (an excruciating scene). He is thrown out of the Cowan house when Michelle finds a pair of Deborah's panties in his coat pocket. 'You have the body of an old man,' Michelle tells him, 'the life of an old man, the past of an old man, and the instinctive force of a two year old.'

I have had, in the past, little time for this kind of sex-obsession in American fiction. But *Sabbath's Theater* makes sex meaningful in a way John Updike's novels do not. In Updike's work, for all its theological gesturing, sex is remarkably unmetaphysical. Sex is innocent of higher meaning; it is only a wrangle of textures, the pretext for Updike's soothing phrases. Sex exists for Updike as grass does, or the metallic sheen of an air-conditioning unit. This is not philosophical at all, but a rather boring paganism, which finds the *same degree of sensuality in everything*. In Roth's novel, by contrast, sex is absolutely connected to nihilism. *Sabbath's Theater* is disciplined and generously subsidized by philosophical tradition – we might expect as much from a novel whose hero has been working on a puppet adaptation of Nietzsche's *Beyond Good and Evil*, and who wants to kill himself because he has seen that life is 'stupid . . . Anyone with any brains understands that he is destined to lead a stupid life *because there is no other kind*.' We recognize the ring of that hammer, hear Nietzsche in it, and those wild uprooters Louis-Ferdinand Céline and Thomas Bernhard. It is the sound of a voice stinging itself in trances of negation, the sound of logical vandalism. Sabbath is a creature of this tradition, and Roth uses it with considerable philosophical precision.

Unlike most of his American contemporaries, Roth has been influenced by European nihilism. He has called Céline 'my Proust'. Roth is attentive, though not didactically or programmatically, to certain motifs of the nihilistic tradition. Chiefly, Sabbath has what Nietzsche recommended his 'free spirits' should possess: 'exaggerated honesty'. He sees through his own life, sees through all life, sees the useless dangle of it, the frayed threads on the back of the plausible brocade. Driving weepily to New York, fleeing his marriage but hardly himself, he gets lost, and universalizes blackly. Perhaps this is what life is like: 'a coffin that you endlessly steer through the placeless darkness, recounting and recounting the uncontrollable events that induced you to become someone unforeseen'. Jonathan Swift once wrote his own obituary, in the form of a poem. Likewise, Sabbath (without mentioning Swift, of course) sketches a merciless obituary of his own wasted life as *The New York Times* might do it. Wittily – this is a funny, funny book – he imagines sub-headings: 'Pig or Perfectionist?', 'Did Nothing for Israel'. Nihilism, which replaces life with death, inverts everything. Sabbath, the Monk of Fornication, turns morality's homburg back to front. 'I'm not big on oughts', he cries, as he attempts to lure Norman Cowan's wife into her own guest bedroom, thereby dispatching Kant's Categorical Imperative. When Michelle Cowan murmurs about fidelity, Sabbath turns fidelity into a sin. 'A world without adultery is unthinkable. The brutal inhumanity of those against it. Don't you agree? The sheer fucking depravity of their views. The *madness*.' Yet even if life is a sickness, the knowledge will not bring health, merely a deeper sense of sickness. At his bleakest moments of self-searing, Sabbath knows that he knows nothing: 'no lucidity to be derived from any of this. Rather, there was a distinctly assertive quickening of the greatest stupidity.'

When this poor trapped beast goes to New York for the funeral of a friend who has killed himself, his sickness becomes acute. Roth's allusions to *Lear* become explicit. Sabbath is homeless and friendless, accompanied, so he imagines, by the ghost of his mother, to whom he talks about his life. It is here that the novel begins to toll its backward peal, becomes the casing to the heavy clapper of memory, which moves ceaselessly between Sabbath's anarchic present and his happy past. Homeless, he is Lear thrown out of his daughters' palaces, and in New York he recites lines from the play: 'I am a very fond and foolish old man . . . You do me wrong to take me out o' the grave.' He rants to the ghost of his mother, and fingers the past: the small town on the Jersey shore where he grew up, his beloved elder brother shot down by the Japanese, his mother who never recovered, the official telegram from the Army, the streets full of soldiers and hawkers, the warm nervous conspiracy of family life to which Roth returns so often, so captively, and so beautifully, in his fiction. In New York, at Norman Cowan's home, Sabbath stands at his window and thinks of hurling himself out of it. He cannot do it. He seeks the grave but, as much, he seeks the graves of his family, and goes on wistful mental travels.

The novel, at this point, is 150 pages old. From this moment, the prose races on a thousand feet and does not stop until the last word. The writing, like Henry Roth's in *Call It Sleep*, speeds along a line of grief, lapsing in and out of stream-of-consciousness. These next 300 pages are an astonishment and a scourge, and one of the strangest achievements of fictional prose that I have ever read. Sabbath cannot kill himself, and wants to; hates life, but loves it well enough to think another minute of consciousness preferable to nullity. On the streets, in borrowed clothes (but clutching in his pocket young Deborah's panties), he mingles with the bums and beggars:

> So passeth Sabbath . . . a caricature of himself and entirely himself, embracing the truth and blind to the truth, self-haunted while barely what you would call a self, ex-son, ex-brother, ex-husband, ex-puppet artist without any idea what he now was or what he was seeking, whether it was to slide headlong into the stairwells with the substrata of bums or to succumb like a man to the desire-not-to-be-alive-any-longer or to affront and affront and affront till there was no one on earth unaffronted.

In this frailty of self, Sabbath tearfully elegizes his dead family, and resurrects them; he longs for death, but would as happily be the victor over it. Beautifully, his inversions veer from nihilism towards the utopian:

> What if they were *all* alive . . . Morty. Mom. Dad. Drenka. Abolishing death – a thrilling thought, for all that he wasn't the first person, on or off a subway, to have it, have it

desperately, to renounce reason and have it the way he did when he was fifteen years old and they *had* to have Morty back. Turning life back like a clock in the fall. Just taking it down off the wall and winding it back and winding it back until your dead all appear like standard time.

Standing in Deborah's bedroom, searching for inflammatory snapshots of Norman Cowan's daughter, he comes upon her college notes on Yeats's poem 'Meru', which Deborah has copied out in full. Sabbath is moved by Yeats's depiction of a world in which man is driven to destroy his own greatnesses:

> Ravening, raging, and uprooting that he may come
> Into the desolation of reality:
> Egypt and Greece, good-bye, and good-bye, Rome!

Under it, Deborah has quoted her professor: 'Yeats was at the verge beyond which all art is vain.' Something like this is true of the next 300 pages of this novel, which burst through stained-glass to a brutal transparency of report; whose racing sentences seem to renounce slowing and local ardours the better to catch the wing of truth.

2

Some of Roth's previous novels have been forged 'confessions' so as to muss our idea of the truth. But *Sabbath's Theater* draws its great power from our feeling that truth is not confessed, or even postmodernistically 'confessed', but revealed. There is almost nothing of Philip Roth in Mickey Sabbath; and there is everything. Sabbath's anguish, his life-reckoning and death-reckoning, his wail of finitude, have the pressure of the writer's deep engagement. Sabbath's seriousness moves us. Sabbath is pathetic, like most of us, because he knows himself well enough for judgment but not well enough for correction: 'A really trivial, really shitty life.' He poisons everything he touches, but this begins with himself: 'Everything runs away, beginning with who you are, and at some indefinable point you come to half understand that the ruthless antagonist is yourself.'

Roth wants to shock, and like Céline he delights to trample on fresh meadows. But those who only register shock at Sabbath's foulness end up simply describing him – which is a tribute to his tremendous reality. *The New York Times*'s critic complained that Roth describes 'in lewd detail, all of Sabbath's sexual high-jinks', and that these read like 'the depressing gropings of a dirty old man'. Indeed they do; and Sabbath admits as much. When he arrives at Norman Cowan's house, he realizes that 'he unnerved Norman no less than if he had been a tramp whom Norman had foolishly invited to spend the night. That he, Sabbath, could inspire such feelings of course entertained him. But it was hideous as well.' Everything flows from Sabbath's quiddity, or does not.

Misogyny always flickers in the nihilist vision, because woman – see Nietzsche – is seen as a timid obstacle to man's metaphysical lawlessness. Woman is convention, in this vision. In Roth's work, certainly, women do seem to exist to indulge or to obstruct the free play of the phallus. Some of Roth's earlier novels have an air of self-congratulation about them. *My Life as a Man* strikes one as misogynistic because even though the narrator passes himself off as flawed ('The broken shall succor the broken'), he lords his completion over difficult or inexperienced women. He teaches them lawlessness ('Then there is the painful matter of the elusive orgasm: no matter how she struggled to reach a climax, "it" never happened'). Sabbath fills his own novel, but he does not control it. And what does Sabbath have to teach a woman? He himself needs tuition. His relationship with Drenka, though interestingly kinky – troilism, voyeurism, lesbian guests – is bracingly balanced: Drenka more than matches him. Certainly Sabbath finds it difficult to look at women without, as it were, scanning their sexual skeletons first. But that is because sex is very important to him. The women with whom he engages – Drenka, Michelle Cowan, a woman at

his wife's rehab unit whom he tries to pick up – are solidly
realized. They are not just clouds of male desire.

While sex has seemed simply a challenge in some earlier
Roth novels, a part of the Céline-influenced programme of
ceaseless shock, sex in *Sabbath's Theater* at least has a personal
inflection, and a metaphysical dignity. Yes, even a kind of
dignity, owing to the philosophical desperation that fills it. Sex
is not a challenge here, it is an endless defeat. No self-
congratulation hangs from it. Sabbath uses sex as part of his
nihilistic war against decency and sobriety. Yet one should recall
the place of sex in the nihilistic vision: it has a meanly absorptive
function. Since the soul is dead, in the nihilistic scheme, it is the
body that registers the soul's wounds. And the body at sex –
seen under the eye of mortality – is a poor, rutting, animalistic
thing. Sabbath's invocation of sex's 'satanic side' is, at least,
double-edged. Satan does not come into things where the stakes
are low or unserious. *Sabbath's Theater* is a great tribute to the *via
negativa*.

Of course, Roth has been fleeing from the sublime since
Portnoy's Complaint. It startles us to return to *Goodbye, Columbus*,
his first book, and to savour the high-minded restraint, the tiny
rounding of each fine phrase, the dab at traditional 'pathos'.
This is some way from the loose, brawling extremities of the
later Roth voice. Ever since Roth was attacked for being anti-
Semitic and self-hating, he has enjoyed spitting at decency.
When Hermione Lee asked him in 1984 if he wrote with a
reader in mind, he replied: 'I occasionally have an anti-Roth
reader in mind. I think, "How he is going to hate this!" That
can be just the encouragement I need.' In *My Life as a Man*, the
Roth-like writer Peter Tarnopol mocks the pallid Wasp
gentilities of his 1950s literary education, the family out of
which *Goodbye, Columbus* emerged. Tarnopol must decide
between traditional sublimity and the anti-sublime. He fears that
'maybe I am turning my art into a chamber-pot for hatred, as
Flaubert says I shouldn't, into so much camouflage for self-
vindication – so if the other thing is what literature is, then this

ain't . . . I'll try a character like Henry Miller, or someone out-and-out bilious like Céline for my hero instead of Gustave Flaubert – and won't be such an Olympian writer.' Likewise, in *The Ghost Writer*, the Roth-like writer Nathan Zuckerman feels he must make a similar choice. Recalling Stephen Dedalus, he throws down a gauntlet to himself. He decides that sex will be his rebellion, his flaming addition to Jewish high-mindedness: 'When I came upon Babel's description of the Jewish writer as a man with autumn in his heart and spectacles on his nose, I had been inspired to add "and blood in his penis," and had then recorded the words like a challenge.'

There has, occasionally, been something puerile about this rebellion (though *The Ghost Writer* never errs). A slick of self-satisfaction sits on top of this rather deliberate grime, in particular a complacency at Jewish inappropriateness. Watch those Jews shred Jane Austen all over the Newark streets! ('The seven Christian critics in the seminar would hardly dare to speak when the three dark Jews . . . got shouting and gesticulating at one another over *Sir Gawain and the Green Knight*.') At such moments, Roth's novels seem to be playing themselves, clattering out manifestos for their outrageousness, mimicking a self-argument – Céline or Flaubert, which shall I be? – which, one feels, has actually been foreclosed.

Sabbath's Theater certainly promotes its own idea of what art should be, as found in the young Sabbath's New York enterprise, the Indecent Theater, 'where the atmosphere was insinuatingly anti-moral, vaguely menacing, and at the same time, rascally fun . . . an unseemly, brilliantly disgusting talent that had yet to discover a suitably seemly means of "disciplined" expression.' We would be naïve not to hear a Rothian self-description in this. Clearly, neither Roth nor Sabbath will be much interested in seemliness. But since self-argument has been surrendered in this book, so has the need to propagandize and to convince. Mickey Sabbath is beyond argument. In *My Life as a Man*, Peter Tarnopol's wife tells him: 'You are not in the virtue racket.' But Sabbath is not in the convincing racket; he is not in any racket; and neither, therefore, is the novel, for Sabbath *is* the novel; he fills it spreadingly, like a CinemaScope effigy on a television screen. Past quarrelling with himself, his lovers, or the reader, he exists only to be confirmed by defeats. For where some of Roth's self-arguing characters – and novels – have been urgent but not quite serious, Sabbath is deadly serious. His nihilism is too bitter to need props, to need the anxious verbal netball of Roth's usual modes. Sabbath screams, singly and envelopingly.

Sabbath's grossness, his racist rants, will doubtless provoke the usual imprecations; but it should be clear that the novel's offence is not political, but metaphysical. Sabbath's offences are against life. They have not worked if they do not disgust. Sabbath is on a crusade: to set the world to wrongs. Roth is not simply delighting in his avoidance of correct thinking or 'disciplined expression'. He is blaspheming, with all the grandeur that blasphemy implies. *Sabbath's Theater* mounts an anti-theological theology. Blasphemy is more profound than rudeness, because it ascribes value to what is blasphemed. Sabbath's negative engagement with the world is a kind of homage to its cruel power. His cruelties remind us of the world's. Unlike satire, which rests its case once its target has been speared, nihilistic blasphemy can never be completed, since it seeks to overturn life itself; it is not over until life itself has ended. Only death can remove Sabbathean outrages. Céline wrote in a letter: 'I'm still a few hatreds short, and I'm sure they exist . . . When the world changes its soul, I'll change my form.' Likewise, Sabbath is unappeasable: 'My failure is failing to have gone far *enough*! My failure is not having gone *further!*'

If this novel shocks, it is not because of what Mickey Sabbath does with women's underwear. What is shocking is to have life written off like a debt. Sabbath wants to spoil life for us, to make it seem not worth living, metaphysically superfluous. Vileness in art has usually been cautionary or cathartic: the absence of good in the work of art excites our desire for the good; or we lose our vileness in the work's exaggeration of it. But Roth wants to adjust our very idea of the good. Obviously, if we no longer know what the good is, our literature can hardly advise us of it (not least because the kind of morality inscribed in the idea of the cautionary tale is not worth having: *Lolita* would not be a great work of art if it merely told us that paedophilia is wrong). The exposing of this may well be sacred, even as it inverts the sacred. 'What if the mass for the dead were read over the living?' asks Beckett in *Molloy*.

3

Sabbath seeks not only his grave. He also seeks his family's graves; and so he leaves New York for New Jersey and his hometown by the sea. He wants to buy his own grave. So begins the novel's tearful final hundred pages, as the book leaves *Lear* for *Hamlet*. (The section is called 'To Be Or Not To Be'.) Like Hamlet, Sabbath strolls among the graves meeting the mortal constituents, the democrats of death. His parents are here, his brother also, but crammed into a ground so thickly planted that it is like a bed of nails. Roth offers a page filled only with gravestone names: 'Our beloved mother Minnie. Our beloved husband and father Sidney. Beloved mother and grandmother Frieda. Beloved husband and father Jacob.' So it goes on and on, the endurance of those who have not endured.

And again like Beckett, Roth cannot resist a cemetery joke. The gentile caretaker of the Jewish cemetery, Mr Crawford, who has worked there long enough to talk himself about 'shvartzes', is one. Crawford cannot find Sabbath the plot he wants, next to his family, but he finds him somewhere else, and consoles him by elevating what has been levelled: 'Yeah, but you're across from a very fine family. The Weizmans.' Sabbath buys the plot. Then he drives into town to visit his old cousin, a man called Fish. Sabbath feels stirred, weepy, late. He finds Fish at home, sitting in his living room. Fish is 100 years old, 'a mere mist of a man'. Sabbath is struck by his endurance: 'The incapacity to die. Sitting it out instead. This thought made

Sabbath intensely excited: *the perverse senselessness of just remaining, of not going.*' Roth's sensitivities, his ironies, quiver in these scenes. For Fish cannot recall Sabbath, though Sabbath tells him that he and his brother Morty, when children, used to help him go round the streets selling vegetables. Sabbath has spent more and more of the novel in memory. He realizes that if he asks Fish questions, prods him gently, persists with him, he will get some kind of retrieval.

Persistence, he tells us, is the secret. The reader jolts: persistence is precisely how Sabbath has defined sexual seduction. And suddenly one realizes that Sabbath is not seducing Fish, but memory itself. The man is chatting up temporality. He is wooing the past; and since this is *his* past, wooing himself. It is the sad onanism of self-memory. At this gorgeous point in the book, a chandelier of gathered moments, all the novel's collected tensions and themes, hangs over this scene to light a strange and new path. It is exquisite. In a moment, Sabbath expels his nihilistic antibodies, and turns sex not into death but into the recovery of life. This is Sabbath's finest inversion, the redemption of all his nihilism: that he might, as he dreamed, turn life back like turning back the clock at fall, and exchange not life for death, but death for life. The inversion of nihilism's inversions. Roth is supremely tactful here. He does not spell any of this out. It is simply implied in his climactic return of the idea of 'persistence'. Certainly, old Fish lives a kind of living death, but it is, wonderfully, a continuous present, for Fish, befuddled, imagines that Sabbath's father is still alive, and somewhere in town. 'He sent you over here? Or what?' he asks. 'Yeah', Sabbath replies about his father. 'He sent me over here.' 'Isn't that remarkable', sighs old Fish.

Sabbath steals a carton of his brother's army mementos from his cousin Fish, and, deeply moved, he wanders down to the seashore. He takes out his brother's memorial flag: 'There he unfurled it, a flag with forty-eight stars, wrapped himself in it, and in the mist there, wept and wept . . . And all from only a single carton. Imagine, then, the history of the world. We are immoderate because grief is immoderate, all the hundreds and thousands of kinds of grief.' Roth's prose, moving on its thousand racing feet, is so mobile here, so absorptive. With what ease it leans back into the middle of the book and plucks out Yeats's apparently discarded poem, and then Fish's gently extravagant adjective, 'remarkable'. Sabbath sees that he cannot bring back the past, and that even the small change of his childhood has been spent: 'The boardwalk was gone. Good-bye, boardwalk. The ocean had finally carried it away ... Remarkable. Yes, that's the word for it. It was all remarkable. Good-bye, remarkable. Egypt and Greece good-bye, and good-bye, Rome!'

Partially redeemed, partially purged, but as unhappy as ever, Sabbath goes on his hate-strewn way. He leaves New Jersey and returns to his wife. 'And he couldn't do it. He could not fucking die. How could he leave? How could he go? Everything he hated was here.' With characteristic relentlessness, and with compassion, this profound novel ends as it might well begin again, in the basement of the soul.

Julian Barnes and the Problem of Knowing
Too Much

Two landscapes, one American and one English, from roughly
the same period. The American landscape is seen by Willa
Cather, in *My Antonía* (1918), and the English landscape is seen
by E. M. Forster, in *The Longest Journey* (1907).
In a celebrated moment in Cather's story, her narrator sits by
a window in Lincoln, Nebraska. He is a student. 'My window
was open, and the earthy wind blowing through made me
indolent. On the edge of the prairie, where the sun had gone
down, the sky was turquoise blue, like a lake, with gold light
throbbing in it.' The man is reading Virgil's *Georgics*. He is
bluntly halted by a line of the poetry: 'for I shall be the first, if I
live, to bring the Muse into my country.' This is a moment of
soft revelation for the narrator. It is also the means by which
Willa Cather establishes her own originality, the obligation she
might feel, as a novelist of the West, to bring the Muse into her
country. But at no point does Cather say this, or even play with
direct statement. Instead, she rustles with suggestion, letting us
know, as if this moment were like the prairie itself, that we are
on the verge of a discovery that can hardly be voiced. Her
narrator comments: 'We left the classroom quietly, conscious
that we had been brushed by the wing of a great feeling . . .'
In *The Longest Journey*, Forster's hero, Rickie, sits on a hill in
Wiltshire. Forster comments: 'Here is the heart of our island:
the Chilterns, the North Downs, the South Downs radiate
hence. The fibres of England unite in Wiltshire, and did we

condescend to worship her, here we should erect our national shrine.' Rickie reflects on how much he loves 'these unostentatious fields'. Then he pulls out a volume of Shelley, and recites a poem. Though the poem annoys him, it is clear that in some way Shelley consecrates this moment and this piece of land.

Both passages are characteristic of their authors, and perhaps characteristic of the literary traditions that produced them. Cather's land is ancient – as ancient as Virgil's soil – but anciently unknown. It is unliterary. If literature is brought to plough it, then this imposition will be a strenuous and artisanal task, with 'an earthy wind blowing through'. Just as Cather's narrator leaves the classroom quietly, so does her writing. It swerves away from the academic, away from knowledge, away from cleverness, away from the merely known. Its window is open. Yet the writing trembles hugely, with an earnestness towards truth, and an aroused plainness.

Forster's English landscape is not unknown, but already sacred. Forster can condescend to the idea of erecting a national shrine precisely because the land is already its own shrine, hallowed and binding. England is known, named, literary. Forster's writing is cosy, prissy-clever. It has a contract with the reader, to whom Forster makes direct address ('our island'). It is slackly written – the word 'fibres' is at once lame, in a literary sense, and awkwardly hints at moral fibre or backbone. Cather is suggestive, stroking the not-said; Forster is explicit, and eager to clear things up. Where Cather's theme is unbreathed, rising like a bird to brush its subject, Forster elbows aside his protagonist, and delivers one of his King's College hearthside chats. Where Cather respects a mystery, Forster engulfs one.

Now both novelists have their own powers and their own feeblenesses, and are so different from each other that a pairing, let alone a comparison, is perhaps invalid at any moment other than in this doubled reflection on landscape, and in any place other than inside the death row of literary criticism. Cather, in poorer books, can be weakly reticent, and Forster, at his best, can be powerfully talkative. Explicitness, and a zeal for the explanatory, is no necessary impediment in a novelist. One of America's greatest contemporary writers, Saul Bellow, is a rich explainer, yet one of the greatest twentieth-century English novelists, Virginia Woolf, had a horror of the explicit. Nevertheless, these two passages surely represent two different approaches to description, and I will go further and claim that Cather's seems to me a kind of perfection, and Forster's a kind of ruination. In Forster's passage, one hears a certain tone – literary, a little fussy, meddlingly foreclosing – that has sounded again and again in English writing since Forster's day. The cognitive neatness, the fondness for direct statement, the fat hand with theme and symbol, the knowingness – all can be found in the works of William Golding, of Ian McEwan, of Angela Carter. A contemporary novelist such as A.S. Byatt sounds hardly different from Forster when she indulges her intolerable urge, like him, to speak over her characters, and tell them in effect, as Matthew Arnold described the early Romantic poets, that they *do not know enough*: 'Mr Rose, had he had access to the whole elaboration of this pleasing metaphor, with its roots in folklore and childhood culture, hallucination and dream, might, or might not, have understood something about Marcus that he did not already understand.' (*Still Life.*)

And this is the sound of Julian Barnes, who, despite his reputation as 'a novelist of ideas', his interest in France, and his Anglo-American suavity, is a thoroughly English writer, squarely in Forster's descent. Like Forster, he is brisk with mystery, gently pedantic, undeniably clever, and certainly cosy. He is Forster without Forster's grand liberalism, and without the moving uncertainties of *A Passage To India*. He has adapted Forster's penchant for interrupting his texts (Woolf complained that Forster was like a light sleeper who was always getting up to come into the next room) into a mode of direct address with his readers. He is entirely literary, and fond of literary games. Like Forster, he has an essentially neat mind; he clears up his intellectual mess as he goes along. Life, in Barnes's books, is a picnic of the mind. Barnes spreads a cloth, and then presents mysteries, riddles, and games for our ingestion. Actually, under sceptical investigation, these riddles and games begin to look like simplicities that are merely camouflaged as fiendish complexities. His fiction is beguiling because it is confident about the known and jauntily undaunted by the unknown.

Barnes is rather celebrated for the fat and waxy health of his 'ideas'. But his fiction is addicted to fact. It proposes riddles and mysteries which then, in a quiet spirit of self-satisfaction, it solves. Of course, his solutions are not announced as such. Often, they are announced as further complications. But in Barnes's world, mysteries are clearer for their enunciation as such. Perplexity need never cause real pain. Talk clears the air, and is preferred to silence. And so, when Barnes tells us that something is complicated, or paradoxical, it does not sound complicated or paradoxical any longer. 'But then the quotidian is often preposterous, and so the preposterous may in return be plausible', as the narrator of one of the stories in his collection, *Cross Channel,* helpfully offers. Barnes smooths his world into summation. Nothing in this world escapes summation, not least those moments which he tells us are escaping summation.

Is this the gift of hard simplicity? Or is it not in fact the trick of easy difficulty – merely the first half of the escape artist's act, when he is facilely imprisoning himself? Certainly, Barnes likes to entangle himself. His usual method is to select a simplicity and turn it into a riddle. What he seems to do, in such a circumstance, is to complicate something. But his complications do not cross his simplicities at any moment; they run parallel to them. His novel *A History of the World in $10\frac{1}{2}$ Chapters* is a concertina of riddles, but it is dedicated, in all its expansions and contractions, to the production of an easy and solving music. One of its contractions – its half-chapter – is called 'Parenthesis', and it has become celebrated, for it is a full-throated contemporary song of love, when such proclamations are rare. (It appears in anthologies of love, and suchlike.) In 'Parenthesis', the novel's narrator, speaking with the authority and range of the real Julian Barnes, attempts to probe the mystery of love. The

probing is entirely typical of Barnes's procedures. First, we must
overpower a simplicity, and make it seem more difficult to itself.
'Let's start at the beginning. Love makes you happy? No. Love
makes the person you love happy? No. Love makes everything
all right? Indeed no.' Love is not the simplicity we thought it
was, says Barnes. (But this simplicity is his making, not ours. His
repeated 'No's' are apparently stern corrections to phantom
questions. How many of Barnes's readers think that 'love makes
everything all right'?)

Next, Barnes fakes – the word is not too strong – the motions
of argument. Having established his mystery, he offers deeper
mysteries. But the mysteries he offers are as simple as the simple
misapprehensions he thinks he is defeating. We think that the
heart is a simple organ, Barnes asserts. (Do we?) But 'the heart
isn't heart-shaped.' Barnes provides some stubborn facts about
the heart, such as that in a child, 'the heart is proportionately
much larger than in an adult', and that 'after death the heart
assumes the shape of a pyramid'. Barnes's narrator visits the
butcher, and buys an ox's heart. He dissects it 'with a radiologist
friend'. The result of these labours: the heart is not a simple
organ, says Barnes. Internally, it is complex and bloody and
messy. One should note the motion here: again, we are being
warned against simplicity in a manner that is itself simplifying.
That the half-chapter's final message about love is, at the end of
these mental labours, childishly solving, and cosily fenced, is not
a surprise: 'Love won't change the history of the world . . . but
it will do something much more important: teach us to stand up
to history, to ignore its chin-out strut . . . How you cuddle in
the dark governs how you see the history of the world.' How
you cuddle! But that is exactly what Barnes offers his readers: a
kind of intellectual cuddle, not in the dark, but in good,
cleansing daylight.

This is not a prose of discovery, but of the idea of discovery.
This is why, although he enjoys metaphor, and uses it
abundantly, his metaphors do not deepen or complicate his

world. Comparing his wife's easy sleep with his own restless-
ness, the narrator in 'Parenthesis' confesses: 'I admire her
because she's got this job of sleeping that we all have to do,
every night, ceaselessly, better worked out than I have. She
handles it like a sophisticated traveller unthreatened by a new
airport. Whereas I lie there in the night with an expired
passport, pushing a baggage trolley with a squeaking wheel
across to the wrong carousel.' Set aside the childish, entirely
unaffecting nature of this metaphor. Note merely that curiously,
although Barnes wants us to compare the order of one approach
to sleep with the disorder of the other, both are subsumed
within the simplifying order of his metaphor. The wife's
serenity sounds as easy as the husband's anarchy, because both
have been trivialized.

This is one of Barnes's intellectual habits. Two opposing ideas
are selected; but as they collide, they each expose the absurdity
and vulnerability of their opposing extremity. This is neat
enough to watch, but seems easy, for what is difficult is not the
vulnerability of extremity, but the troublesome solidity of what
is in the middle, of what is not extreme. This is what Hans
Castorp painfully learns in *The Magic Mountain*; it is indeed the
very fabric of Mann's novel. As the Fool warns King Lear:
'Thou hast pared thy wit on both sides and left nothing i' th'
middle.' So has Barnes. One of his short stories, 'Junction', is
about the building of the Rouen–Paris–Le Havre railway line in
the 1840s. The story tidily deploys and tidily solves, while
pretending not to. The rail-building interests Barnes because the
line was largely built by English navvies, and is thus one of the
'Cross Channel' entanglements of the French and the British
that provides his book of stories with its title-theme. 'Junction'
generates a collision between the opposition of scientific
triumphalism (the railway) and religious obscurantism (a local
curé's belief that the line is preparing not the path of French
travellers, but the way of the Lord). Barnes nicely exposes the
weakness and the comedy of both extremities. The story is
charming, and zany with fact.

Cross Channel ends with a story called 'Tunnel', which is about an 'elderly English gentleman' who takes the Chunnel train from London to Paris, in the year 2015. He reflects on many of the themes and some of the situations in the book's preceding stories. We suspect that this reflective gentleman may well be Barnes himself. As indeed he is. The story ends, happily enough: 'And the elderly English gentleman, when he returned home, began to write the stories you have just read.' Earlier in this story, Barnes meditates on something that one of his narrators has already announced: the preposterousness of ordinary reality, and hence the ordinariness of the preposterous. The elderly author, thinking about the trick reality plays on the creative imagination, remembers a woman seen frantically searching her handbag at an airport. What had she lost? Surely, the writer thinks, it could not be something humdrum, like lipstick or camera film. Perhaps it is a 'contraceptive item whose absence would imperil the holiday?' The woman is in his party, and days later, after obsessing about it, he asks her what she had lost at the airport. Her boarding card, she replies. The author is deliriously happy at the foolishness of the quotidian, and is uncertain which delights him more, 'the excess of his misprisions or the primness of the truth'. This is nicely phrased. But note that both positions, his misprisions, and the truth, are excessive in their ways. The author's imagination, which invented all kinds of disasters for the frantic lady, is excessively imaginative; and the truth, which muzzled imagination with its quiet actuality, is excessively quiet. The misprision is too great a misprision, and the primness is too prim. And both are a little ridiculous, and somewhat trivialized. Both have been caricatured, and what is being enjoyed here is not the *deep* comic surprise of ordinariness (as in Chekhov, say), but the mere pantomime of banality.

So Barnes's fiction caricatures truth while playing games with it. Many of these games have to do with fact. Barnes is in love with facts – true facts, false facts, funny facts, ironic facts. *Flaubert's Parrot*, Barnes's first great success, is an attractive enough meditation on fact. Barnes takes the details of Flaubert's life, and stretches them until they no longer have the dependable silence of facts, but the smart reply of riddle or paradox. He likes to enslave facts with a sense of their own constructedness. For example, it is well known that when Flaubert and his friend Du Camp climbed the largest pyramid in Giza to watch the dawn, Flaubert found, attached to the top of the pyramid, a calling card that said *Humbert, Frotteur*, and an address in Rouen, Flaubert's own town. Barnes notes that this seems to us one of the great modern ironies. Yet, Barnes goes on to explain, Flaubert's friend Du Camp had planted the card there the night before; and Flaubert had himself brought the card from Rouen to Egypt. Was Flaubert planning his own traveller's ironies? Barnes, it seems, destabilizes fact, makes the familiar less familiar than we had imagined it to be.

But despite Barnes's postmodern compound eye – the writer, locust-like, seeing around and behind all truths – he is old-fashionedly in love with the surety of fact. In this, he displays his Englishness. He is not a European Pyrrhonist so much as an English empiricist – more precisely, a rogue empiricist, for whom facts, real ones and faked ones, are all pieces of information. *Le Figaro* has praised Barnes for 'the abundance of original thought, the wealth of information' in his work. (Who reads fiction for a 'wealth of information'? Original thought puts 'information' on a diet, rations it.) It is hard to tell if he is feeding us true or false information. And this is the point. Some of it seems benignly verifiable, such as the information that Flaubert likened himself to a camel, and that '*chameau*, camel, was slang for an old courtesan. I do not think this association would have put Flaubert off.' Noting that Flaubert also likened himself to a bear, Barnes's narrator gushes forth bear-information: 'William Scoresby, the Arctic explorer, noted that the liver of the bear is poisonous – the only part of any quadruped known to be so. Among zoo-keepers there is no known test for pregnancy in the polar bear. Strange facts that Flaubert might not have found strange.'

But some of Barnes's facts are more obscure. The elderly English gentleman in 'Tunnel', for instance, remarks, as the train passes through Lille, that he could get off and visit 'the last surviving French slag-heap'. But the story is set in 2015. Is this Barnes's prediction of where France's last slag-heap will be situated? Much of Barnes's fiction deals in historical information – about Victorian railways, or an English cricket team that was preparing to travel to France in 1789, while revolution breaks. Most readers will be sure about the Rouen-Paris railway, but unsure about the eighteenth-century cricket team. In Barnes's style of narrative, however – and this is the important point – there are no such things as ruined facts, for all that he goes around happily destroying them. For the facts that Barnes explodes or complicates have the *same status* as the true facts (like the building of the French railways) that he leaves alone. That is, all his facts startle so as to soothe.

How? First, they offer the riddle of their strangeness – cricket was last played at the Olympics, in 1900, in Los Angeles, according to Barnes – and then the impregnability of their existence, which is itself a kind of solution to their strangeness. Even when we suspect the accuracy of certain facts, they are still soothing, because they connect us to the known world. Even inaccurate facts have a kind of empirical electricity for Barnes, because they connect him to a larger informational zealousness. Wrong facts connect us to the world of true facts because they contain within themselves the seed of their own correction, the ghost of their own accuracy, in the same way as a good parody says something true about its object. Wrong facts, in the Barnes world, may be seen as parodies of true facts; and just as soothing. This is because Barnes is a cognitive meliorist, for whom the world is, despite his games, old-fashionedly knowable. When we learn, in *Flaubert's Parrot*, about the complicating ironies of that calling card at the top of the Egyptian pyramid, we complicate our knowledge; but not very much, and it is always better, in Barnes's world, to know more than to know less. It is knowingness as an aesthetic. However he muddies the waters, he always ferries us across. Helpfully, he points out that the waters are now very muddy, because he has stirred them up, but he is still ferrying us.

In fiction, this regime of fact is, necessarily, despotic. Of course, all fictional description contains fact, and description is explanation. Facts cement narrative's relationship with the known. The writer must then make a revolution with this description-explanation. In Barnes's fiction, however, facts are separated from description and handed out like coins to the reader. His writing does little with them, descriptively. All this information comes from the known world, and merely passes through Barnes's writing on its way to the reader, who is also in the known world. It is as if Barnes's prose is merely a host to this passage. As a result, his fiction is one of tidy statement. He likes to order his themes even as he proclaims that he is scattering ideas all over the floor. In his story 'Experiment', Barnes has fun with the jauntiness of his factual load: a narrator tells us about the strange tale of his Uncle Freddy, who as a young man in Paris in 1928 once took part in André Breton's Surrealist Group's researches into sexuality. The hearty Englishman, sitting next to Breton and Queneau, and forced to intellectualize, Gallic-fashion, about the commonsensical business of sex, is a fine *donnée*, and is amusing. But it is precisely the jauntiness of fact – did an Englishman really participate in these famous sessions? – which imprisons the story, and makes it a revolving conceit rather than a grasped truth. 'Experiment' is itself an experiment, controlled, sealed, and finite.

This tidiness is a peculiar problem of English fiction in this century. A writer like D. H. Lawrence, who bullies his reader but who also bullies himself, whose prose is a violent bloom of awkwardness – such a writer is the exception in modern English fiction. Kipling, whose stories have a vigorous reticence, is a different exception to the English zeal for plain-speaking. Barnes's story 'Evermore', about a woman's lifelong mourning for her brother, who was killed in the First World War, is strongly reminiscent of two Kipling stories on a similar theme,

'The Gardener', and 'Mary Postgate'. In 'Evermore', we learn of Miss Moss, an ageing proof-reader, who makes obsessive visits in her antique Morris Minor car to the French war cemetery where her brother lies. She cannot forget him, and has dedicated her life to remembrance. It is a touching story. When Barnes is most like Kipling, he comes closest to defeating his own intellectual tidiness, and to producing something that discovers grief, rather than something which tells us about grief. But even here, Barnes will not let his material flow its own way. He cannot resist bustling around. Where Kipling's two stories about a woman's grief subtract, Barnes's story over-supplies. Kipling seems to tell us everything about Mary Postgate, except about her obsessive hatred of the Germans. Barnes cannot help informing us that Miss Moss's life was 'devoted . . . entirely to her own commemorations'. Miss Moss is given to ask herself the kinds of rhetorical questions, perfectly expressed, that only characters in stories ask themselves, such as: 'Was it a vice to have become such a connoisseur of grief?' We are told about her 'voluptuous selfishness of grief', a phrase whose own luxuriousness condescends, somewhat, to Miss Moss. And this sentimentality of explicitness: 'She claimed no understanding of military matters. All she claimed was an understanding of grief.' The story is themed. Its own devotion to commemoration does not make clearer its protagonist's devotion, but drowns it. By the end, Barnes is interrupting, like Forster, and talking directly to the reader – making his own appeal, literalizing the theme of remembrance: 'if this [forgetting the First World War] happened to the individual, could it not also happen on a national scale?'

Narrative must discover. The facts that it 'discovers' already exist, of course; but great fiction is not daunted by the prior existence of the world. Great fiction appears to discover facts by giving us the impression that our reading of the text completes the bottom half of a discovery whose plaintive stalk the writer has merely uncovered. Fiction should seem to offer itself to the reader's completion, not to the writer's. This whisper of conspiracy is one of fiction's necessary beauties. Perhaps this illusion of discovery, the uncovering of a world which is related to, but not continuous with, the known world, is fiction's greatest beauty: fiction's false bottom. It cannot be said enough: this is not, as in the fiction of Julian Barnes, the false bottom of fact, by which we learn one certainty only to have it replaced by another, brighter, or more complicated certainty. It is the false bottom of truth, whereby we learn many things, all of them bottomless. Fiction must not stroke the known but distress the undiscovered. A literature of fact, of knowingness, like Barnes's, like too much recent English fiction, knows too much and speaks too much. But a literature that discovers, that dares to know less, is always on the verge of what is not sayable, rather than at the end of what has just been said.

W.G. Sebald's Uncertainty

Anxious, daring, extreme, muted – only an annulling wash of contradictory adjectives can approach the agitated density of W.G. Sebald's writing. For this German who has lived in England for over thirty years is one of the most mysteriously sublime of contemporary European writers. When his book *The Emigrants* appeared, one immediately recalled Walter Benjamin's remark in his essay on Proust, that all great works found a new genre or dissolve an old one. Here was the first contemporary writer since Beckett to have found a way to protest the good government of the conventional novel-form and to harass realism into a state of self-examination.

His book *The Rings of Saturn* is yet more uncanny than *The Emigrants*. In it, a man who might be Sebald walks around the English counties of Norfolk and Suffolk. The book is curlingly set in the present, but this man is something of an old-fashioned journeyman, a turnpike-pounder, as if from a nineteenth-century tale. The book is divided into ten bending and opaque chapters. The narrator alights upon certain natural and man-made features: a town here, a village there, a strange piece of the coast, a church, and several country houses. Like *The Emigrants*, it is amphibiously slippery, neither quite fiction nor travelogue, and yet always absolutely artistic.

In *The Emigrants*, Sebald told the stories of four men, each of whom had been menaced by twentieth-century history. The book was not really about the Holocaust, as American readers have claimed, and it was most certainly not about Nazism.

Sebald's subjects were victims of slightly different kinds of upheaval or catastrophe: two were casualties of Nazism, and two of exile, and all, like nineteenth-century fictional characters, had had their lives eaten at by sadness, by a kind of internal wasting sickness which Sebald superbly evoked. The two exiles furnished, perhaps, the most mysterious tales: Dr Henry Selwyn was a Lithuanian Jew who arrived in England as a child at the turn of the century. When Sebald met him in the 1970s, Selwyn was at the end of his life, and was quietly demented. He had retreated from his country house to live in a stone folly of his own making in his garden. He shot himself dead a few years after telling Sebald his story. The other exile, Sebald's Great-Uncle Ambros Adelwarth, left Germany in the early years of the century, and worked for a long time as a butler for a Long Island family called the Solomons. Ambros want mad, and died in an Ithaca asylum in the early 1960s. Three of these characters actually existed, and one was partly based on the British painter Frank Auerbach, yet *The Emigrants* reads like fiction – and *is* fiction – because of the care and patterning of Sebald's narration, because of its anguished interiority, and because Sebald so mixes established fact with unstable invention that the two categories copulate and produce a kind of truth which lies just beyond verification: that is, fictional truth.

On its own, this would not be remarkable, of course. What is remarkable about *The Emigrants* and *The Rings of Saturn* is the reticent artificiality of Sebald's narration, whereby fact is taken from the real world, and made fictional. This is the opposite of the trivial 'factional' breeziness of writers such as Julian Barnes or Umberto Eco, who take facts and superficially destabilize them within fiction, who make facts quiver a little, but whose entire work is actually in homage to the superstition of fact. Such writers do not believe deeply enough in the fictional to abandon the actual world; they toy with accuracy, are indeed obsessed with questions of accuracy and inaccuracy, for even inaccurate facts, to such writers, have a kind of empirical electricity, since they connect us to a larger informational zealousness. This informational neurosis makes their fiction buzzingly unaffecting. Facts are a sport for such writers, a semiotic superfluity, ultimately quite readable.

For Sebald, however, facts are indecipherable, and therefore tragic. Sebald works in exactly the opposite way to Barnes or Eco. Though his deeply elegiac books are made out of the cinders of the real world, he makes facts fictive by binding them so deeply into the forms of their narratives that these facts seem never to have belonged to the actual world, and seem only to have found their proper life within Sebald's prose. This, of course, is the movement of any powerful fiction, however realistic: the real world gains a harsher, stronger life within a fiction because it receives a concentrated patterning which actual life does not exert. It is not that facts merely *seem* fictive in Sebald's work; it is that they actually *become* fictive even though they remain true and real (for instance, it is true that Sebald's great-uncle left Germany in the early years of the century). They become fictive not in the sense that they become untrue or are distorted, but in the sense that they become newly real, in a way parasitical of, yet rivalrous to, the real world.

In addition to the delicacy of his patterning, Sebald invests his narrations with a scrupulous uncertainty. Again, although he wants us to reflect on this uncertainty, his self-reflexive procedures differ from much postmodernism in important respects. Sebald's reticence is more than teasing; it is the sound of anguish. Sebald's narrators, in both *The Emigrants* and *The Rings of Saturn*, are somewhat proximate to Sebald: they are German men who live in England, and who teach. Yet they are also voices in pain, and their pain is that they do not seem to know themselves, and cannot be known by the reader because they are apparently incapable of revealing themselves. In *The Rings of Saturn*, for instance, the narrator appears to be half-mad, wandering around Suffolk and Norfolk collecting stray information. An uneasy comedy is never far away. When this narrator stops in Southwold, he tells us: 'Whenever I am in Southwold, the Sailors' Reading Room is by far my favourite haunt.'

Beckett is the most obvious influence here, and in both writers uncertainty is always raised to a metaphysical power. Self-reflexion in such writers is the text pinching itself to see if it actually exists.

Consider Sebald's use of photographs, which, in different hands, might easily degenerate into a glib game of spot-the-truth. In both *The Emigrants* and *The Rings of Saturn*, uncaptioned photographs are included, most of which seem to relate to a place or an incident in the text, but some of which do not. It seems likely that Sebald borrowed this idea from Stendhal's autobiography, *The Life of Henri Brulard*, throughout which Stendhal litters his own often unreliable drawings and diagrams. But Sebald uses his photographs solemnly, elegiacally, and rarely jauntily. If one passage can suggest the frail beauties, the dreamy suggestiveness and the soft pain of Sebald's work, it might be a passage from *The Emigrants*, in which Sebald is walking with his Uncle Kasimir, on the beach in New Jersey. He has come here to gather information on the strange and sad life of his great-uncle. Uncle Kasimir looks at the sea:

> I often come out here, said Uncle Kasimir, it makes me feel that I am a long way away, though I never quite know from where. Then he took a camera out of his large-check jacket and took this picture, a print of which he sent me two years later, probably when he had finally shot the whole film, together with his pocket watch.

Under this paragraph, Sebald prints a photograph of a man who looks a little like the author, standing on a beach. But the photograph is so murky that it is impossible to tell. We are encouraged to look at the photograph, which then turns us away from itself, converting the passage, very movingly, into a meditation on visibility. The book's deep theme, after all, is visibility: how we see the past, and how it sees us. Sebald has arrived in New Jersey partly to look at old photographs of his great-uncle. His Uncle Kasimir has been standing on the beach 'gazing out at the ocean', trying to see something he cannot articulate – the past, perhaps. And then come these two sentences, whose literary care is immense: the blurred photograph reminds us that we cannot read this narrator; the tiny, pregnant detail about how it took Uncle Kasimir *two years* to shoot the rest of the film suggests a life without photographs, a life without much sense of its own visibility. And the detail of the pocket watch closes the scene like a still life, like a skull in a Renaissance painting, suggesting Time vainly controlled (by the writer who has assembled these constituents) and also lost (by these characters).

In both books, Sebald's language is an extraordinary, almost antiquarian edifice, full of the daintiest lustres. He is helped in this by an English poet, Michael Hulse, who renders Sebald's German into English. Sebald then powerfully treads his own English into Hulse's, sometimes rewriting entire passages. One of the oddest effects of this prose is a quality of melodrama and extremism running alongside a soft mutedness. Sebald's melodramatic side, one suspects, comes from the mid-nineteenth-century German tale, such as was written by Adalbert Stifter. Often, in *The Rings of Saturn*, Sebald's narrator finds himself on a desolate heath, or caught in a storm, like the narrator of Stifter's tale 'Limestone'. (Often, Sebald's English prose is almost indistinguishable in diction from Stifter's in English translation.) There is a quality of the Gothic about Sebald, written up in dementedly patient locutions: 'I stuck to the sandy path until to my astonishment, not to say horror, I found myself back again at the same tangled thicket from which I had emerged about an hour before . . .' Speaking of Belgium, Sebald's narrator notes that that country seems physically scarred by the memory of its vicious colonialism in the Congo; he allows himself a rant, which sounds deliberately antiquarian:

And indeed, to this day one sees in Belgium a distinctive ugliness, dating from the time when the Congo colony was exploited without restraint and manifested in the macabre atmosphere of certain salons and the strikingly stunted growth of the population, such as one rarely comes across elsewhere. At all events, I well recall that on my first visit to Brussels in December 1964 I encountered more hunchbanks and lunatics than normally in a whole year.

One notes again the desperate comedy, and the strongly artificial, even dumbfounding, prose. A sentence like 'the macabre atmosphere of certain salons' exists in its own register of rhetorical excess; it does not really refer to anything outside language. What salons are these? Indeed, for all the apparent quietness of Sebald's prose, exaggeration is its principle, an exaggeration he has undoubtedly learned in part from Thomas Bernhard. Sebald's pessimism is Bernhard-like, too; as the narrator puts it here: 'In reality of course, whenever one is imagining a bright future, the next disaster is just around the corner.'

Bernhard exaggerates the grotesque; Sebald, by contrast, exaggerates the elegiac. But where Bernhard uses a Nietzschean hammer, Sebald's exaggeration is squeezed through a dream-like reticence. This effect does not resemble any other writer. On the one hand, the narrator of *The Rings of Saturn* tells us often that the world is dwindling, that nothing is as it used to be: there are fewer herring in the sea; all the elms that used to sway in England's woods and gardens have died, victims of the terible Dutch elm disease; all the country houses Sebald visits in East Anglia were once thriving and are now either defunct or have become popular museums. Yet on the other hand, this narrator donates this information narrowly, slipping it to us by way of the dreamiest indirections. Early in the book, for example, the narrator reaches a beach: 'I reached Benacre Broad, a lake of brackish water beyond a bank of shingle halfway between Lowestoft and Southwold. The lake is encircled by deciduous woodland that is now dying, owing to the steady erosion of the coastline by the sea. Doubtless it is only a matter of time before one stormy night the shingle bank is broken, and the appearance of the entire area changes.'

The coastline of East Anglia is subject to severe erosion, and this causes the narrator to remember the story of one Major George Wyndham Le Strange, whose obituary he has recently come across in a local newspaper. This Le Strange was one of the British soldiers who liberated the camp at Belsen in April 1945. As with so many of Sebald's subjects, this event appears to have corroded his normality. The narrator tells us that Le Strange retreated from life, letting his large house and grounds fall into ruin, and sharing his life only with a cook, to whom he left the estate when he died. The narrator moves away from this story, and says:

> As these things were going through my mind I was watching the sand martins darting to and fro over the sea. Ceaselessly emitting their tiny cries they sped along their flight-paths faster than my eyes could follow them. At earlier times, in the summer evenings during my childhood when I had watched from the valley as swallows circled in the last light, still in great numbers in those days, I would imagine that the world was held together by the courses they flew through the air.

This is very beautiful, and its strangeness is what is beautiful. We know nothing about this narrator. He has, so far, revealed little about his childhood, about its location; we assume it to be roughly contiguous with Sebald's. (Germany in the 1950s; Sebald was born in 1944.) But suddenly, this man who has told us nothing about himself, delivers this: 'At earlier times, in the summer evening during my childhood when I had watched from the valley . . .' He speaks of these 'earlier times' as if they were already familiar to us, as if we had dreamed them. And then follows this mysterious, utterly unfounded lament: 'as swallows circled in the last light, still in great numbers in those days . . .' But why would the swallows have disappeared? Why would they have been so abundant 'in earlier times' – whenever exactly those times were? Slowly the reader gathers the beautiful complexity of Sebald's elegy. This narrator mourns not only for what is lost (the swallows), but for what he has had to leave out of his own narrative. *All that has disappeared from his life is what has also disappeared from the narrative.* This is why neither we, nor he, can make sense of these backward glances. Reticence becomes the very stutter of mourning. This resembles a careful attenuation, almost a reversal, of Proustian retrospect: in Sebald, we are defined by the terrible abundance of our lacunae. And so the narrator who tells us that as a child he believed that the world was held together by the courses the birds took through the air, is now simply holding his life together by the strange courses his sentences take.

Rather than other books, it is a film that most resembles Sebald's lovely combination of opacity and extremity: Werner Herzog's *Caspar Hauser,* to which Sebald silently alludes in *The Emigrants* (his work is saturated in reference). In that film, Caspar is asked by his mentor why nothing has been going right since he escaped from the prison he was kept in for the first twenty years of his life. 'I have the feeling,' says Caspar – dreamily, modestly, but also grandiloquently – 'that my life since that moment has been a great fall.' All of Sebald's characters have experienced some kind of 'great fall', beginning with the narrators of his books.

Like Caspar Hauser, the narrator of *The Rings of Saturn* dreams of the desert, and is something of a brilliant child, wandering around a landscape both real and imagined, at a finely bemused angle to all knowledge. As he tramps through East Anglia, he communicates with the dead, and ponders the strangest information, with which he is insanely profligate – the destruction of trees, the habits of the silkworm. He communicates to the reader in a language of exceptional beauty, whose diction is also imprisoned, as if only just escaped from the nineteenth century: 'The day was dull and oppressive, and there was so little breeze that not even the ears of the delicate quaking grass were nodding.' Or: 'The water in the gutter gurgled like a mountain stream.' Always, an alienated dreaminess pervades everything. The narrator visits a family called the Ashburys in Ireland. They live in a crumbling mansion: 'The curtains had gone and the paper had been stripped off the walls, which had traces of whitewash with bluish streaks like the skin of a dying body, and reminded me of one of those maps of the far north on which next to nothing is marked.' He is attracted again and again to all that is dwindling and passing. At Somerleyton Hall, he sees nothing but grasses and weeds where once was a thriving estate: 'It takes just one awful second, I often think, and an entire epoch passes.' It is just the same at Sudbourne Hall, where the flamboyant Sir Cuthbert Quilter once held sway. At Dunwich, on the coast, Sebald tells us that one of the most important ports in Europe during the Middle Ages now lies underwater: 'All of it has gone under, quite literally, and is now below the sea . . .'

Sebald tells the stories of eccentrics and fantasists, many of whom resemble the first subject of *The Emigrants*, Dr Henry Selwyn, the Lithuanian who reinvented himself as the perfect Englishman, but who ended his days living in a stone folly in his garden and eating only his own garden vegetables. We encounter the memory of Edward Fitzgerald, the translator of the *Rubaiyat*, who retired at an early age to a 'tiny two-roomed cottage on the perimeter of the estate, and there he spent the next fifteen years, from 1837 till 1853, leading a bachelor life.' There Fitzgerald read and wrote, becoming increasingly eccentric. 'For decades he had eaten a diet of vegetables, offended as he was by the consumption of large quantities of rare meat which his contemporaries considered necessary to keep one's strength up, and now he altogether dispensed with the chore of cooking, which struck him as absurd, and took little but bread, butter and tea. On fine days he sat in the garden surrounded by doves, and at other times he spent long periods at the window . . .' Sebald narrates Fitzgerald's abrupt death superbly; it is a sign of how nineteenth-century is Sebald that his lives so often end with fully-told, full-blown deaths. Swinburne, the poet, is also of interest to Sebald's unhappy narrator, for Swinburne, like Fitzgerald, essentially retreated from life, and lived quietly in Putney. He 'reminded a visitor', writes Sebald, of a 'silkworm'; and it is entirely characteristic of Sebald's writing that this last fact might be invented, and that the 'visitor' might be Sebald himself.

The true subject of *The Rings of Saturn* is death. In the first section of the book, Sebald writes about (and incorporates passages from) Sir Thomas Browne's *Urn Burial*, which is about the complicated artefacts that human beings surround themselves with in death. The country houses which Sebald describes again and again in this book are like the Pyramids and pagan graves that Browne described: they are mausolea. But Sebald is always deeply self-examining, and he feels the need to include his own book among these mausolea. The silkworm is Sebald's emblem for this, and it appears throughout the book. The artist is like the silkworm, suggests Sebald, killing himself as he produces his fine thread of silk. The book ends with a moving passage, in which Sebald compares the worker at a loom to the writer or scholar. Both, he writes, are manacled to their work. An old loom, he writes, resembles a cage, and reminds us that 'we are able to maintain ourselves on this earth only by being harnessed to the machines we have invented.' Writers and scholars, like weavers, tend to suffer from 'melancholy and all the evils associated with it'. And this is understandable, writes Sebald, 'given the nature of their work, which force[s] them to sit bent over, day after day, straining to keep their eye on the complex patterns they created. It is difficult to imagine the depths of despair into which those can be driven who, even after the end of the working day, are engrossed in their intricate designs and who are pursued, into their dreams, by the feeling that they have got hold of the wrong thread.'

In this sense, we are all artists, or death-artists: in a plane from Amsterdam to Norwich, the narrator looks down and notes that one never sees people on the ground, only buildings, cars, objects: 'it is as if there were no people, only the things they have made and in which they are hiding.' Sebald is hiding in this book, of course. All of us create edifices in which to hide; these then become our mausolea.

Elegy, in England, is easy to buy, especially of the country-house kind. But what distinguishes Sebald from most English elegists is the deep unease of his elegy – its metaphysical, Germanic insistence. Sebald does not just see a Romantic-political decline in England, as say Larkin did; he sees a decline of which we are not just the inheritors but the creators, too. This, I think, is because he believes in a kind of eternal recurrence. He does not say exactly this; but his book suggests that in every historical moment we have already been here. Standing in a camera obscura on the fields of Waterloo, he looks down on the old battlefield, and remarks that history is always falsely seen: 'We, the survivors, see everything from above, see everything at once, and still we do not know how it was.' Now, 'survivors' is an odd word. How can *we* be the 'survivors' of Waterloo? We were not there. Typically opaque, Sebald proceeds in mournfully shuffled sentences touched with comedy, never underlining anything. But I take him to be suggesting that we are always the survivors of a history that we attended in a previous incarnation. Sebald's subjects, in both this book and *The Emigrants*, can escape nothing; they are always 'survivors', even of events which they never directly experienced. The virus of history infects even the inoculated. This is why the two exiles in *The Emigrants* suffer in similar ways to the two direct victims of Nazism. They are all survivors of a kind. In Sebald's world, one can be a refugee by birth, born under the sign of Saturn. This explains why so many of his characters feel like Mrs Ashbury and her daughters, the eccentric Anglo-Irish family who have escaped from life, who live in their rotting mansion and consider breeding silkworms. About them, Sebald writes that they 'lived under their roof like refugees who have come through dreadful ordeals and do not now dare to settle in the place where they have ended up.' Mrs Ashbury, sounding just like Caspar Hauser, tells the narrator: 'It seems to me sometimes that we never got used to being on this earth and life is just one great, ongoing, incomprehensible blunder.'

Sebald's pessimism is not really metaphysical, despite being touched by the wing of eternal recurrence. It is aesthetic. In the same way that Sebald's facts appear to exist only in the fictional form that Sebald gives them, so Sebald's pessimism is a mood that can only express itself in the forms of his own books. That is to say, in patterned fragments, haltingly, uncertainly. This mood is a kind of nineteenth-century melancholia, a tendency rather than a system. Outside Sebald's books, in précis, this mood would amount to little. Inside these pages, it lives vividly; and so each book by Sebald becomes a test-case of itself, and of the artistic, for each book is indescribable except in its own terms.

Sebald's quality of elegy is quietistic. Life is a 'blunder' partly because it also seems a dream, and it seems a dream because it is dreaming us, not the other way around. The special beauty of Sebald's peroration on how the weaver and the writer are haunted by the idea that they have got hold of the wrong thread is that Sebald admits into his own books the condition of being beautifully mistaken. Sebald and his characters are haunted by the incomprehensible, the indecipherable, the wrong turn. And Sebald includes his own thread, his own course, in this category. These intensely patterned books might, after all, be in search of the wrong pattern. They are themselves silken errors. But how will we know?

The Broken Estate: The legacy of Ernest Renan and Matthew Arnold

1 The Nineteenth Century

'As soon as a religion seeks help from philosophy, its doom is inevitable', wrote Heinrich Heine, in his vibrant, playful little book *Religion and Philosophy in Germany*. 'Trying to defend itself, it talks its way further and further into its perdition. Like any other absolutism, religion must not justify itself.' Heine was right. In Europe, the high moment of Christianity's talking its way into perdition arrived in the middle of the nineteenth century, which was also the high moment of the novel's progress. This was when historical biblical criticism began to treat the Bible as if it were a biography or even a novel, and when, in turn, writers such as Ernest Renan and Matthew Arnold began to treat Jesus as if he were the hero of a novel. (Renan did, in fact, write fiction.) Novelists, meanwhile, began to treat Jesus as if he were the hero of a mystery-tale. There was a new interest in the lean Jesus of reality, as opposed to the fuller Jesus of faith. Kramskoi painted his lifelike *Christ in the Wilderness*. Renan, Gogol and Melville all travelled to Jerusalem in the 1850s and 1860s. In literature, this secular tilt freed the writer, and produced several fine, uncanny works. Balzac wrote an extraordinary story in 1831 called 'Christ in Flanders', set in the Middle Ages, in which Christ appears as a mysterious stranger on a boat, and calms a storm. In *De Profundis* (1897),

Oscar Wilde apotheosized Jesus as the greatest artist, and described the gospels as 'the four prose-poems about Christ'. Later still, D.H. Lawrence wrote 'The Man Who Died', a Nietzschean fantasy in which Jesus does not die on the cross but survives at the last minute. All these visions are characterized by their great interest in the real. Indeed, the genre of the 'mysterious stranger', the Christ-like visitor who suddenly appears and shatters domestic reality – a genre that also includes Tolstoy's 'What Men Live By', and the last part of Flaubert's 'The Legend of St Julian Hospitator' – takes the interaction of the divine and the real as its very subject. Insofar as the men and women in these stories spend their time trying to uncover the true reality of their visitor they are actually applying themselves to the 'mystery' of the incarnation, that impossible imbrication of the godly and the human. That is the true mystery of these visitations.

But the moment at which Jesus became the hero of a novel, of a 'prose-poem', he also became fictional. The old estate broke. Jesus lost his divinity, became only an inspiring fantasist. We may wonder what use Jesus is if he is a figure no different from Socrates on the one hand, and Daniel Deronda on the other. Why should we heed his difficult words, what is the flavour of his command once the taste for his authority has evaporated? Secularists perhaps relish that point in intellectual history at which Christianity loses its theological prestige, and begins to fall into the secular ranks. Yet, intellectually, a new pettiness was the first replacement of the old, divine Jesus, and it is hard not to lament the passing of actual belief when it is replaced with only a futile poetry. Christianity was not, of course, shovelled away; it was coaxed into sleep by nurses who mistakenly thought that they were healing it. Indeed, it might be said that in the last forty years of the nineteenth century, until Nietzsche's decisively cancelling work began to dominate, the feeblest evasions and weak-mindedness passed for theological rethinking.

Ernest Renan and Matthew Arnold are the chief nurses of the

sleep of nineteenth-century Christianity, and in their work one finds much false medicine. Renan was born in Brittany, in 1823, and was sent to Paris to train as a Catholic priest. But he abandoned his calling in 1845, and lost his faith at around the same time. In his *Cahiers*, he wrote in that year: 'It is scientifically obvious to me that the orthodox interpretation of the Bible is impossible to sustain.' He became a Professor of Hebrew at the Collège de France in 1862, and a year later published his very influential book, *La Vie de Jésus*. In it, Renan presents a kind of biography, or novel, of Christ's progress. He treats Christ's claim to be the son of God as merely a claim, and the resurrection as a legend created by 'credulous' followers. Jesus, suggests Renan, was a teacher of a beautiful, utopian poetry whose disciples pushed him towards a Messianic fanaticism alien to his nature. Matthew Arnold, who committed the later part of his life to the redefinition of Christianity, met Renan several times, and considered the Frenchman to be close to his own theological ambitions. In *Literature and Dogma*, 'Puritanism and the Church of England', and the volume *Last Essays* (1870), Arnold requested a religion of rationality, compatible with the new advances in science (neither he nor Renan took seriously the Gospels' claim that Jesus performed miracles), in which the test of membership would not be the evangelical one of belief, but the secular Victorian one of 'right conduct'. In 'St. Paul and Protestantism', Arnold argues that Paul did not mean that Christians would undergo an actual resurrection, but that Paul wanted Christians to die to sin on earth, and then to rise to life-in-Christ on earth. Arnold writes that 'religion is that which binds and holds us to the practice of righteousness'. In healthy opposition to Cardinal Newman's iciness, sin is not central to Christianity: 'sin is not a monster to be mused on, but an impotence to be got rid of.'

Both these writers are moving, because it is moving to witness an emergency renovation that is doomed. But Renan and Arnold were slayers of Christianity. Both writers, while believing themselves the saviours of Christianity, removed its self-justification as a religion, its claim to be true. Both doubted Jesus's claim to be the son of God, doubted his supernatural capacities, doubted resurrection and thus the idea of heaven, and doubted the very idea of God. Neither, however, could quite admit this, and both therefore twist themselves into the most exquisite evasions. A sour disingenuousness hangs over both writers. For both of them, God appears to be a force which lives inside us, and which lived most vividly inside Jesus, but which is no longer an external, and actually-existing, power. Arnold, in the preface to *Last Essays*, argues that 'for a man to obey the higher self, or reason, or whatever it is to be called, is happiness and life for him; to obey the lower is death and misery.' To do this, men must 'fasten and rest upon certain examples, precepts, and sayings, to which they perpetually recur'. Jesus becomes a role model, and God a noble pulse, beating inside us, but not outside. Notice how Arnold slides, as he advises that 'to serve God, to follow *that central clue in our moral being* [my italics] which unites us to the universal order, is no easy task.' Likewise, Renan is slippery. Jesus is a great moral teacher, a utopian poet, but his dreams of a kingdom of God have no real relevance to modern man. Thus it is that Renan is unable to define exactly what Jesus commanded and promised. On the one hand, the invention of Christianity was a great glory of humanity: 'Never did so much joy fill the breast of man. For a moment Humanity in this the most vigorous effort she ever made to rise above the world, forgot the leaden weight which binds her to earth and the sorrows of the life below. Happy he who has been able to behold this divine unfolding, and to share, were it but for one day, this unexampled illusion!' On the other hand, this rising above is an 'illusion', and Renan, like Arnold, can only redefine Christianity by internalizing it. The best Christian, he writes in his *Vie de Jésus*, is one 'who shall reproduce *in himself* [my italics] the celestial vision, and, with no millenarian dream, no chimerical paradise, no signs in the heavens, but, by the uprightness of his will and the poetry of his soul, shall be able to create anew in his heart the true kingdom of God!' As with

Arnold, religion has become good conduct and poetry. It is no longer in the precinct of truth.

Renan's book is surpassingly disingenuous on the question of truth. He condescends to Jesus and his early followers, by excusing them from the stringencies of empiricism and scientific accuracy that held sway in modern Europe; yet it is only via this same empiricism, in which Renan certainly believed, that he is able to *excuse* them from empiricism. And it is this empiricism which Renan uses to lay waste to Christianity, though surreptitiously. Jesus may have performed 'miracles', suggests Renan, but likely these were no more than a form of primitive faith-healing. Perhaps Jesus's disciples arrived on the third day, and found an empty tomb; but we do not have to believe in resurrection. 'Had his body been taken away, or did enthusiasm, always credulous, create afterwards the group of narratives by which it was sought to establish faith in the resurrection?' Jesus 'believed himself the son of God . . . But it must be remarked that these words, "superhuman" and "supernatural", borrowed from our petty theology, had no meaning in the exalted religious consciousness of Jesus. To him nature and the development of humanity were not limited kingdoms apart from God – paltry realities subjected to the laws of a hopeless empiricism.'

Here is Renan's characteristic manoeuvre: he calls nine-teenth-century standards of accuracy 'petty' and 'hopeless', and urges us to get beyond our literalist timidities so as to embrace Jesus's 'exalted' nature. Yet, using exactly this petty empiricism, Renan declines to believe in Jesus's supernaturalism! For, if Renan must only get beyond his own timid pettiness, why cannot he believe in actual miracles? And there is no doubt that Renan judges Jesus's world by the standards of mid-nineteenth-century France. For he calls Jesus's divinity a 'falsehood' while trying to argue that we must get beyond the idea of falsehood:

> It is easy for us . . . to call this falsehood, and, proud of our timid honesty, to treat with contempt the heroes who have

accepted the battle of life under other conditions. When we have effected by our scruple what *they have accomplished by their falsehoods* [my italics], we shall have the right to be severe upon them. At least, we must make a marked distinction beween societies like our own, where everything takes place in the full light of reflection, and simple and credulous communities, in which the beliefs that have governed ages have been born.

This is rather repulsive, is it not? Renan appears to think that he is being fair and just to Jesus's world, and lectures us on the importance of not being too 'severe'. Yet his own condescension is the greatest severity possible. Warning us not to judge this society by modern standards, he does exactly that, in deciding that Jesus's divinity is a 'falsehood'. And yet he praises himself for *not* doing that, and pompously warns us against his own intellectual habits! The result is to reduce Christianity to a magic, an Eastern superstition apparently beyond the reach of Western science, but in actuality beneath its notice. 'We little understand, with our cold and scrupulous natures, how anyone can be so entirely possessed by the idea of which he has made himself the apostle. To the deeply earnest races of the West, conviction means sincerity to one's self. But sincerity to one's self has not much meaning to Oriental peoples, little accustomed to the subtleties of a critical spirit.' Here Renan comes very close to calling Jesus an untrustworthy Oriental trader, a Jewish confidence-trickster.

But what are Renan and Arnold left with, if Jesus was merely a beautifully deluded shaman? They are left with precepts, teachings, examples. Nervously aware that they have killed off Christianity as a faith, they must reinstate it as a religion, as a guide-to-life, as a poetry. They were not alone in this response; the poeticizing of non-divine religion was a characteristically nineteenth-century gesture. Even bitter Flaubert could write, with nonsensical illogic, in 1857: 'What attracts me above all else is religion. I mean all religions, no one more than another.

Each dogma in particular is repulsive to me, but I consider the feeling that invented them as the most natural and poetic of humanity.' Thus it is that Arnold and Renan idealize Christ's teachings even as they reduce the authority of those teachings. Stripping Jesus of his claim to be the son of God, they turn the worship of this diminished orphan into a sickly poetry. Renan makes Jesus sound like Dostoevsky's idiot, Prince Myshkin, a holy fool dribbling fine phrases. Referring to the Sermon on the Mount, he writes that 'his preaching was gentle and pleasing, breathing nature and the perfume of the fields.' Jesus, says Renan, was 'the great consoler of life', even though it was on the Mount that Jesus issued his most impossible, his most unconsoling, his cruellest demands. It was here that he enjoined us to love our enemies; here he asked us not merely to cultivate a Renan-like uprightness of will, but perfection itself: 'be ye therefore perfect, even as your Father which is in heaven is perfect.' Yet Renan's Jesus is a poet, an 'amiable character, accompanied doubtless by one of those lovely faces which sometimes appear in the Jewish race'. And although Renan cannot quite decide what Jesus demands of us, he knows that 'he founded the pure worship of all ages, of all lands, that which all elevated souls will practise until the end of time' – whatever that is. Arnold, too, praises Jesus for his 'attractive poetry of hopes and imaginings'. More schoolmasterly than the effusive Renan, he remarks on 'the fitness of the character and history of Jesus Christ for inspiring such an enthusiasm of attachment and devotion'.

Since Jesus is no longer the Messiah, being a Christian is no longer a trial of belief, but a poetry that brushes our moral fibres the right way – towards conduct in the world. Arnold decides that conduct is 'three-fourths of life', and that Christianity, since it enforces good conduct, is 'the indispensable background, the three-fourths of life'. The Church of England, Arnold famously declared, is 'a corporation for purposes of moral growth and practice'. Yet both writers are then forced into pragmatism, forced to justify the social and emotional *efficacy* of Christianity.

Were Christianity simply true, its effect on the world could not be a way of measuring its truth. 'Success' would be immaterial. But Renan and Arnold do not believe it to be true; its 'truth' lies only in its usefulness. It is painful to see them wallow in the most primitive consequentialism. Both are defensively triumphalist, and entirely circular. Christ is a better moral example than Socrates, says Arnold. Why? Because Christ has inspired love and ardour over centuries, and Socrates has not. 'History has proved' this. In other words, Christ is a better example . . . because he has proved to be a better example. In the end, both writers merely *assert* that Christianity is greater than the other religions – because Christianity has so galvanized the white man. Arnold, in his politic way, merely hints at this, with his use of the clubbable euphemistic verb, 'counts': 'And we know how Jesus Christ and his precepts won their way from the very first, and soon became the religion of all the part of the world which most counted, and are now the religion of all that part of the world which most counts.' Renan is more brutal: 'It is neither the ancient Law nor the Talmud which has conquered and changed the world . . . the morality of the Gospels remains the highest creation of human conscience . . .' Christianity, he writes elsewhere, 'has become almost a synonym of "religion". All that is done outside of this great and good Christian tradition is barren.'

There we have it: Christianity is not a God-given religion, because it is the 'creation of human conscience'. We made it up. And yet we still need what both Arnold and Renan call 'religion'; and the best form of this 'religion' is Christian morality. And the proof of this assertion? Christianity's *success* in the world. Such thinking, which does not deserve to be called thinking, with its clownish contradictions and repulsive evasions, positively *deserves* Nietzsche's decisive hammer. And Nietzsche did bring his hammer down on Arnold and Renan. Such people, he wrote, were atheists who wanted to be honoured for *not* being atheists. Renan, wrote Nietzsche in *Twilight of the Idols,* 'misses the point with painful regularity'. He was a writer, he says in *Beyond Good and Evil*, 'in whom every other minute some nothingness of religious tension topples a soul which is in a refined sense voluptuous and relaxed'. Such people 'have got rid of the Christian God, and now feel obliged to cling all the more firmly to Christian morality'. Yet 'when one gives up Christian belief one thereby deprives oneself of the *right* to Christian morality . . . Christianity is a system, a consistently thought out and *complete* view of things. If one breaks out of it a fundamental idea, the belief in God, one thereby breaks the whole thing to pieces: one has nothing of any consequence in one's hands . . . Christian morality is a command: its origin is transcendental; it is beyond all criticism, all right to criticize; it possesses truth only if God is truth – it stands or falls with the belief in God.'

So, fortunately, ended the brief reign of 'three-fourths of life'.

2 The Evangelical Struggle

Mankind is growing out of religion as out of its childhood clothes.

– Schopenhauer, *Parerga and Paralipomena*

The child of evangelicalism, if he does not believe, inherits nevertheless a suspicion of indifference. He is always evangelical. He rejects the religion he grew up with, but he rejects it religiously. He has buried evangelical belief but he has not buried the evangelical choice, which seems to him the only important dilemma. He respects the logical claustrophobia of Christian commitment, the little cell of belief. This is the only kind of belief that makes sense, the revolutionary kind. Nominal belief is insufficiently serious; nominal unbelief seems almost a blasphemy against earnest atheism.

My childhood, which was a very happy one, was spent in the command economy of evangelical Christianity. Life was centrally planned, all negotiations had to pass by Jesus's desk.

Sometimes it seems that my childhood was the noise around a hush, the hush of God. And at times an actual hush: I recall episodes when my parents talked quietly and on their own about someone they knew who had 'lost his faith', and the solemn vibrations that would fill the house at these times, as if a doctor were visiting. Similarly, my childhood was marked by the deaths of friends of my parents who were members of their congregation, people for whom the full evangelical panoply – prayer, the laying on of hands, anointing with oil – did not seem to have worked.

The church to which we belonged was part of the Church of England, but during the 1970s it had been 'renewed' and now considered itself 'charismatic'. These code words seem dated now; then, they meant that the church felt itself to have been visited by the Holy Spirit, and to be making fresh use of what St Paul in I Corinthians called 'spiritual gifts' or 'the manifestation of the Spirit': speaking in tongues, dancing in the spirit, ecstatic worship, healing, miracles, prophecies. This movement, with its late eighteenth- and nineteenth-century roots, took hold of many parts of the Church of England during the 1970s, and was a casualty of its own explosiveness, for it broke up congregations into those who had been mildly renewed and those who had become fanatical. Eventually the fanatics left the Church of England and established the 'house church' movement. From the outside, the church I attended with my parents and siblings was conventional enough: a stout medieval fortress with a square tower and the usual gaudy strip-cartoon windows, fixed to a slight hill in a university town. But wonders occurred inside. I saw people shivering with ecstasies, people clutching at God with their hands raised. I saw people dancing in the aisles, whirling and writhing. It was explained afterwards to me that these dancers were 'taken with the Spirit'. There was one young woman who was a persistent dancer, and I recall being disappointed that she was one of the least attractive women in the congregation (at thirteen, this was important). I was disturbed by how many adults broke into tears during these services. One man spent entire services shaking like a machine. I never saw his eyes dry. He always looked as if he were painfully giving birth to something unwanted. I began to associate Christianity with crying, and with a form of sublime punishment. The sick were prayed for. Repentant sinners gave testimonials. A visiting preacher who brought his guitar into the pulpit with him – a strange Picasso-effect, this disjunction – told us that if we had not committed ourselves to Christ we were in terrible danger. For who could tell – we might walk out of the church and be hit by a car, and then where would we be? After the service, people came up to me and asked me how I had done in my school exams. If the answer was good, there would be an earnest hug, and a bellowed 'Praise the Lord!' There was nothing too small for the Lord's attention.

There were many good and kind people in this church. Nevertheless, it was perhaps the wrong kind of religion for a child because it excited in me two childish responses: fear and slyness. I feared being called out to give testimonials to the congregation. At times, we would all have our heads bent in prayer, and the vicar – incongruously, a gentle Oxonian with the voice of a classics master – would announce that he was certain that there was someone here who 'had not turned to Christ'. His voice scathed me like a searchlight. With the self-consciousness of adolescence, it was always I who had not turned to Christ. The fear produced slyness, or suspicion. 'They desired to make me truthful; the tendency was to make me positive and sceptical', writes Edmund Gosse in *Father and Son*, his moving account of his evangelical childhood. I noted that in this church no sick person was ever healed of anything, despite the laying on of hands, the prayers. Indeed, one of the kindest and gentlest people in the congregation died of cancer, despite the enormous prayerful effort to save her. My parents told me that God had called her. I concluded that prayer either did not work (for it could not be that people were not praying hard enough) or that God had decided not to answer this particular prayer. Either way, prayer seemed a fool's game, and it seemed that one of the cardinal promises of the New Testament – 'If ye shall ask any thing in my name, I will do it' (John 14) – was not a promise. Faith might move mountains, but in an invisible mountain-range. And I noticed that when people were speaking in tongues, a state of ecstasy in which people intoned in a verbal shuffle, instead of producing a nonsense version of English they seemed to produce a tourist's imitation of Hebrew, a stirring of throaty 'ch' and 'sh' sounds, a noise as if they were saying the Scottish words 'Loch Shiel' over and over again. The idea seemed to be that this was more 'religious', an oral memory of Jerusalem.

The theology of this church tended towards literalism, but a literalism of the spirit rather than of the word: intelligent evangelicalism. This was a church in a university town. Nobody believed that Genesis was creation's blueprint, but most believed that it was a divine allegory of creation's divine beginning. The Bible, in Protestant custom, could be argued over locally as long as certain general truths were not compromised. This nest of truths opened out thus: God made us; the Bible was God's revealed word; Jesus was God made man; Jesus was resurrected, thereby conquering death. Jesus died for our salvation, and if we believe in him we will have eternal life. We will not always understand why some things are as they are, but we must have faith. Evangelicalism is most impressive, perhaps, for the intensity which it bestows on our decision to choose, and the consequences that flow from this. If we choose to accept Jesus as the saviour, then our lives will be in sublime revolution, every molecule adance, every minute scrutinized. This is what such believers mean when they talk of commitment. It is like entering prison: you must turn out your spiritual pockets and hand over all your inner belongings, even your shoelaces. They take their intensity – fairly, it seems to me – from Jesus's encounter with Nicodemus, as told in John 3. Jesus tells the puzzled Pharisee, Nicodemus, that to see the kingdom of God a man must be born again. Bemused, Nicodemus wonders how a man can be born twice, and Jesus replies that that which is born of the flesh is flesh, and that which is born of the spirit is spirit.

What is both magnificent and oppressive in evangelicalism is the apprehension of momentousness, and the belief in divine realities. It is an appalling contract. If you believe in Jesus's claims, then everything flows from this, and your life has been changed. Nothing could be more important. And once you have signed this contract, then certain dividends follow, dividends that have reality: God's love, the guidance of the holy spirit, eternal life, Christ's active presence in your life, and the promise of eternity.

Alongside this ardent Christianity ran another, more relaxed style of worship. For several years I sang as a chorister at the very old and very beautiful cathedral which dominates the town in which I was born. Singing was a training and a discipline. Evensong was sung every day, and on Sunday, three services, Matins, Holy Communion and Evensong. Monkishly, I had to board at a school that sat in the lee of the great church. We were two minutes' walk from the cathedral cloisters. Here, time was ruled and divided by the quarter-hour chimes of the great cathedral clock, those chimes whose metal judder could be heard everywhere in the school, even in the dormitories, and which, though mournful in sound, nevertheless, being themselves a tune, reminded one every fifteen minutes of music, and thus of the source of happiness. For this was happiness. To sing Palestrina and Victoria, Gibbons, Tallis, Byrd, Purcell in such a building, whose stone columns had a stony, vast smell, was an experience never to be repeated or regained, a lost garden. At a quarter to four every afternoon, the twenty-four choristers lined up at the door of the school. We were dressed in black cloaks, fastened with a clumsy silver clasp, and we wore black mortar-boards with indolent tassels that lolled this way and that. These mortar-boards resembled prototypes of hats. We were two dark disciplined lines; from far above, from an aircraft, say, we must have looked like tracks left by an invisible vehicle. From here we processed to the cathedral, to the service we had to sing.

Inside, candle-flames shivered slightly, the wood of the pews was tense to the touch, the huge organ pushed waves of sound to every corner of the dark building. We choristers rather pitied those few loyal worshippers who appeared every day: a terribly thin and pompous student from the university, who always wore his old school tie; a devout and hobbled old lady who supported herself, curiously, with three sticks (one stick for the left leg, and two sticks for the right); a man who always slipped in five minutes late, seemingly at exactly the same time every day, as if he were the victim of an obsessive disorder. We pitied them because they were not singing. Music was our only concern; it entirely dominated our sense of worship. During the lesson, or during the sermon, we would doze in our tall choir stalls, or read the sheet-music of our next performance. We were vaguely aware that a form of religious liturgy surrounded us, a rather pleasant, lax, aesthetic liturgy. But it impinged little. We approached these daily performances self-obsessedly, as technicians. We had ears only for our own sounds.

These were the two very different versions of Christianity around me at this time. In the school term, the cathedral; in the holidays, the evangelical church. I did not choose between them, but strove to pass by both of them. At the age of fifteen or so, I sat down with a notebook and tore myself away from belief in God. It is a process that brings great unhappiness to others, but not to oneself. It is like undressing. You are so quickly, so easily free. One writes down four or five objections to belief in God. Before one has read any atheist or sceptical philosophy one finds that one has apparently invented the old, old objections to God – the problem of evil and suffering in the world, the senseless difficulty of faith, the cruelty of heaven and hell, the paganism of Jesus's 'sacrifice', one's own lack of religious experience. It is probably because these objections are so obvious and so old that atheism, as a philosophical tradition, is generally underpowered. Literary and philosophical atheism moves between a rather charming serenity and a spirit of gauntlet-throwing naughtiness. The naughtiness produces personal defiances, disobediences, and challenges laid down to God: John Stuart Mill saying: 'If I go to hell for it, then to hell I will go.' The serenity treats religion as if it were, almost self-evidently, nonsense – think of Stendhal, Russell, even Hume. For Stendhal, to judge from his fiction, the priests are hypocrites, therefore religion is a lot of hypocritical nonsense. Nietzsche is the great wild exception to this, and Camus is the great calm exception: both of them, in their intense dismantling, judge the true challenge of belief in God, and labour to kill it philosophically. Both of them realize that God cannot be destroyed by 'philosophy' as such, but only exchanged for a form of rival belief, a belief that God does not, cannot, exist. The philosophers are right: *The Myth of Sisyphus* is poor philosophy. But what of it? It is not philosophy, but a tract aimed at evacuating God, and a promise to live by the moral rigour of that evacuation. Camus cannot *know* that God does not exist; he believes it. So it is that believers, actual Christians such as Dostoevsky, offer the very deepest objections to their own belief. Dostoevsky's parable of the Grand Inquisitor, in *The Brothers Karamazov*, is, for me, an unanswerable attack on the cruelty of God's hiddenness. In my early twenties, it proved decisive. Kierkegaard writes in *Works of Love* that the true Christian preacher 'should not hesitate, aware of *the highest responsibility*, to preach *in Christian sermons* . . . AGAINST Christianity'. He meant, of course, the better to protect Christianity's hard challenges from the softened challenges of the established churches. But it was Kierkegaard's devout mutilation of himself, his repulsive masochism, his belief in the absolute impossibility of imitating Christ, that finished off, in my mid-twenties, what I had begun for myself at fifteen, and finally rid me of religious belief.

True atheism understands the obligations of the negative revolution it has begun. My own position might be summarized thus: I can see no way in which it is a good thing for humans to have accidentally and pointlessly evolved on an earth which they must inhabit (irrespective of my own local happiness). Life-under-God seems a pointlessness posing as a purpose (the purpose, presumably, being to love God and to be loved in return); life-without-God seems to me also a pointlessness posing as a purpose (jobs, family, sex and so on – all the usual distractions). The advantage, if it can be described as one, of living in the latter state, without God, is that the false purpose has at least been invented by man, and one can strip it away to reveal the *actual* pointlessness.

3 The Twentieth Century

In fact, Nietzsche did not end the reign of 'three-fourths of life'. Arnold and Renan have their heirs: theologians who believe that God can be rationally argued for, believers who value the Church only for its contemporary success, non-believers who have given up God, but refuse to surrender the categories of God. A few years ago, for instance, Paul Johnson, a Catholic layman, wrote *The Quest For God*. His book is part of a noble tradition, both Anglican and Catholic, in which laymen have written devotional treatises. The layman explains his love of God, and his fondness for his ecclesiastical tradition. The apex was reached more than three hundred years ago when Sir Thomas Browne published his marvellous *Religio Medici* in 1643, and Johnson's book hardly reverses that slide. It is written in the quasi-judicial style of conservative journalists, in which syntactical pomposity substitutes for the motions of true thought, and in which no sentence is exactly slipshod, nor exactly alive.

But the book, for better and worse, gives a picture of a typical Catholic mind at the end of the century. In its pragmatism, Johnson's Catholicism resembles Arnold and Renan's 'belief'. He does not argue, in the evangelical way, that religion is true and that you should believe in order to win your salvation, though what is most simple and most attractive in his book is premised on this quiet certainty. Instead he argues for the strength of the Church against the weakness of its opposition. This is a part of Cardinal Newman's argument, in his *Apologia Pro Vita Sua*, that the Catholic Church is 'a great remedy for a great evil'. Johnson is more sanguine than Cardinal Newman about the fate of modern evil. He thinks secularism has come to naught, and that this is why Christianity, and especially Catholicism, is growing in our time. He admires the Pope, as a firm bulwark. It is all about holding firm, defeating evil, the correction of man. As in Newman's book, the word 'love' hardly appears here.

This medicinal idea of the Church as a remedy for evil is unstable. It gives primacy to evil, and makes religion a reaction. It raises the unwelcome question of whether, were evil to cease, the Church should not also cease. The antibody, after all, lives off the virus. For evil is not the front door to religious belief. Yet Johnson's sanguine version of Newman's pessimism seems not far from an apparent satisfaction that evil has not damaged religion and that *therefore* religion is a great good. His message: religion has survived, in part, because the alternatives have failed. Johnson seems not to realize that the danger of this argument is that it makes religion one of those alternatives – it becomes an alternative to the alternatives. The Godlessness of totalitarianism is Johnson's test-case because his book's argument rests on it: the argument that when God is absent humans wither into confusion (as in atheism or humanism or socialism) or commit terrible evil (as in Nazism and Communism). In his chapter on why evil exists in God's world, he equates secularism with moral relativism, and religion with what he calls 'absolute morality'. Though he does not say so, this is sometimes called, in Christian ethics, the Divine Command Theory. But God was not absent in Nazi Germany. Ordinary Christians, the very believers who, in Johnson's vision, crew the little craft of morality, did little to avert evil and in many cases furthered it. Since religion, in this case, did not stop evil, why should we believe that religion, in another case, would promote goodness?

In a stroke, Johnson's presumed connections between religion and 'absolute morality' are broken. This is a Christian prejudice that, even without the example of Nazi Germany, ought to be affronted by the counter-evidence. Most atheists and sceptics have been morally conservative. God-fearing Europe – say before the death of David Hume in 1776 – does not seem to have been obviously more moral than God-questioning Europe.

Like Arnold and Renan, Johnson has a developed sense of the obligations of belief and almost no sense of the obligations of unbelief. He knows that if God exists, 'our life then becomes a mere preparation for eternity and must be conducted throughout with our future in view.' He is right about this. But he thinks that if we decide God does not exist, there are 'no commands to follow except what society imposes upon us, and even these we may evade if we can get away with it. In a Godless world, there is no obvious basis for altruism of any kind, moral anarchy takes over and the rule of the self prevails.' This inability to take unbelief seriously infects his defence of Christianity. His book is replete with an air of self-evidence. Having consumed all the secular alternatives, he does not see the need to stir from his chair to prepare the religious feast: he lounges in the afternoon of argument. Since it is self-evident to him that all opponents of Christianity are mad, evil, or silly, then it is also self-evident to him that Christianity is the opposite of this. And that is that. Though he defines, at the beginning of his book, the Christian choice as one of great momentousness, he does not seem to feel that this choice needs urgent defence. Hence his rather idle pragmatism, which, although he does not intend this, undermines what is not pragmatic in Christianity. He writes: 'It is because sensible men the world over, at all times, have recognised and accepted the inevitability of mighty death, that they have turned to God to explain its significance. Without God, death is horrific. With God, death is still fearsome, but it can be said to have a meaning and a hope. The great strength of Christianity has always been that it brings men and women to terms with death in a way which offers them comfort and an explanation.'

No, the great 'strength' of Christianity is not that it offers medicines, but that it is true. Health comes from *this*. Johnson's ecclesiastical cynicism – where 'strength' means only 'strength for the Church' – suspends what is most powerful about Christianity: its claim to be true. Instead, like Arnold and Renan, he offers the milder language of success: does it work for you? He secularizes religion and demonizes secularism. In doing so, he makes Christianity vulnerable where it should be strongest. If Christianity can be defended as merely a set of advantages, then it can be attacked as merely a set of disadvantages by rival advantages, most of them secular. If Christianity is only a therapy-service, a matter of comfort and consolation, then why not something more powerful than its withered ardour? (Drugs, love, literature, etc.) Christianity can be sold as a set of gifts but it cannot be proved by these gifts. It is true or it is not true. This is its 'defence'. To defend its success is not to defend it at all. Indeed, it is to cross into the other camp. David Hume, in *The Natural History of Religion*, attacks religion in exactly the way Johnson defends it, as a therapy offering comfort and solace: 'The primary religion of mankind arises chiefly from an anxious fear of future events.' Unwittingly, Johnson turns religion into the very superstition that Hume so disliked.

Or take Richard Swinburne, who teaches the philosophy of religion at Oxford, and who believes that God's existence can be rationally argued for, and rationally believed. He is a logical successor to the Matthew Arnold who wanted religion to proceed by 'reason' rather than 'assumption'. (See Arnold's *Literature and Dogma*.) But rationalism and God are not friends. For it to be rational to believe in God, God must be rational, or we would not want to believe in him. Sure enough, Richard Swinburne, in his books, usually sets about describing a God who resembles Richard Swinburne – cool, intelligent, decent, bookishly abstracted, and distinctly limited in power. Because his God is rational, Swinburne must make him limited in power, because God's omnipotence is far from rational; it is literally incomprehensible. A God who could do anything could do evil things or order us to do evil things. The early Church father, Origen, from whom Swinburne borrows, dealt with this like a true theologian: circularly. He simply asserted that God would not do evil things: 'We also assert that shameful things are impossible to God, for if they were it would mean that God is able to cease to be God.'

Similarly, and just as unconvincingly, Swinburne 'asserts': he makes up God's mind for him. He tells him just what the extent of his powers is. He anthropomorphizes God and then oppresses him with his own humanity. God is a source of moral obligation, he has written. He orders us to do our duty. 'But God clearly cannot make things which are our duty no longer our duty; he cannot make it right to torture children for fun . . . for it is wrong to command what is wrong.' Well, yes it is, if Swinburne's idea of what is 'wrong' happens to coincide with God's. But why should it? What if God had an entirely different, entirely incomprehensible idea of right and wrong? It is interesting that Swinburne's example here of incomprehensible command is torturing children, for he seems to be anxiously repressing a celebrated example of God's power to command something horrible. It seemed to involve not the torture but the possible death of a child: Abraham's commanded sacrifice of his son Isaac.

Swinburne's work is scattered with phrases like the one above, in which he tells God what he can and cannot do. 'We owe God a lot. Hence (within limits), if God tells us to do certain things, it becomes our duty to do them.' God apparently has 'the right' to allow people to do evil to each other. But 'it would, of course, be crazy for God to multiply evils more and more . . .' 'One might expect' God to intervene in history every so often. Indeed, 'it would be odd to suppose that God' intervened only invisibly. Equally, although there is much good on earth, 'it would be odd if God did not plan something greater and longer for those humans who want it.' In other words, 'it would be odd' if heaven did not exist. 'It would be odd': nothing stronger than that? If it were only 'odd' that heaven did not exist, presumably, for Swinburne, it is only – what shall we say? – 'not odd', or 'rather agreeable' that heaven does exist. Swinburne, busily constructing his own rational and agreeable God, a kind of Oxonian version of a Golem, precisely conforms to the complaint of one of the greatest of all atheists, Ludwig Feuerbach, that God is merely the projection of human desires and schemes. Certainly, the spectacle of a God who could so easily be known and bossed around by Richard Swinburne is the best possible argument against the likelihood of his existence.

Only when Christianity is understood as a set of truths, with a set of promises and obligations dependent on those truths, does it retain uniqueness, and a command structure. The 'great strength' of biblical Christianity is that we need it. We are told, unequivocally, that we need Christianity not only as comfort and consolation, but to save ourselves. 'Oddity' hardly comes into it. We need eternal life, or we are lost. Theologies which deconstruct this need eliminate Christianity's uniqueness, hence its power, hence its existence.

This is apparent in the work of Don Cupitt, a fellow of Emmanuel College, Cambridge and an Anglican priest, whose books have been responsible for the growth of a movement in the Church of England called the Sea of Faith. One of its members, a soft-spoken parish priest from Sussex called Anthony Freeman, wrote a book a few years ago in which he argued that God is not a supernatural external force, but a power inside us (*God In Us*). The Sea of Faith priests like to talk as if they have dealt with the problem of religious unbelief in our time by deconstructing God's existence. In fact, they are merely rationalists who have lost their faith and who are not as clever, most of them, as Arnold or Renan or even Richard Swinburne, and not as brave as the friend of my parents who admitted to losing his faith.

It is difficult to keep pace with Don Cupitt's changes of skin. He has been a poststructuralist, a Christian Buddhist, and now calls himself, I think, a Kingdom Christian – he believes that we must make God's kingdom here on earth. Why we would bother to do such dark and lonely work is anyone's guess, since Cupitt, like Freeman, assumes that we create our own God. For Cupitt, language is all, and there is no creator outside language, or outside our world. Truth does not come from the other room; we make it up. Freeman suggests that when we pray we do a kind of meditation; Cupitt speaks of Christianity as something 'recognized as the highest form of creative self-realization'. 'The task', writes Cupitt, 'is to learn to practise religion just for its own sake, disinterestedly, and to become a creator rather than a passive recipient of religious meaning and value. A world in which people have become active creators of religious value is what I mean by the Kingdom of God.' Every word in these two sentences is feeble or contradictory. If we are 'practising a religion' (whatever that means) for its own sake, who decides, other than Cupitt, that this is a 'task' we *must* begin? Orthodox Christian faith is precisely not a matter of being a passive recipient. Faith – the belief in what is not visible to us – involves a decisive activity of belief. However, practising religion for its own sake sounds exactly like an enormous relaxation. Christ, seen thus, becomes the representative of some rather decent principles and goals, but indistingishable, one imagines, from worshipping Socrates or John Lennon.

Cupitt and Freeman and the Sea of Faith priests have dismantled God but kept intact the language of religious obligation. In place of the savagery of truly disillusioned knowledge, they prefer the serenity of partial illusion. If we pretend to believe, they seem to say, then things will go better for us. Cupitt speaks the language of obligation; it is just that, like Swinburne, the commands are his own rather than God's. Christ tells us that we must believe, or we are lost. Clearly, much flows from a belief that we are created by an 'actually-existing God'. Cupitt's suggestions, by contrast, are scribbled, as it were, only on an internal memo, and all he offers us is rapid promotion within the company of man. 'We need to cultivate an inner scepticism,' he writes; 'but Christianity still needs an inner discipline'; 'we need to learn a kind of Buddhist inner simplicity'. And all he offers are his own beatitudes: at the end of his book *The World To Come*, he asks how we are to live in a postmodern age, when God has been deconstructed away. 'Four guiding principles become fundamental . . . Truth, disinterestedness, creativity and love.' But what is 'fundamental' about these principles? This is not the door of command which is written about in the Book of Revelation. We stand at Cupitt's diminished lintel, being called by Cupitt. Just as Johnson's pragmatism collapses into David Hume's atheism, and Swinburne's rationalism collapses into Feuerbach's atheism, so Cupitt's religion collapses into Camus's atheism. Cupitt's four principles remind me of nothing so much as Camus's three guiding principles at the end of *The Myth of Sisyphus*: 'my revolt, my passion, and my freedom'. I prefer Camus's stoicism to Cupitt's disguised stoicism, because Camus's stoicism seems to me to be based on an accurate assessment of the difficulty of living in a world without belief and without apparent purpose.

The shallowness of Cupitt's atheism produces the shallowness of his solution to atheism. He never seems to realize that his own commands are merely his own commands. His atheism is without depth because it will not see the consequences of its actual depth; and correspondingly, his new 'religion' is without depth because it refuses to accept the consequences of its limitations.

4 The Problem of Evil

The problem of evil and its existence in the world is, for many people, the real affront to belief in God. This was the hot crux that obsessed me, that tormented me when I was a child, and which broke open my religious adherence. People do evil things to each other and cause each other pain; equally, we live in a world of natural uncontrollable pain and suffering – earthquakes, cancer, mental and physical handicap. The existence of this pain is an obstacle to belief because it seems either to limit God's power or to qualify his goodness. Either God cannot control this evil (and then he is not all-powerful) or, in some way, he wants it to exist (and he is not good). Theology has a number of answers, none of them satisfactory. God's ways may be incomprehensible to us. (This is Job's message.) Various theologians have argued that we will be paid back in full in heaven for everything we have lost on earth. And connected to this is the less specific consolation that out of harm comes good; for we are part of God's divine plan, and even if we do not know why we are suffering, we must be suffering for a final absolute good. Most people of any sensitivity find this idea unacceptable, if not repulsive, because it is not clear why happiness must be only approached belatedly by the path of suffering rather than tasted originally.

The more sophisticated defence is that for us to act at all as moral agents we must have free will, and this must entail the freedom to do evil things as well as good things. Origen argued that without Judas's evil, Christ could not have been crucified; and without the pain visited on Christ, we would not be saved by his resurrection. Doing good in a world in which we could not do evil would be literally meaningless; the light needs the shade. Augustine is the best developer of this defence. Often, this defence becomes monstrously immoral. Richard Swinburne, for instance, borrows the free will argument but adds to it a twist. If free will is a good thing – and clearly it is, for it enables God to watch us grow morally – then to suffer is a good thing for it allows the person who is doing bad things to you to exercise the obvious good of free will: 'Being allowed to suffer to make possible a great good is a privilege, even if the privilege is forced upon you . . . it is an additional benefit to the sufferer that his suffering is the means whereby the one who hurt him had the opportunity to make a significant choice beween good and evil which otherwise he would not have had.' Elsewhere, Swinburne writes that terminal illness, such as cancer, at least offers the victim the great good of choice – 'whether to endure it with patience, or to bemoan his lot'.

Swinburne's theodicy is interesting because it is a greedy man's salad. Essentially, he loads every single traditional defence of God onto his plate and mixes them. Thus, our pain is incomprehensible. (All theodicies end up at this point of incomprehension: they have to. As an atheist, one grows fond of this repetitive weakness, as one might cherish a dog with a limp.) But, says Swinburne, we must have free will. Moreover, our pain is good for us, because we are part of the larger progress to heaven. This progress involves our education as moral beings. Partly we are educated by our use of free will; and partly we are educated by our sacrifice to someone else's free will. And though we can't understand any of this, in the end all this is contributing to the greater good. Though Swinburne's argument seems monstrously cynical, it is in fact a logical development of his belief that free will is the greatest good we can have. Swinburne makes the decision that our suffering, however great, must be superseded by the greater importance of free will.

There are several powerful objections to the free-will argument. First, as the seventeenth-century sceptic Pierre Bayle has it, why would God bestow a gift that he knows in advance will be abused in such a manner that it will only serve to bring about the ruin of the person to whom it is given? What mother, asks Bayle, would let her daughter go to a ball if she knew in advance that at the ball her daughter would be seduced and raped? Bayle is penetrating, but the free-will arguers are likely to reply that the only possible world in which we might have meaningful relations with each other, and with God, is a world with free will, which inevitably means a world in which we are free to do horrible things to each other. This reply is surely weak: such an argument is always premised on the idea that a world without free will would be a more awful thing, would be a bigger sacrifice, than the world as we know it, which is merely full of pain and evil. Free will, to such defenders, is the highest good, higher than human happiness. But how on earth – literally – would we know? Would a world without free will be a poor, limited place? Suppose that humans had never known pain or evil. Suppose that for all recorded history humans had had the capacity to do *only* good things to each other. It is unlikely that such a world would seem to us poor and limited, because we could not know what the alternative – a world with plenty of free will – would be like. Similarly, if no species had ever developed hearing, intelligence and culture might have evolved around the other senses, and none of us could feel the lack of something that had never existed. God, presumably, *could* have created such a world – indeed, such an Eden would be a perfect laboratory for him to observe the enactment of Jesus's first two commandments: Love thy God and love thy neighbour. Such a world would be heaven, and God could have created heaven on earth. In other words, free will is clearly important for humans *as we are currently constituted*. But it is not clear that human free will is necessarily important for God, for God might well have created a world in which humans were somewhat less free but also somewhat less evil and hence somewhat less in pain.

Theodicy must lead back to the question of why we were created at all. If we were created to share in God's creativity, and to worship God, it is not clear why humans had to be constituted in the only form we know, which seems a radically imperfect and painful one. The same might be said for this world; as Schopenhauer puts it, we can be certain that this world is not the best of all possible worlds, and is in fact a kind of hell for most people. And besides, continues Schopenhauer, even if Leibniz were right, and this world were the best of all *possible* worlds, God created both the world 'and also the possibility itself; accordingly, he should have arranged this with a view to its admitting of a better world'. (Perhaps the only answer to why humans were created in the form they have is deeply satanic, or Gnostic: God was incapable of creating something other than himself. We are formed in God's image, and therefore God is just as evil as we are . . .)

This objection to the free-will argument seems decisive to me. It raises the most uncomfortable questions about why God, so far as we understand him, created the world. If heaven was not created on earth, then earth is a testing ground for heaven. The free-will idea rests on this. But there is something more. For a world without freedom would be a world in which God controlled all our actions. Crucially, it would be a world in which God spoke directly to us without the need of faith. We would all believe. Faith is, apparently, part of the test visited upon us. I have always found Philip's cry to Jesus in John 14, piercing: 'Philip saith unto him, Lord, shew us the Father, and it sufficeth us.' But the Lord does not show us the Father. It seems obvious to theologians like Richard Swinburne that a world of limited freedom and absolute transparency of knowledge, in which not one of us is in any doubt about our creator, would be a limited, useless place. But it would not, presumably, be useless to God. It is what heaven would be like; and why, before heaven, must we live? Why must we move through this unhappy, painful, rehearsal for heaven, this desperate ante-chamber, this foreword written by an anonymous author, this hard prelude in which so few of us can find our way?

Acknowledgements

Acknowledgements are due to *The New Republic*, *The London Review of Books*, *The New Yorker*, *The Los Angeles Times*, *The Republic of Letters*, and *The Guardian*, where some of this material first appeared. A part of 'What Chekhov Meant By Life' appeared in *Best American Essays 1998*. A section of 'The Broken Estate' was delivered as a sermon at Worcester College, Oxford. The author is grateful to Association d'Art de La Napoule, and offers particular thanks to two editors, Martin Peretz and Mary-Kay Wilmers.

Index

Index